INTERNATIONAL STUDIES OF THE
COMMITTEE ON INTERNATIONAL RELATIONS
UNIVERSITY OF NOTRE DAME

Beleaguered Tower

Beleaguered Tower:

The Dilemma of Political Catholicism in Wilhelmine Germany

RONALD J. ROSS

UNIVERSITY OF NOTRE DAME PRESS
NOTRE DAME · LONDON

Library of Congress Cataloging in Publication Data

Ross, Ronald J   1935 -
   Beleaguered tower.

   (International studies of the Committee on Inter-
national Relations, University of Notre Dame)
   Bibliography: p.
   Includes index.
   1.   Germany -- History -- William II, 1888–1918.
2.   Deutsche Zentrumspartei. I. Title. II. Series:
Notre Dame, Ind. University.   Committee on International
Relations. International studies.
DD228.5.R65   322'.1'0943   74-12568
ISBN 0-268-00547-8

Manufactured in the United States of America

CONTENTS

To My Parents

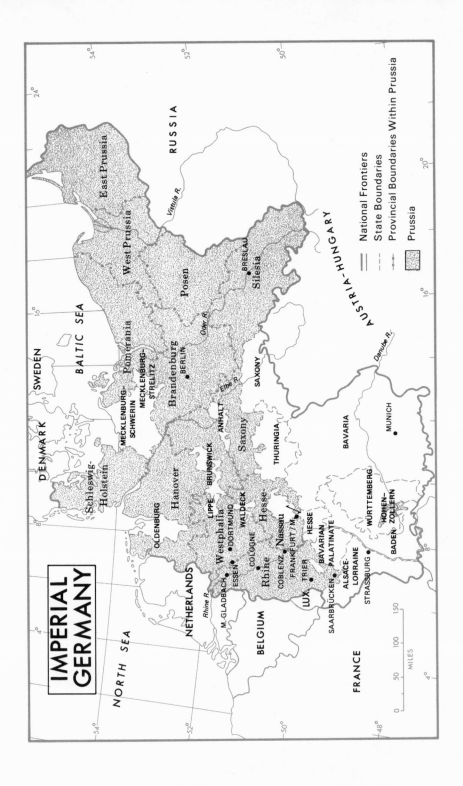

IMPERIAL GERMANY

National Frontiers
State Boundaries
Provincial Boundaries Within Prussia
Prussia

NORTH SEA

BALTIC SEA

SWEDEN

DENMARK

Schleswig-Holstein

NETHERLANDS

BELGIUM

FRANCE

RUSSIA

AUSTRIA-HUNGARY

East Prussia

West Prussia

Pomerania

MECKLENBURG-SCHWERIN

MECKLENBURG-STRELITZ

Posen

Brandenburg

BERLIN

Silesia

BRESLAU

SAXONY

Saxony

ANHALT

Hanover

OLDENBURG

BRUNSWICK

LIPPE

WALDECK

Westphalia

DORTMUND

Hesse

THURINGIA

BAVARIA

MUNICH

WÜRTTEMBERG

HOHEN-ZOLLERN

BADEN

Nassau

COLOGNE

Rhine

COBLENZ

FRANKFURT/M.

HESSE

BAVARIAN PALATINATE

ALSACE

LORRAINE

STRASSBURG

SAARBRÜCKEN

LUX.   TRIER

ESSEN

M.-GLADBACH

Rhine R.

Vistula R.

Oder R.

Elbe R.

Danube R.

MILES

0   50   100   150

PREFACE

   Symbols are often synonymous with political parties and movements. No one fails to equate the swastika with National Socialism
or the hammer and sickle with Communism. But other emblems,
while less familiar, are equally significant. Political Catholicism in
Germany, for example, also attached great importance to a symbolic device. During the time of the German Empire and the Weimar
Republic, the Centrum party [*Deutsche Zentrumspartei*], a political
movement for Roman Catholics, adopted as its emblem the image
of a fortress tower. A more appropriate symbol could scarcely have
been devised. Representing a religious minority (one-third of the
population) in a state dominated by Protestants, and having under-
gone the rigors of confessional persecution during the Kulturkampf
(Otto von Bismarck's conflict with the Roman church and political
Catholicism in the seventies and eighties), the Centrum party constituted a fortified political sanctuary for Germany's Roman Catholics.
   But the Centrum "tower" was not assailed by external enemies
alone; during the post-Bismarckian or Wilhelmine era (c. 1890–
1914/18) of the German Empire, the Centrists fell prey to internal
factional strife. Such conflict was not to be unexpected, for the
Centrum party was a unique phenomenon. In sharp contrast to
other German political parties—National Liberals, Progressives,
Social Democrats, Conservatives, and Free Conservatives—which
were relatively homogeneous in their social composition, the Centrum was remarkably diverse. Other parties might have their differences, but, as Bismarck noted, the Centrum had "not merely two
souls" but "seven," all reflecting "the colors of the political rain-
bow from the extreme right to the most radical left."[1] Composed
of socially disparate elements and interests (Germans and Poles, industrialists and workers, aristocrats and peasants, and a wide range
of the middle classes), the Centrum party was held together with
only the utmost difficulty by a common religious faith. Whereas

the party acquired extraordinary political cohesion in the course of the Kulturkampf, the termination of that struggle dissolved those confessional ties which were essential to the unity of the party.

As systematic governmental repression gave way to less overt discrimination, social, economic, and political questions took precedence over religious issues. Inner cleavages, suppressed because of the exigencies of the church-state conflict, became sharper. Centrist policy tended to polarize less around ecclesiastical and religious issues *per se* as new socio-political considerations began to intrude more and more into the foreground. Although the party endeavored to represent and somehow harmonize diversified interests within its own ranks, it was confronted with a tactical dilemma. The Centrum faced essentially two choices. On the one hand, it could seek to de-emphasize its confessional identity and purport to be a purely political party. This would exorcise traditional Protestant fears regarding the party's ties to Rome and facilitate the working of Centrist legislation through the national and state parliaments. On the other hand, it could adopt an intransigent pose, immuring itself as it were in a beleaguered citadel, and seek to infuse strength into its ranks by raising the cry of religious persecution. In short, the Centrum had to decide if it was a political party or a religious interest group; it had to choose between secularism and sectarianism. Both options were self-defeating. Without its sectarian penumbra, the party jeopardized its internal unity. If, however, the Centrum comported itself as a sectarian organization, it relegated itself to political isolation. The choice between sectarianism and secularism exposed the party to rifts of considerable dimensions, splitting the Centrist rank and file along its social faultings. Thus the Centrum "tower" was undermined from within. Besieged from without, divided by factional bickering from within, the Centrum was a beleaguered tower.

Wilhelmine Germany's religio-political conflicts and the Centrum party's internal development and strife have been accorded little of the attention they deserve.[2] Forgetting the importance of religious hostility, historians have tended to ignore the persistence of many issues of the Kulturkampf, even though Bismarck ceased his attack on the Roman church in the eighties.[3] Although the diplomatic agreement of 1887 between Berlin and Rome officially settled outstanding church-state problems, it did not terminate anti-Catholic prejudice. Systematic repression merely gave way to indirect discrimination. The end of the Kulturkampf also did not regulate or solve the question of how the Roman Catholic population should fit into a religiously mixed society which was dominated by Prot-

estants. Less concerned with ecclesiastical matters, the basic complaint of Roman Catholics in this new situation was directed against
social and political disqualifications which denied them equality of
civil rights in Wilhelmine society.

If the termination of the Kulturkampf did not end religious discrimination, neither did it deprive the Centrum party of its *raison
d'etre*. No longer preoccupied with the defense of the church's interests, the party instead concerned itself with the unequal status
of Roman Catholics in Wilhelmine Germany. This cause, known as
the "Parity Question," was dedicated to the elimination of discrimination in the laws of the Empire and the states, in governmental
service and the professions, and in politics. My analysis of the Centrum in the quarter century preceding the First World War turns on
the discussion of this "Parity Question." It provides a Wagnerian
leitmotif for the entire study. From this leitmotif several secondary
themes unfold to form a more comprehensive picture of the problems plaguing the Centrum party and its auxiliary organizations in
the post-Kulturkampf era. Lacking the relative social homogeneity
of other parties, the Centrum itself was beset with a "parity question" of its own. The party's efforts to achieve equality for Roman
Catholics within Wilhelmine society were paralleled by the attempts
of classes and interests within Roman Catholicism itself to integrate
into their own confessional community on the basis of parity.

Although I examine a number of theoretical and practical issues
facing the Centrum party and its partisans, I attempt to go beyond
a mere discussion of clearly defined frictions and disputes in order
to place them in a broader perspective. The "parity question" writ
small confronting political Catholicism, it is argued, mirrored the
same issues facing the German nation as a whole—the integration
on the basis of equality of religious and social minorities. But there
is still another reason for my concern with this topic. The conjunction of religion and politics is an important component in any discussion of the larger and more significant "German Question," the
failure of liberal democracy to develop satisfactorily in Germany.[4]

To deal with these complex socio-political problems clearly, it
has been necessary to avoid a narrative and chronological approach.
This is, moreover, neither a religious history nor a study of political
Catholicism's role in the Reichstag and in the state diets. It does
not aim at completeness as a party history, but is intended as a
contribution toward understanding the religio-political problem
in the German Empire. My study concerns itself with sectarianism
not as a system of religious beliefs, but as a significant factor in

Germany's social and political history. With reference to the peculiar problem of religion and interest-group politics, this study has
several aims. First of all, it draws attention to the abiding importance of religion in German politics. Second, it discusses the pervasiveness and the intractable character of anti-Catholicism in Wilhelmine Germany. Third, it assesses the impact of the "Parity Question" on the Centrum party's factional disputes and political stance.
Fourth, following an examination of the Centrum's tactical choice
between a sectarian or secular image for the party, it places these
issues in the context of the Church of Rome's confrontation with
secularism and the growing de-confessionalization of the Centrum
party. Fifth, this investigation relates these conflicts to still another
quest for equality (this time within Roman Catholicism itself) as
workers endeavored to attain "parity" with other Roman Catholic
interest groups. Sixth, it explains the reasons for the success of the
political, nonsectarian image of the Centrum. And finally, this study
gives attention to the impact of these problems on German society
as a whole. Although the Centrum represented a religious minority,
it exercised an amazing degree of power and influence. But in the
furtherance of that power, the party collaborated with antidemocrat-
ic forces, inhibited political and social reform in Imperial Germany,
and revealed the inherent contradictions or dilemmas within German
political Catholicism.

*   *   *   *

In the preparation of this book, it was necessary to confront certain orthographical problems regarding the proper spelling of cities
and towns. Territories important to this study and which were once
part of the German Empire have changed political hands. Alsace-
Lorraine and Silesia, for instance, are now part of France and Poland. Accompanying this political shift came a change in spelling
or names for numerous communities. In order to maintain historical
accuracy and consistency, however, I deemed it best to adhere to
the German nomenclature. The capital of Silesia therefore is identified as Breslau, not Wroclaw, its present Polish appellation. Other
Silesian cities, communities, and towns also retain their German or-
thography in this book. Similarly, the French city of Strasbourg is
identified as Strassburg, the German spelling.

For the sake of clarity, an anomaly in German spelling must also
be noted. Although it remained without interruption under German

control, one municipality underwent a recent orthographical change. The present town of Mönchengladbach, a textile center located some fifty-six kilometers northwest of Cologne, was known variously as München-Gladbach or M.-Gladbach in Imperial Germany. To maintain consistency, I have again discarded the current and retained the old spelling.

NOTES TO PREFACE

1. Quoted in Felix Rachfahl, "Windthorst und der Kulturkampf," *Preussische Jahrbücher*, CXXXVI (Apr.-June 1909), 71.

2. For recent historiographical trends concerning Wilhelmine Germany, see John Snell, "Imperial Germany's Tragic Era, 1888-1918," *Journal of Central European Affairs*, XVIII (1959), 380-395, XIX (1959), 57-75; and James J. Sheehan, "Germany, 1890-1918: A Survey of Recent Research," *Central European History*, I, 4 (Dec. 1968), 345-372.

3. The basic work on this subject—Karl Bachem, *Vorgeschichte, Geschichte und Politik der Deutschen Zentrumspartei*, 9 vols. (Cologne, 1927-1932)—despite the richness of its material and the comprehensiveness of its scope, is informed by emotional overtones and partisanship which limit its usefulness. More recently, following a period of neglect, attention is once again being given long-forgotten religio-political problems in Wilhelmine Germany. Good examples of this renewed interest are Rudolf Morsey, "Die deutschen Katholiken und der Nationalstaat zwischen Kulturkampf und erstem Weltkrieg," *Historisches Jahrbuch*, XC (1970), 31-64; Klaus Müller, "Zentrumspartei und agrarische Bewegung im Rheinland, 1882-1903," in *Spiegel der Geschichte: Festgabe für Max Braubach*, edited by Konrad Repgen and Stephan Skalweit (Münster, 1964), pp. 822-857; Dan Silverman, "Political Catholicism and Social Democracy in Alsace-Lorraine, 1871-1914," *The Catholic Historical Review*, LII (Apr. 1966), 39-65; Manfred Stadelhofer, *Der Abbau der Kulturkampfgesetzgebung im Grossherzogtum Baden, 1871-1918*, Vol. III: *Veröffentlichungen der Kommission für Zeitgeschichte bei der Katholischen Akademie in Bayern* (Mainz, 1969); and John K. Zeender, "German Catholics and the Concept of an Interconfessional Party, 1900-1922," *Journal of Central European Affairs*, XXIII (Jan. 1964), 424-439. One should also consult Karl Buchheim, *Ultramontanismus und Demokratie: Der Weg der deutschen Katholiken im 19. Jahrhundert* (Munich, 1963) and especially the introductory chapter of Rudolf Morsey, *Die Deutsche Zentrumspartei, 1917-1923*, Vol. XXXII: *Beiträge zur Geschichte des Parlamentarismus und der politischen Parteien* (Düsseldorf, 1967). These publications notwithstanding, there is no reason to revise Sheehan's conclusion that "the Catholic Center is the least well studied of the major German parties." See "Germany, 1890-1918," 349.

4. An excellent discussion of the "German Question" is found in Ralf Dahrendorf, *Society and Democracy in Germany* (Garden City, N.Y., 1967), pp. 3-17.

ACKNOWLEDGMENTS

I have incurred many obligations in the writing of this book. My study of religion, politics, and society in Imperial Germany was begun as a dissertation under the direction of Professor Gerald D. Feldman of the University of California, Berkeley. For his many kindnesses and constant encouragement I owe an immense debt of gratitude. In addition, I am grateful for the helpful suggestions and incisive criticisms offered by Professors Russell H. Bartley, Wolfgang Sauer, Paul Seabury, James J. Sheehan, and Philip Shashko.

To the University of Wisconsin-Milwaukee I also owe many thanks. My work was facilitated by a Research Travel Grant and through the efforts of the Library to obtain for me materials difficult of access. Equally valuable was the contribution of Mr. Donald G. Temple and his assistants in the university's Cartographic Services Laboratory. With meticulous care they prepared the maps for this volume.

My indebtedness to individuals and institutions in Europe is no less great. In Germany and Poland I am indebted to the directors and staffs of the *Bayerisches Hauptstaatsarchiv* in Munich, the *Bistumsarchiv* in Trier, the *Bundesarchiv* in Coblenz, the archives of the German Foreign Ministry in Bonn, the municipal archives of Cologne and Mönchengladbach, the state archives in Coblenz and Münster, the *Stegerwald-Archiv* in Cologne, the *Archiwum Archidiecezjalne* in Wroclaw, and the *Biblioteka Śląska* in Katowice. Although more people overseas have helped in the completion of this work than I can ever acknowledge, I especially wish to thank Bishop Wincenty Urban for his assistance and the many kindnesses shown to me and my wife while we were his guests in the Episcopal Archives of Wroclaw. I should also like to thank particularly Dr. Wolfgang Löhr of the *Stadtarchiv* in Mönchengladbach for his invaluable bibliographic advice.

And finally, I wish to acknowledge a debt to my wife, Dawn Louise Ross. She helped this work to completion by copying documents and typing various versions of the manuscript. To her, my warmest thanks.

Needless to say, none of these persons or institutions bears any responsibility for errors in fact or interpretation in this book. All its shortcomings are my own. What merits it might have are due largely to their assistance.

1: CONFESSION AND COMMUNITY

> Das aber muss ich aussprechen, der Unglaube
> wächst, und das Katholische wächst auch. Und
> das Katholische, das ist das Schlimmere. Göt-
> zendienst ist schlimmer als Unglaube.
>
> Tante Adelheid[1]

The nature and character of the Roman Catholic community's external relations with the rest of German society was the result of that country's peculiar social development, territorial changes, and intractable political conflict.

Ever since the Reformation the German people have been divided on the all-important question of religious belief. With a population two-thirds Evangelical and one-third Roman Catholic, "no other major state of the world," the trade-union leader Adam Stegerwald could declare in 1912, "reveals a similar strong percentage of adherents of both confessions as Germany." Under the circumstances, he concluded, sectarian animosities "react much more strongly upon public and economic life" in his homeland "than in almost all other large states."[2] Although Stegerwald was a Roman Catholic, many Protestants shared his view and concern. Even the *Deutsche Zeitung*, a newspaper having ties with the Evangelical League, declared in 1905 that "neither Liberal nor Conservative, plutocracy or Social Democracy" were the "decisive contrasts" in German society. More important was the *"hard-fought* [religious] *struggle* since *1517."*[3] This broad division between Protestant and Roman Catholic, together with the sectarian enmity that existed between these creeds, remained of consequence throughout Germany's modern history and necessitated arrangements to render superfluous confessional strife.

It is surely one of history's ironies that Protestantism did not triumph everywhere in Germany, the country which witnessed the beginnings of the Reformation. The achievement of successful reli-

1

gious reform in Germany was due more to the decision of the
princes than of the people. The Reformation, moreover, was introduced at the territorial level, in such places as Brandenburg-Prussia,
Mecklenburg, or Saxony. But the nation as a whole remained divided. This division, the result of an incomplete religious revolution, kept confessional enmities alive which in turn provided an
ideological underpinning to traditional regional political rivalries.
Interaction, both hostile and cooperative, between Protestantism
and Roman Catholicism established a framework in which much
of the history of modern Germany was played out. Pronounced
sectarian differences came into conjunction with other problems
inhibiting that country's breakthrough into a modern political and
social order.

Recent efforts to explain Germany's failure to modernize its
constitutional life and to democratize its society generally presup-
pose a failure regarding the political and industrial revolutions.[4]
The basic theme of this argument is that Germany was denied a
successful popular revolution "from below," a true popular upheaval sweeping the whole nation, with its motive force provided
by the masses. Attempts to achieve such a fundamental revolution—as in the Peasant War of the sixteenth century, the upheavals
in 1848, and the insurrection of 1918—all resulted in utter and
complete failure. And yet Germany was changed and modernized.
Because of insufficient social development and the overriding necessity to force the pace of change to make the state more effi-
cient and effective, reform in its German context appeared as "revolution from above," carried out by the government itself. The
revolution from above was not such a complete upheaval that it
created a radically different state. Fundamental traditions, admittedly in a modified manner, were continued. This revolution from
above was not a mere episode in German history. It was an event
or phenomenon which occurred again and again. What it entailed
was an improvement in the social and political order under the direction of a disinterested, supra-party agency acting as a supreme
arbiter. While neither appreciably extending the range of political
freedom nor encouraging the active participation of the masses in
political affairs, such reform represented a kind of "incomplete
revolution"—change designed to fend off the social consequences of
successful revolution thereby leaving the traditional elites in power.
This was a peculiarly German phenomenon.[5]

If Germany did not have a thorough-going political revolution
which transferred power from one social class to another, the

country nevertheless was revolutionized in an economic sense. The transition from the estates system to a modern society, which had affected western Europe first, after the Wars of Liberation (1813–1815) began to affect Germany as well. But in Germany it worked itself out in a different way. In the West the existence of a capitalist economic system and the industrial revolution provided the motive force for social change. Through these factors there took place a shift in economic power from the aristocracy to the middle classes. The middle classes used their newly acquired economic strength to seize political power. In Germany, economic development was impeded by political fragmentation into several states as well as by other factors. As a result, the shift in power from one class to another was not as perceptible as in the West. Industrialization in Germany was the result of economic policies of bureaucratic reformers whose objective, as in the case of political reform (or even the Reformation), was to strengthen the state. But even here the nature and character of this kind of industrial revolution was such that it was not accompanied by its social corollary, the emergence of a wealthy, self-confident, and numerous middle class. Economic development, largely under the auspices of the state itself, led to an unbalanced development of German society. Germany emerged a capitalist nation with but a few capitalists. Hence industrial capitalists did not exist as a serious political force.

This two-dimensional "revolution from above" produced a peculiar amalgam of revitalized authoritarianism and modern industry, leaving the country economically progressive but socially and politically backward. Under these conditions, Germany was unable to break through to social and political modernity.

Such arguments, however, ignore still another "incomplete revolution" in Germany—the religious. Neither the Protestant Reformation nor the Roman Catholic Counter Reformation emerged entirely victorious within Germanic Central Europe. In that respect, Germany's religious experience was quite unlike that of other countries—England and France, for example—that subsequently made the transition to liberal parliamentary government. In the former country the Reformation was successfully implemented, whereas in the latter the Counter Reformation, though not without resistance, was brought to completion. Germany, on the other hand, witnessed a stalemate between Protestant and Roman Catholic. This situation, too, was a cause of the aberrations of German evolution.

The significance of the religious dualism in Germany was not

simply that the possibility for sectarian friction was ever present.
Confessional dualism meant that Germany, in attempting to cope
with political and social questions, invariably had to grapple with
the additional problem of irreconcilable religious interests, which
encumbered the solution of other questions. England and France,
to continue the comparison, made the transition to modernity and
liberal, parliamentary political systems largely because they passed
through the traumatic experiences of national unification, religious, political, and socio-economic upheavals in sequence and, as
a result, with success. England, already a united country, had its
religious Reformation in the sixteenth century, its political revolution in the seventeenth, and its industrial revolution in the eighteenth and nineteenth centuries. France's experience was similar.
It too was a unified nation before it passed through a religious crisis which ended with the victory of the Counter Reformation and
the reestablishment of confessional uniformity in the late sixteenth
and seventeenth centuries. Beginning in 1789, a political revolution
wrenched France out of its traditional past and permitted the
country to develop in the direction of social and political modernity. Not until this development was relatively stabilized did the
French have to face their next ordeal, the socio-economic troubles
associated with industrialization. In the case of both England and
France a particular pattern can be discerned: their "moderniza-
tion" proceeded in progressive stages, allowing for the consolida-
tion of each change; moreover, their confessional revolution or
counterrevolution was complete in that sectarian minorities did
not continue to exist in numbers strong enough to inform policies
regarding subsequent crises in society.[6]

Unlike other nations, the Germans faced the conjunction of several problems at the same time. Germany's religious failure indicated that the ever divisive confessional issue continued to inform
political and social issues in that country. Because of this situation,
the Germans confronted all their problems—national unity, politi-
cal-constitutional, industrial, and social—simultaneously in the
nineteenth century.[7] These circumstances could not fail to ad-
versely affect Germany's development toward modernity. Comprising one of the chief elements within this matrix, of course, was
that nation's religious dualism.

Following the Reformation there existed within the Germanic
cultural area an approximate equality in numbers between Protestant and Roman Catholic. Because neither sect could attain ascendancy over the other, some means had to be devised by which reli-

gious conflict could be rendered unnecessary.[8] The most significant of these arrangements were the Peace of Augsburg and the
Treaty of Westphalia.

The Peace of Augsburg in 1555 did not result in a basic and fundamental agreement about religious beliefs. But it did stipulate
that the two major creeds were permitted to coexist in Germany
as equals. As a collective entity, then, not as individuals, the Lutherans attained a tentative recognition and equality of rights with
the Roman Catholics.[9]

What was begun in the Peace of Augsburg was elaborated upon
by legal specialists during the subsequent decades. By the early
seventeenth century the prevailing opinion among Protestants, formulated and rooted in secular ideas of justice, was to view religious peace as an order based on confessional parity in which both
faiths, as corporate entities, were equals, each enjoying the same
claim to legitimacy. Aware that the Protestants were outnumbered
not in the general population but in the various Reich institutions
(the Imperial Supreme Court, for example), the Lutheran party resisted decisions based on a majority vote in religious issues. They
demanded instead the convening of a special committee composed
of equal numbers of Protestants and Roman Catholics to insure
equality of treatment for the two religious parties.[10]

Corporate equality as a means of neutralizing sectarian conflict
was reflected in the negotiations leading to and embodied in the
Treaty of Westphalia itself. That the peace congress sat for seven
years, between 1642 and 1648, in two separate but equal conclaves in the province of Westphalia symbolized the concept of religious parity between the warring factions. Whereas all previous
efforts to secure permanent equality of confessions failed, the
Treaty of Westphalia for the first time explicitly recognized the
principal of equality between the major creeds (Protestant, which
by then included Calvinist and Lutheran, and Roman Catholic) of
the German Empire. Reinforcing this confessional parity was the
fact that the treaty embodied the concept of reciprocity in all special cases of dispute. Even the membership of the Supreme Court
was at last apportioned on the basis of religious parity.[11] With this
treaty, therefore, a new, permanent, ordered system was created
permitting the principal faiths to coexist as corporate equals down
to the Seven Weeks' War, a time span of nearly two centuries.

Within this context, however, parity was raised to the point of
parody. An extreme case was offered by the Hanovarian town of
Osnabrück. Ever since the Treaty of Westphalia, Osnabrück was

distinguished by a constitutional peculiarity. Delicately balanced
between a predominantly Roman Catholic cathedral chapter and a
Protestant estate-assembly, a political solution was achieved whereby the office of territorial Prince-Bishop alternated between Catholic and Protestant incumbents.[12] Such an arrangement epitomized
confessional parity between the religious beliefs.

As long as no changes were introduced to upset the confessional
equilibrium of this system, there was harmony and an absence of
sectarian conflict. Not that there was no enmity between the religious faiths. But that hostility was directed outward where it could
be handled by treaty and institutional arrangements. Within the
territorial states religious minorities were virtually nonexistent and
hence no source of concern. If the German Empire was divided
along sectarian lines, the separate states were confessionally homogeneous, the result of such principles as *jus reformandi* and *cujus
regio, ejus religio* which permitted the territorial prince to implement the reformed faith or to reimpose the dogmas of the Roman
church on his population. The assertion of this princely prerogative resulted in uniformity of religious belief within the frontiers
of the territorial state. Until this confessional homogeneity began
to break down at the territorial level, corporate equality was possible. But with the territorial changes beginning in the eighteenth
century, states with confessionally mixed inhabitants were formed,
giving equality a triple meaning in Germany. Anxiety was expressed not simply for corporate equality, but for a numerical
equilibrium between the creeds, and equality in treatment for the
adherents of the different faiths within the regional states, a concern which resulted in a new parity question.

The first of the German territorial states to confront this problem was Prussia.[13] Not until the acquisition of Silesia in 1742 did
Prussia cease to be solely a Protestant state. Until then the Roman
church had no unified organization within the Hohenzollern territories and the number of Roman Catholics was very small. The incorporation of the new province, however, increased the number
of Roman Catholic inhabitants some eightfold. And for the first
time since the Reformation, a Bishop of the Roman creed became
a Prussian subject.[14]

If the essentially Protestant character of Prussia remained undi-
luted and unchanged until the War of the Austrian Succession, the
confessional equilibrium between the major creeds established for
Germany as a whole in the Peace of Westphalia was threatened by
the French Revolution. That revolution was not without its im-

pact on the religio-political situation in Germany. In the Final Recess [*Reichsdeputationshauptschluss*] of the Holy Roman Empire of the German Nation issued in 1803, just before its destruction by Napoleon, numerous tiny principalities were absorbed by their more powerful neighbors. However much it rationalized Germany's political geography, this Recess affected the Roman Catholic church in two ways. On the one hand it mediatized or dissolved the petty ecclesiastical territories, and on the other it secularized ecclesiastical property. Not only did this move change the status of the German episcopate but it deprived the church of much of its material basis. While doubtless a grievous blow for the Roman church, it would be a simplification if mediatization and secularization were simply described as high-handed theft on the part of the state. Both the destruction of ecclesiastical sovereignty and the secularization of the church's wealth diverted the church from its preoccupation with material interests and heightened its concern for spiritual issues. Accompanying the reorganization of Germany and the de-secularization of the church, German Roman Catholicism experienced a spiritual regeneration. Whereas in the eighteenth century the church was morally lax and overly concerned with temporal matters and viewed more or less as an extension of the state, Roman Catholicism during the early decades of the nineteenth century underwent a transformation. The Roman church turned away from its moral indifference and scepticism and increasingly resisted the subordination of church to state.[15]

The Final Recess also contained provisions regulating the relationship between the Christian creeds. Freedom of religion was guaranteed in all the German territories as of the confessional situation in February 1803. What this signified was that the year 1803 was substituted for the religious arrangement established by the Treaty of Westphalia. This guarantee was especially important for the inhabitants of those territories that passed under the sovereignty of rulers belonging to a different faith.[16]

Following the defeat of Napoleonic France, the Congress of Vienna also made an effort in 1815 to safeguard the religious peace in Germany. Article 16 of the Federal Act, the legislation which established the German Confederation, established freedom of conscience. But such a provision failed to fully establish parity and tolerance. Close reading of Article 16 reveals that it neither permitted the existence of every sect in all the German states nor placed the Christian creeds on the same legal footing. Furthermore, it failed to concede to the adherents of the chief faiths the

same measure of freedom regarding conscience and the practice of
their religion. What Article 16 did guarantee was full legal equality
for the individual adherent of the Christian faiths in matters of citizenship and political rights. Such rights included a personal claim
to individual freedom of conscience, but they did not embrace the
notion of corporate religious freedom for sectarian organizations.
Nor for that matter did the article extend the right to practice
one's faith publicly.[17]

All this indicated that existing provisions to regulate the religious peace were inadequate. And yet confessionally mixed populations necessitated some means to insure peaceful coexistence between the creeds. This was all the more urgent because a shift in
the ideological climate increased the likelihood for sectarian conflict.[18] The decline of the Enlightenment and Rationalism was accompanied by a revival of religiosity which came into conjunction
with the confessional dualism created by territorial changes. Such
a situation demanded religious toleration and equality.

Prussia, the first German state to lose its confessional homogeneity, was thus the first to face this problem. Actually a tolerant
stance in the Hohenzollern lands was prefigured by the existence
since 1613 of a Calvinist dynasty and a Lutheran population. The
existence of other religious beliefs was also countenanced for pragmatic reasons. Out of military necessity, Friedrich Wilhelm I permitted Roman Catholic spiritual exercises for soldiers of that
creed recruited from non-Evangelical regions lying outside Prussia's frontiers. Dictating similar ecclesiastical dispensations was the
king's plans for the establishment of royal arsenals, the staff of
which would have to be composed or ordnance experts recruited
from Roman Catholic Liége.[19] These dispensations, however, fell
short of real toleration and equality.

Toleration received its formal recognition in the General Law
Code of 1794 which specifically guaranteed individual freedom of
conscience. This was supplemented by subsequent decrees. In order to ease the assimilation of the Rhineland, for instance, a guarantee of religious freedom was contained in the Patent of Possession
issued by Prussia in 1815.[20]

But toleration was not equality. Toleration amounted to no
more than forebearance. It was not viewed as an inalienable right
and was subject at any time to revocation. Genuine parity denoted
equality of rights or "equality of treatment for the different religious confessions." This transcended what is commonly under-
stood by the term "nondenominational." Equality of this kind

called for "separate and equal" coexistence between Germany's religions.[21] Only under those conditions could confessional minorities exist within society and enjoy parity in status with the majority of the population.

Formal recognition of equality in this special sense was never fully attained in Prussia. Complaints about alleged discrimination as a result increased after 1815. But accelerating progress in the direction of equality were the revolutions of 1848.[22] Although the ecclesiastical parts of the Frankfurt constitution went far toward granting equality, that document died with the failure of the revolution. In spite of this failure, however, the Berlin government, in a conciliatory gesture to forestall further trouble, issued a constitution for the Hohenzollern kingdom. Included in that document were certain provisions which guaranteed ecclesiastical privileges and further narrowed the state's autonomy in church matters.[23] As adopted in 1850, this constitution ushered in a period of unprecedented autonomy for the Roman church in Prussia, a situation which had no parallel in any other European state down to 1871.[24]

These changed circumstances—confessionally mixed territories, the inability to accommodate a religious minority on a fully equal basis, and rising sectarian feeling—necessitated painful readjustments on the part of both the governments and the various religious groups. This process led inevitably to sectarian friction and open church-state conflict.

Indicative of the uneasiness between the major creeds was the dispute concerning the incorporation of the Rhineland into Prussia, a kingdom popularly identified as the bastion of Protestantism, following the Congress of Vienna. Seeking to accelerate the assimilation of the newly acquired province, the population of which was two-thirds Roman Catholic, the Prussians sought to effectively neutralize Cologne, the natural capital for the Rhineland, as a cultural and political focal point. Scrupulously avoiding Cologne, the Prussians located the administrative apparatus and the military command in Coblenz, the university in Bonn, and the Land Captaincy, together with the Art Academy in Düsseldorf, decentralizing the administrative and cultural organs in the newly acquired territory and checking any possibility that Cologne might rival the Hohenzollern capital as a second, Roman Catholic "Berlin."[25] Whatever the degree of sectarian animosity in this policy, such an action, when added to other discriminatory activities, estranged the Roman Catholic population from the rest of Prussian society.

Other developments also encouraged the Rhenish Roman Catholic population to ascribe confessional motives to Berlin and to complain of discriminatory practices. In its personnel policy, for instance, the government betrayed a marked preference for Evangelicals. Despite its Roman Catholic majority, the Prussian Rhine Province never had an *Oberpräsident* of that creed during the entire nineteenth century. Nor did overwhelmingly Roman Catholic districts like Cologne and Trier—with the exception of a few weeks during the revolutionary disturbances in 1848—have a *Regierungspräsident* of that faith. Numerous Roman Catholic communities never had a *Landrat* of that denomination. And during the *Vormärz* there were even cases of Roman Catholic towns where the mayor was the only Protestant, having been appointed to the post by the Prussian government.[26] Discrimination of this kind belied Berlin's claims that religious equality existed in Prussia.

Personnel grievances concerning Roman Catholics were not restricted to the Rhenish area. Prussian Roman Catholics complained that their coreligionists were virtually unrepresented among civil servants in the upper echelons of the administration. Dissatisfaction was also expressed because no ambassadors to foreign states were adherents of the Roman faith. And although Roman Catholics were represented within the army officer corps, few, it was said, were promoted to the senior grades. Only Count August Neithardt von Gneisenau, a national hero and Roman Catholic, attained the rank of general. It was widely believed by his coreligionists that if not for his heroism in the Napoleonic wars even he would never have risen beyond the rank of captain or major.[27] Under the circumstances Roman Catholics concluded that though they were tolerated they were not treated as the equals of their Protestant fellow citizens in Prussia.

These conclusions were reinforced by subsequent experience. The governmental decrees of February, May, and July 1852 imposed restrictions on alien clergy functioning in Prussia, particularly on their missionary activities in predominantly Protestant areas. Simultaneously, Berlin forbade the attendance at the Collegium Germanicum in Rome by clerics of Prussian citizenship.[28] Issued by Karl Otto von Raumer, the Prussian Minister of Culture, these orders were designed to curb proselytism and maintain the confessional peace. This latter aim, however, was vitiated by the fact that Prussian Roman Catholics coalesced into a confessional parliamentary organization (known as the Catholic *Fraktion*) to defend their interests. What Roman Catholics held to be unequal treatment from their government led to parliamentary conflict along sectarian lines. By 1859, this Roman Catholic group in the Prussian Landtag adopted the name Centrum, a label it retained until the party ceased to exist in 1866-1867.[29]

Also testifying to the persistence of the confessional issue, especially the strained relations between Roman Catholic and Protestant, were the expressions of anti-Catholic sentiment during the Austro-Prussian conflict. As early as May 1866 anti-Catholic tendencies intensified, manifesting themselves in the newspaper press. The *Norddeutsche Allgemeine Zeitung*, for example, referred to the Habsburgs as "the mortal enemy of the Evangelical church," a sentiment that found reinforcement in the Conservative *Kreuzzeitung's* pronouncement "that a religious war is brewing, perhaps as bloody as the Thirty Years' War 200 years before." Similar views were shared by the educated classes. In his inaugural address, the Rector of the Prussian University of Greifswald spoke of an imminent "Gustavus Adolphus ride through Catholic territory," an opinion that his audience greeted with enthusiasm. Similar sentiments met with the approbation of broad sections of the Prussian bureaucracy, a collective group which in any case never fully reconciled itself to carrying out those constitutional provisions of 1850 guaranteeing religious rights.[30] All this, together with the propensity to herald Prussian military successes over Austria and Bavaria as the victory of Protestantism, indicated that the external relations of the Roman Catholic community with the rest of German society were subjected to strain.

Austria's defeat at the hands of Prussia in 1866 portended serious dislocations for German Roman Catholics living outside Habsburg control and further threatened the Roman Catholic position within Prussia. The dissolution of the German Confederation, the displacement in the balance of power in Germanic Central Europe from Roman Catholic Austria to Protestant Prussia, could not but signify a serious defeat for the adherents of the Roman church within Germany.[31] Austria, with a ruling dynasty closely identified with the Roman faith, constituted a bulwark for Roman Catholics against the intolerance of their Evangelical countrymen. Its exclusion from German affairs, together with the establishment—albeit temporary—of autonomy for the South German states, relegated the Roman Catholic population to permanent minority status, casting doubt about the future of religious equality. Within the new North German Confederation not only did the Hohenzollern kingdom achieve an unassailable position of hegemony but eight million members of the Roman faith faced twenty million Evangelicals, a ratio of 2:5. While numerical parity between the two creeds did not exist in Prussia before 1866, the existence of constitutional guarantees and the presence of Roman Catholic states within the Confederation neutralized most Roman Catholic fears, even if it did not mute all complaints and conflict. Without Austria, however, or even in the absence of the predominantly Roman Catholic South German states, there was no longer an effective counterweight to the Protestant interest.[32]

Although the Franco-German war of 1870–1871 resulted in the adhesion of the South German states to the Prussian-led North to form the German Empire, the new political alignment did not restore the confessional equilibrium of the German Confederation. Reduced to minority status—one-third of the population—the Roman Catholic community was neither concentrated in one area nor evenly distributed throughout the nation. Large numbers were to be found in the South and Southwest where Bavaria and Baden were overwhelmingly Roman Catholic. Württemberg, despite its essentially Protestant character, also had a sizable and influential Roman Catholic minority. Prussia, on the other hand, though predominantly Protestant, shared with the German Empire as a whole the distinction of possessing a Roman Catholic community that comprised one-third of the total population. While this confessional minority did not constitute a monolithic bloc, in specific localities Roman Catholics actually were in the majority. For example, the Rhenish districts and Westphalia in western Prussia were largely Roman Catholic in confessional composition. Adherents of the Roman faith were also to be found in large numbers along Prussia's eastern frontiers. Even if we exclude for purpose of analysis the province of Posen because it was overwhelming Polish in ethnic population, Silesia—Upper Silesia in particular—possessed a sizable Roman Catholic population of German extraction. This geographic dispersion made for the heterogeneity of both the German and Prussian Roman Catholic population, a circumstance that not only underscored the regional and local diversity of Roman Catholicism in Germany, but also impeded the formation of a unified Roman Catholic stance. A multiplicity of local interests, therefore, reinforced the significant disparity in numbers between the two major Christian faiths.

Subsequent events alienated Roman Catholics even more from the general community. Not infrequently, publicists chose to interpret the events of 1870–1871 as the ineluctable consequence of Protestant principles. Informed by an anti-Catholic bias, these interpretations indiscriminately attributed Germany's past misfortunes to the Habsburgs, the Jesuits, the papacy, or more generally,

the Counter Reformation. Anti-Catholicism was rampant. Writing in
March 1872 Lord Odo Russell, the British Ambassador to Berlin,
was impressed by the degree of hostility toward the Roman faith.
Enthusiasm greeting Bismarck's measures against the church in the
early stages of the Kulturkampf, he said, exceeded even the joy
surrounding the declarations of war against Austria and France.[33]
Recent literature in 1870–1871—Conrad Ferdinand Meyer's novels
and stories about Ulrich von Hutten's last days or the period of the
Thirty Years' War and Gustavus Adolphus—bore witness to anti-
Catholic prejudice. Ludwig Anzengruber's *Der Pfarrer von Kirchfeld*
(1870), an attack on the Roman church's narrow-minded dogmatism, was also indicative of these deep-seated confessional tensions.
Even more popular than these stories, however, were Wilhelm
Busch's satirical anti-Catholic cartoons *Der heilige Antonius von
Padua, Die fromme Helene,* and *Pater Filucius.* Nowhere was this
animus more graphically portrayed than in the sketches and verse
of Busch. Despite the worst lapses of taste, he gave expression to
the deep-seated hostility toward the pious philistinism so widely
associated with Roman Catholics.[34]   On occasion, this animosity
erupted into open violence as, for instance, in August 1869, when
rioters attacked a small Roman church and orphanage in the Berlin
suburb of Moabit. Anticlericals even used this incident to demand
the abolition of monasteries and other religious foundations.[35]
Alienating Roman Catholics even further was the fact that all too
often apologists for the new German Empire, Bismarck included,
injudiciously spoke of the "Protestant Kaiser." Such a dignity, in
the minds of Roman Catholics, was not rooted in the "sacred" and
medieval concept of universal monarchy,[36] but in nationalism, a
basis both temporary and corrosive of religious tradition and belief.
Moreover, the title accentuated the apprehension that they, as a
community, were extraneous to this society. In their opinion, a
Protestant Empire offered little prospect for religious parity.

   The changed circumstances of the confessional situation, the result of territorial changes, led not only to increased sectarian friction, but at times to serious religio-political clashes. Of these, the
most important were the "Cologne Troubles" and the Kulturkampf.

   Giving evidence of the strained relationship between Roman
Catholic and Evangelical in Prussia were the so-called "Cologne
Troubles."[37]   This conflict had as its focal point the problem of
mixed marriages, a question of vital importance to the principal
German creeds.[38] Fearing the possible defection of its members,
together with the potential loss to the faith of children resulting

from a confessionally mixed union, the Roman church traditionally
has opposed such marriages. But under the leadership of Count Ferdinand August von Spiegel, since 1825 the Archbishop of Cologne,
church policy was characterized by a compliant attitude regarding
mixed marriages.

Spiegel's conciliatory attitude was not supported by the entire
Roman Catholic community. Chafing since 1815 under an arrogant
and predominantly Protestant bureaucracy and military,[39] many
Roman Catholics perceived in such mixed marriages what they
thought was a "scheme" to "Protestantize" the Rhineland, thereby
facilitating its assimilation into Prussia. The massive influx of Protestant officials from the eastern provinces of the Hohenzollern
lands, together with the rising number of confessionally mixed marriages—the latter encouraged by the archbishop's accomodating attitude—promoted defections from the Roman faith.[40] If equality between the creeds existed in the formulation of the marriage con-
tract, such agreements worked to the advantage of the Evangelicals.

Seeking to resist this trend, Rhenish Roman Catholics were thrust
into the ironic position of opposing the concept of equality in
mixed marriages. Following Count Spiegel's death in 1835, his successor, Clemens August Droste-Vischering, disavowed the previous
working arrangements and chose not to recognize any marriage
where the prospective non-Catholic spouse refused to rear potential
children in the Roman faith. Curiously enough, in the ensuing quarrel between church and state it was the Prussian government which
stood firmly for the equality principle, insisting that the Roman
church consecrate such interfaith marriages even in the absence of
the binding pledges demanded by the ecclesiastical authorities.[41]
Equality of treatment, Berlin argued, was to be meted out to both
creeds.

This conflict over "parity" in marriage, not between the sexes,
but between the sects, led to a religio-political crisis of the first magnitude, attracting public interest and evoking enormous controversy. When Droste-Vischering stubbornly refused to accede to Berlin's
demands, the government lost patience, arrested the obstreperous
prelate in late 1837, and held him under fortress detention.
Prompted by indignation at the arrest of their archbishop, the Roman Catholic community was galvanized into political action, the
first manifestation in Germany of organized Catholicism.[42] The
outstanding expression of their sense of outrage was the famous
tract "Athanasius."[43] Written by Joseph Görres in 1838, this
curious piece of work ignored the contradictions of the archbishop's
position but summarized the grievances of his coreligionists, shifted

the argument away from the dispute concerning equality between the creeds, and emphasized instead the demand for equality between church and state.[44]

Although the "Cologne Troubles" were satisfactorily settled following the accession of Friedrich Wilhelm IV to the throne in 1840 and the establishment of a separate (but equal) department within the Ministry of Culture concerned with Roman Catholic ecclesiastical affairs,[45] latent suspicion and enmity between the faiths did not disappear. While this animosity broke out into occasional open conflict in subsequent years, the most serious religio-political conflict followed the unification of Germany in 1871.

The major religio-political conflict in nineteenth-century Germany was the Kulturkampf.[46] This Kulturkampf, a grandiloquent term meaning the "struggle for civilization," represented a clash between Bismarck and liberalism on the one hand and political Catholicism and the Roman church on the other. Seeking to safeguard their interests in the drastically new circumstances of a confessional imbalance within the recently created German Empire, the Roman Catholic minority, both within truncated Germany and Prussia, coalesced into an organized political movement and reestablished the Centrum party.

Fearing an omnipotent state in which they were the minority, the Centrists placed great emphasis on the question of religious equality. Formulated in the Westphalian town of Soest in October 1870, their political platform included a demand for "the actual implementation of parity for the recognized religions."[47] Anxious to implement this platform, the Centrists demanded legal guarantees which safeguarded the interests of their church and their coreligionists. Two attempts were made, the first in 1867 even before the Centrum was reconstituted, and the second in 1871, to incorporate into the organic laws of the new Germany those paragraphs from the Prussian constitution of 1850 which protected freedom of religion and guaranteed the independence of the churches and their administration.[48] On both occasions these motions were defeated.

Centrist efforts to attain these constitutional guarantees represented a far-reaching attempt by Roman Catholics to regulate, on the basis of equality, the relationship between church and state. This maneuver, coming at virtually the same moment the German Empire came into existence, awakened Bismarck's latent suspicions about political Catholicism.[49] Also encouraging Bismarck to view the Centrum as a threat to the Empire's integrity was his well-founded belief that the party served as a rallying point for such avowedly

hostile elements as Alsatians, Danes, Hanoverian Guelphs, and Poles.
The conjunction of these fears led to the Kulturkampf.

What Bismarck and his partisans attacked was the special status
the Centrists were attempting to obtain for the church in German
society. The government's fundamental object was to separate
church and state and to subordinate the former to the latter. Indicative of this aim was the abolition in July 1871 of the special division for Roman Catholic affairs in the Prussian Ministry of Culture.[50]
Subsequent measures in the Kulturkampf betrayed the same objective. The "May laws," for example, so called because they were first
promulgated in May 1873, introduced educational requirements for
clergy, carefully regulated ecclesiastical appointments, and restricted
the disciplinary power of the Roman church. Other efforts to assert
the state's supremacy over the church followed. Penalties were imposed for noncompliance with the new ecclesiastical legislation. Between 1872 and 1874 several religious orders, beginning with the
Jesuits, were suppressed. And in 1875 the Reichstag passed legislation permitting the expulsion of recalcitrant clergy from German
territory. These measures were also reinforced by the "breadbasket
laws" which terminated state contributions to the church and sal-
aries to the clergy.

Although this punitive legislation failed to break the Roman
church, the Kulturkampf crippled its operations and disrupted its
organization in Germany in general and Prussia in particular. By
1876 almost all Prussian bishops were in exile or prison. And among
the 4,600 parishes in 1880, about 1,100 (involving some two million
Roman Catholics) were without their pastors.[51] The whole experience contributed to the estrangement of the Roman Catholic community from the rest of German society. The memory of the Kulturkampf was seared into the collective consciousness of Roman
Catholics and the fear of its recrudescence exerted considerable influence on their subsequent political behavior.

Bismarck's fears regarding political Catholicism did not subside
with these parliamentary successes. During the Kulturkampf the
Centrum party moved from strength to strength. In 1871 the party
garnered 724,000 votes and secured 63 seats in the Reichstag. Three
years later, in the midst of the Kulturkampf, the Centrum's vote
nearly doubled to 1,446,000 and 91 deputies were sent to Berlin.
This trend persisted. Although obtaining fewer votes (1,341,000) in
the general elections of 1877, the Centrists nonetheless secured 93
parliamentary mandates. This rapid growth, followed by relative
stability, could not long be ignored by Bismarck.

When the Kulturkampf demonstrated that the government could neither neutralize the church nor extirpate the Centrum party, Bismarck took advantage of a papal offer of reconciliation to bring the church-state struggle to an end. The Chancellor pointedly refrained from purely parliamentary discussions and entered instead into direct negotiations with the Roman Curia (the governing body of the church) to end the Kulturkampf and, if possible, relegate the Centrum to client status. While these discussions led to a gradual abatement of the Kulturkampf, they did not result in a final settlement until 1887. Even then, the end of the Kulturkampf brought incomplete relief and satisfaction. Although the diplomatic agreement between Berlin and Rome officially settled outstanding church-state issues, it neither deprived the Centrum of its basis for existence nor reestablished a harmonious relationship between the religious creeds within Germany. It also did little to efface the accumulated residue of ill will and failed to redress all the major grievances (particularly those pertaining to alleged bias and discrimination) of the Prussian Roman Catholic community. This diplomatic accomodation was but a palliative, tending to treat the symptom rather than the root of the confessional problem in Imperial Germany.

2: A SILENT KULTURKAMPF

*Down to the lowest servant only Protestants
can be appointed here.*

Edgar Loening[1]

"As we all know," admitted Chancellor Bernhard von Bülow in
the midst of one of Wilhelmine Germany's periodic religious disputes, "unresolved conflicts remain left over from the time of the
Kulturkampf."[2] Systematic governmental repression of the Roman
church and its adherents during much of the Bismarckian era subsequently gave way to less overt discrimination usually referred to
by Roman Catholics as a "silent" or "creeping" Kulturkampf.[3]
Their basic and universal complaint in this new situation, summed
up in what was called the "Parity Question," reflected aggrieved
confessional feelings concerning the persistence of social and political disqualifications which thwarted Roman Catholic efforts to secure a position equipollent in Wilhelmine society. Testifying to the
existence of such discrimination and prejudice were numerous vestiges of repressive legislation and practices.

* * *

With the end of the Kulturkampf not all the legislation against
the Roman church—some of which antedated the Kulturkampf itself—fell into abeyance.[4] Of the remaining Imperial statutes the
most noxious, in the opinion of the Centrum, was the Jesuit Law.
Passed by the Reichstag in 1872, it comprised three clauses which
(1) suppressed the Jesuit order and its affiliates, (2) exiled or restricted the movements of its membership (about 600 to 800
priests[5]), and (3) invested the Bundesrat with the power to oversee
the execution of these provisions.[6] Continuing agitation by the
Centrum led to the repeal in 1904 of Paragraph 2.[7] Because it was
an incomplete victory the matter refused to disappear from the

18

public view. The remaining clauses of the Jesuit Law (not expunged until April 1917) and the wrangling frustrations of a twenty-five-year-long repeal campaign epitomized for many Roman Catholics the whole issue of legal discrimination.[8]

The Jesuit Law was not the only statute to survive the Kulturkampf. Other laws, particularly at the state level, also refused to wither away—a situation which contributed to Centrist dissatisfaction. Particularly chafing were the civil codes of Brunswick, Mecklenburg, the Kingdom of Saxony, and such "dwarf" states as Coburg-Gotha, Reuss, and Schwarzburg-Sondershausen. The Centrist deputies Ernst Lieber and Franz Pichler enumerated a long list of injustices—the imposition of school taxes for Evangelical institutions, prohibition or restrictions of church services, Protestant domination of ecclesiastical courts—and evoked the memory of every indignity suffered by Roman Catholics in these states.[9] Although these gravamina were more annoying than persecutory, such encumbrances against their creed, like the existence of the Jesuit Law, served to remind adherents of the Roman church that they occupied an inferior position in German society. Hence the charged emotion reserved for the governments' anachronistic and retrograde ecclesiastical statutes. Centrist complaints and strictures, Lieber and Pichler claimed, were directed "against conditions, against legislation, against administrative guidelines" which by any standard must be considered "entirely obsolete."[10]

No less infuriating for the Centrists than the existence of such laws was the stubborn resistance which greeted their efforts at repeal. Increased complaint and criticism were in large measure the result of migrations, chiefly seasonal, of Roman Catholics into areas previously considered homogeneously Protestant. While available statistics do not offer a very accurate indication of their number, the figures cited in the Reichstag permit to some degree an assessment of the nature of the problem. Mecklenburg, for instance, with 7,000 Roman Catholics out of a total population of some 600,000 witnessed the influx of additional adherents of the Church of Rome. Diluting the Protestant character of that state were some 12,000 seasonal workers brought in from Roman Catholic provinces to help with the sugar beet harvest. Owing to the influx of Roman Catholic workers seeking better employment opportunities, Saxony was a similar case.[11] Irritated by the existence of discriminatory laws in these territories, the Centrists sought to denude the statute-books of such legislation. For that purpose, Toleration Bills were introduced into the Reichstag in 1900 and again in 1905.[12] Because

Reich legislation took precedence over state law, such bills were regarded as an unwarranted violation of the federal principle by the
government and were defeated.[13] Similarly, the Centrum party's repeated attempts to restore those paragraphs of the Prussian constitution guaranteeing certain religious freedoms—Articles 15, 16,
and 18—which were repealed during the Kulturkampf, were unsuccessful.[14]

   Parity was frustrated not only by the existence of statutory discrimination. Reinforcing these formal disqualifications was a be-
wildering and tangled skein of informal disabilities which excluded
Roman Catholics from certain categories of employment. As such,
the "Parity Question" was not concerned with bias and discrimination in hiring practices and wage scales in a broad sense. The group
most concerned with the "Parity Question" was the *Mittelstand*.
Although the *Mittelstand* in Imperial Germany included the spectrum of social groups from artisans through small businessmen and
lower managerial employees to the professions, not all were equally
concerned with discrimination against Roman Catholics. That segment of the Roman Catholic *Mittelstand* or middle class most vi-
tally interested in the "Parity Question" were officials in the state
bureaucracy, lawyers, school teachers, university students, and professors. Given the preindustrial origins of these occupations, this
stratum of the *Mittelstand* was not so much interested in findings
regarding the pervasiveness of discrimination in employment and
housing against the Roman Catholic working classes. Nor did the
Mittelstand perceive the "Parity Question" primarily in terms of
ecclesiastical interests. Rather, the middle classes were concerned
with their personal careers, above all with informal discrimination
which excluded Roman Catholics from the civil service and the
academic professions.

   Although nearly one-third of Germany's population was Roman
Catholic, few members of that creed were to be found in the highest
positions of the Reich and Prussia. Ample statistics attested to this
fact.[15] Of ninety such positions—Chancellor, Prussian ministers,
state secretaries in the Reich administration during the quarter century preceding the First World War—only eight were held by adherents of the Roman faith. And two of these individuals, Chancellor
Chlodwig zu Hohenlohe-Schillingsfürst and Karl Heinrich von
Schönstedt, Prussian Minister of Justice, were not members in good
standing with their church.[16]

   Discrimination against Roman Catholics was also widespread in
the Imperial bureaucracy. Only five Roman Catholics, for example,

could be found among the forty-nine senior officials of the Foreign
Office. The Roman creed was also a liability to promotion. In rec-
ommending the appointment of Götz von Seckendorff as Chief of
the Reich Chancellery, for instance, Chancellor Hohenlohe felt it
necessary to stress the candidate's "unconditional reliability," even
though he was an adherent of the Roman church.[17]

Similar discrimination prevailed in the Prussian ministries. A
messenger boy was the only Roman Catholic employed in the Ministry of the Interior. The Finance Ministry also had one adherent of
the Roman church, whereas two could be found in the Ministry of
Ecclesiastical Affairs and Education, a department of obvious great
concern to Roman Catholics. It was alleged that Adolph Förster,
one of these two Roman Catholics in this important ministry, had
he been Protestant, might well have become a director in 1899.
Two years later, when his promotion could no longer be evaded, a
reorganizational scheme was implemented to prevent him from
taking charge of the schools department, an extremely sensitive
post given the confessional climate of Wilhelmine Germany. Only
the Ministry of Agriculture, it is said, employed several Roman
Catholics. Although the figure for the total staff is unknown, five
officials, including the under-secretary, belonged to the Roman
creed. And in 1910 Klemens von Schorlemer-Lieser, a Roman Catholic, became Minister of Agriculture, the only member of that creed
to hold a ministerial position in either Prussia or the Reich at the
time the First World War broke out.[18]

Elsewhere in the Prussian administration the situation was no better. With five provinces possessing populations with Roman Catholic
majorities, Prussia had only one *Oberpräsident* of that creed.[19] The
number of *Regierungspräsidenten* was also disproportionately small.
In 1902, a high point, seven out of thirty-eight positions were in the
hands of Roman Catholics. By 1913 this figure fell to three.[20] *Landräte* were still another example of disparity. Of 485 such officials
in 1910, only sixty-four belonged to the Roman faith.[21] Although
Berlin did appoint Roman Catholic *Landräte*—provided the individual was not affiliated with the Centrum—assignments were restricted
to predominantly Roman Catholic districts.[22] Similar restrictions
were not made for Protestant *Landräte*.

If a bias against the employment of Roman Catholics was obvious
in the bureaucracy at both the national and state levels, it was
equally apparent in the academic professions.[23] Even the government's statistics revealed the existence of discrimination. A particular notorious case was the Kaiser-Wilhelm-University in Strassburg,

a focal point for the "Parity Question" between 1901 and 1903.
According to the Prussian Ministry of Culture, the Strassburg faculty (excluding the Protestant theological faculty) had two Roman
Catholics among seventy-eight Protestant and four Jewish full professors. Among the extraordinary-professors the situation was
scarcely better: four members of the Roman faith, five Jews, and
twenty-six Protestants were to be found.[24] Similar figures were
cited by the Governor of Alsace-Lorraine. Out of 111 lecturers employed by the university, he discovered that whereas eighty-three
were Protestant, fifteen were Jews, and two claimed no religious
preference, only eleven were Roman Catholics. This affront to religious parity was all the more glaring in view of the fact that this
situation prevailed in a territory that was overwhelmingly Catholic.[25]

Even allowing for error and distortion, it was clear that a disproportionately low number of Roman Catholics held academic positions. For all its disparity, however, the Imperial and Prussian governments could with *some* justification defend this situation. They
maintained that the small number of Roman Catholics in both the
civil service and the academic life merely reflected the lack of qualified candidates for such assignments within that denominational
group.[26] Among every 100,000 males for each of the major creeds
in Prussia during the period 1887–1897, for example, fifty-eight
Protestants, 519 Jews, but only thirty-three Roman Catholics became university students.[27]

As early as 1896, the facts concerning this educational lag, especially in the higher schools, were brought to the attention of the
Roman Catholic leadership.[28] Simultaneously, Hermann Schell, an
original, although obscure, philosopher and theologian, confronted
this aspect of the "Parity Question." Without denying the inferior
social status of his coreligionists, Schell treated their social predicament as the symptom of a far deeper malady than mere discrimination: he attributed their status as much to their strict separation
of spiritual matters from the temporal as to prejudice. Equality in
secular life, he argued, required that his coreligionists themselves
establish "parity" between spiritual concerns and material values.
Unless his creed adapted itself to the modern world, Schell concluded, unless it ceased to exalt spiritual values at the expense of
secular considerations, Roman Catholics would remain unrepresented within the governmental administration.[29]

* * *

All this was unpleasant to the Roman Catholic community. Not without reason they continued to believe that they were not allocated their fair share of the posts. They attributed this situation not so much to the lack of qualified personnel, but to prejudice and bias on the part of the traditional ruling elite. Giving evidence of the enduring quality of this anti-Catholic sentiment, reinforcing the conviction that external factors were solely responsible for their disabilities, were the existence of popular agitators and the frequent confessional controversies.

Anti-Catholicism manifested itself in several ways. There was only one significant organization standing against Roman Catholic claims —the Evangelical League.[30] Established in 1886 by liberal Protestants who saw in the rapprochement between Berlin and Rome a defeat of the national state by the Roman Catholic church, the Evangelical League sought both to strengthen the solidarity of German Protestants and to protect themselves against what they considered to be the extensive and far-reaching demands of the Roman church. Capable of sustained and permanent agitation, the Evangelical League maintained a steady stream of invective at the Roman church, its causes, and its adherents. As such, the hectoring tone adopted by this organization, chiefly in its widespread press activities, impeded Centrist efforts to achieve parity for their coreligionists. Among the most important of the League's campaigns was the agitation it directed against repeal of the Jesuit Law.

In addition to the activities of the Evangelical League, permanent agitation on a much smaller scale was carried on by individual critics and polemicists. While anti-Catholic tracts were not uncommon, the Roman Catholic population was to some extent inured to this kind of attack. But during the Wilhelmine era there was one pertinacious adversary—the apostate Count Paul von Hoensbroech—whose caustic jibes and scathing attacks were resented all the more bitterly because he was himself an ex-Jesuit.[31] His connections at the Imperial Court,[32] his links of kinship with the political renegade Count Wilhelm von Hoensbroech-Haag,[33] made Hoensbroech a particularly vexatious agitator.

Most of the significant anti-Catholic agitations, however, were improvised on an *ad hoc* basis, precipitated by public outrage over some particular concession to the Roman Catholics, or some action on the part of Catholics themselves, but which faded away with the passing of excitement. Attesting to the inseparable relationship between the "Parity Question" and religious discrimination were such confessional controversies as the "Strassburg affair," the "Spahn case," the election of a bishop to an academy of scholars, the Trier school incident, and the "academic" Kulturkampf.

Exacerbating tension between Roman Catholic and Evangelical at the end of the last century and the early twentieth century was the so-called "Strassburg affair." It was engendered by the government's attempts to establish a Roman Catholic theological faculty in the Kaiser-Wilhelm-University situated in Strassburg. Although this project was contemplated as early as 1872, the year of the university's founding, owing to the acrimony of the Kulturkampf it was never carried out.

This omission impeded the assimilation of the Imperial Territory into the German Empire. Unable to use the facilities of the new university, the local clergy had perforce to be educated in local seminaries, the affairs of which, in the absence of new regulations, continued to be governed by the Concordat of 1801. According to the provisions of that agreement, the local episcopate had complete jurisdiction over seminary education. Under the circumstances of this arrangement it was impossible for the state to impose academic standards. However much the episcopate's influence might be resented and the rigor of training left wanting, it was the political dimension that was the most important consideration. The existence of such local seminaries meant that the clergy continued to be imbued with a spirit of French culture and patriotism. Having never adjusted to the new political situation prevailing in Alsace-Lorraine after 1870–1871, these seminaries became centers of opposition to the Germanization of the newly acquired territories.[34]

Attempting to rectify this anomalous situation to accelerate the integration of these territories into the German Empire, the government began negotiations with the Curia to establish a theological faculty in the University of Strassburg. These discussions began in 1894, were revived again in 1898, and were brought finally to a successful conclusion five years later.[35]

"The establishment of the Catholic Faculty in Strassburg," said the Alsatian representative to the Bundesrat, "is the most important and most effective innovation which the University has experienced since its founding in 1872." Such a theological faculty would not only "place on an equal footing the religious character of the University," but it would complete the University's organization, placing it on a "parity" with its sister institutions in the Empire, "which already, because they are situated in Catholic states, possess Catholic Faculties, in which students of theology receive a deeper scientific education and a strong spiritual incentive."[36] Echoing the opinions of the German Roman Catholic population, and acknowledging the legitimacy of their demands, he added that it was but "a simple demand for equity that a Catholic Theological Faculty be established in the university of a state wherein five-sevenths of its population belonged to the Catholic religion."[37]

Count Georg von Hertling, the government's special negotiator with the Vatican, was a symbol for the Roman Catholic community of one of their coreligionists who attained "parity" in Wilhelmine society. Not only was he a recognized political leader in the Centrum party, but, as a professor of philosophy in Munich, Hertling possessed a distinguished academic reputation. His prominence in the Görres Society, moreover, an organization that sought the recognition of the academic world for Roman Catholic scholarship, made Hertling the incarnation of the "parity" principle.[38] When in 1899 the count was elected to the Academy of Sciences, a friend wrote in congratulation, ". . . the clumsiness and partiality of former days has suddenly at long last been abandoned." "If only this attitude will last!" he concluded.[39]

This hope proved illusory. Opposition to parity, in the form of a theological faculty in Strassburg, was widespread and diverse. During the parliamentary discussion of the project, the National Liberal Carl Sattler said that he was not opposed in principle to the establishment of a Roman Catholic Theological Faculty in the Kaiser-Wilhelm-University. Indeed, he would be pleased if students of Roman Catholic theology were brought into full harmony with the other students and "in connection with the prevailing free, scientific atmosphere." But for the achievement of this goal, he added, the new Faculty had to be an integral part of the state university, not an enclave dominated by the bishop. "That is the reason," he concluded, "from which my opposition against the steps of the government has come."[40] Sattler, moreover, expressed dismay at the far-reaching concessions to the episcopate and to what he called its "front organization," the Centrum party, predicting that the Centrum would become emboldened by this victory and that more concessions would be made by the government in the future.[41] Karl Schrader, a Progressive, also claimed that the government had surrendered too much authority to the German episcopate. Making reference to previous cases of episcopal interference in academic affairs, he implied that the new theological faculty might also become the center of similar controversy should the hierarchy meddle in the curriculum.[42] Such opposition was not entirely unwarranted. But the Roman Catholic community ascribed this resistance to confessional animosity.

Not all Roman Catholics supported the government's Strassburg

project. Alsatian Roman Catholics demanded parity not only for
their coreligionists, but equality for their territory as well. Nikolaus
Delsor, an Alsatian deputy to the Reichstag, viewed the entire project as but a device by which to "Germanize" the Imperial Territory. He opposed this scheme because it would erode those peculiar
Alsatian characteristics which had developed over the course of history. "There are certain Germanizers who want to take away this
unique character," he said. "Against them we claim the right to be
and to remain Alsatians just as the Bavarians make the claim to be
Bavarians." Because they wanted to place Alsatian traditions on the
same level as those of other social groups, Alsatian Roman Catholics
opposed the Strassburg project as incompatible with the notion of
"parity."[43] For this reason, many Alsatian Roman Catholics isolated
themselves from Germany and refused to send young men from the
province to the university in preparation for administrative careers.
Two Alsatian priests, resenting German reproaches for this behavior,
argued that such an attitude was justified because governmental
positions were restricted as the perquisites of Reich Germans. The
only exception to that practice—and that a travesty of parity—was
the appointment of a Protestant Alsatian as the Imperial Territory's
Minister of Culture.[44]

The "Spahn case" was a *cause célèbre* in turn-of-the-century Germany. Seeking to establish a Roman Catholic Theological Faculty
within the University of Strassburg to accelerate the "Germanization" of Alsace-Lorraine, the Imperial government in its discussions
with the Holy See and the German episcopate was informed that
the university instruction of Roman Catholic theologians required
the appointment from that creed of professors of history and philosophy outside the department of theology. Quite by coincidence,
one of the two chairs of history in Strassburg fell vacant in 1901 as
a result of the departure of a professor to another institution. Under
ordinary circumstances a Roman Catholic could have been appointed to fill the vacancy. Complicating the issue in this particular case, however, was the presence of a Jew—the highly respect-
ed medievalist Harry Bresslau—in the remaining history position. Because the Protestant interest had also to be safeguarded, the authorities attempted to solve the dilemma by the creation of a third chair
of history. Both a Protestant and a Roman Catholic received calls to
Strassburg. Chosen by the faculty to fill the vacated position was
Friedrich Meinecke, later to become one of Germany's outstanding
scholars. As the occupant of the newly created third chair, the government chose Martin Spahn, the twenty-six-year-old son of a

prominent Centrist deputy, who had just completed his *Habilitation* at the University of Berlin. By means of Spahn's appointment, the government sought two goals. First, they hoped to obtain the good-will of the Centrum to use that party to overcome the Holy See's suspicions concerning the Strassburg project. Second, the government sought to placate those Roman Catholics critical of German society because of the "Parity Question." Whatever Berlin's intentions, however, the bulk of the German academic community was outraged. But rather than attack this appointment as an egregious example of political patronage, Spahn's tenure was vehemently contested on confessional grounds.[45]

"A feeling of degradation is passing through German university circles," declared Theodor Mommsen, the doyen of German historians. "Our mainspring is unconditional research," he continued, "that kind of research which neither finds what it is supposed to or wants to discover according to ulterior motives and considerations, serving some practical goal lying outside the limits of science, but rather by what logically and historically appears as correct to the scientific investigator." All this, he concluded, can be "summed up in one word: Truth." Once permitted to intrude beyond the limits of purely theological studies, confessionalism becomes the mortal enemy of the whole concept of the university. Attacking Martin Spahn by implication, Mommsen emphasized that any appointment made outside theology on confessional grounds represented nothing less than the "blow of an axe" against the "mighty tree" of "German science" under whose "shadow and protection we live."[46]

Mommsen's outraged appeal struck a sympathetic chord among his academic colleagues. The new appointment, "purely on a scientific basis," was unpleasant, wrote Meinecke. "Catholic history professors," he continued, "are and remain a monstrosity."[47] The bulk of the faculty of several universitites, Munich, Strassburg, Leipzig, along with a large number of professors from Berlin, Bonn, and Breslau, signed a petition affirming Mommsen's statement.[48] "What we oppose," said Mommsen on behalf of his supporters, "is in no way the representation of the Catholic viewpoint in the German universities or the right to equality of Catholic scholars." Fearing that the concept of "parity" was being transmuted into a crude, mechanical system of quotas, he added: "We simply oppose the crass embodiment of scientific parity" whereby the universities are compelled to appoint "one professor for Protestant and another for Catholic history or philosophy or social science."[49] Roman Cath-

olics greeted such an explanation with incredulity—indeed with
derision—and dismissed it as still another specious argument to deny
them religious and social parity. Although their sense of outrage was
slightly mitigated by the fact that Spahn did retain his position,
even this success was vitiated by revelations concerning the young
professor's affiliations with the professional anti-Catholic Count
Hoensbroech. It was claimed that Spahn offered to write anonymous articles for inclusion in the count's *Tägliche Rundschau*, an
anti-Catholic paper.[50]

If the "Strassburg affair" and the "Spahn case" exacerbated the
"Parity Question," divisions were further deepened between the
Roman Catholic community and German liberals by still another
cultural-confessional controversy. Anxious to assuage the feelings
of Roman Catholics outraged by the controversies concerning
Strassburg and Spahn, the Ministry of Culture encouraged a prestigious scholarly society to elect a prominent churchman into its
ranks. In 1901 Friedrich Althoff, the official concerned with higher
education and chief advocate for the Strassburg project, persuaded
the Society for the Advancement of Science in Göttingen to elect
Prince-Bishop Georg Cardinal Kopp of Breslau, a native Hanoverian,
as an honorary member. The ostensible reason for Kopp's election
was to grant him recognition for his efforts on behalf of historical
research. He had, it appears, allowed scholars access to the episcopal
archives, thereby facilitating research into the history of the medieval church.[51]

Under the influence of the liberal historian Max Lehmann, the
Society for the Advancement of Science initially proved reluctant
to accede to the government's request. While the Society demurred,
Lehmann published an article seeking to demonstrate that the Index
of prohibited books served to circumscribe the intellectual independence of the Roman Catholic scholar.[52] Without once referring to
Kopp by name, Lehmann obliquely attacked Althoff's project. For
if, as Lehmann maintained, one of the bishop's functions was that
of censor, then any bishop was an opponent of unfettered scientific
research as defined by Mommsen.[53] By inference, then, the cardinal's election to the Göttingen organization was scandalous in the
eyes of all liberals.

In spite of Lehmann's efforts, Althoff's persuasive powers suc-
ceeded in wearing down the resistance of the Society and Kopp was
duly elected in February 1902. Lehmann resigned in protest.[54] Although the outcome of the matter, because of governmental pressure, was no doubt greeted well by the Roman Catholic community,

exposure to insulting and deprecating charges offended their sensitivities and reinforced the belief that anti-Catholic attitudes were widespread in Germany's learned professions.

The "Parity Question" was exacerbated by still another case of alleged unfair treatment, this time in Trier. The role of ecclesiastic and secular authorities in the educational process then, as now, was a bone of contention between the Roman church and the state. All the ingredients for trouble, therefore, were present when in 1902 the Prussian government decided to establish a nondenominational Teachers' Academy in the Trier diocese.[55] Even though liberals defended this decision in economic terms—better education provided the opportunity for better jobs and eventual "parity" with non-Catholics[56] —such a move was perceived by Bishop Michael Felix Korum and the local Roman Catholic population as an affront to the notion of religious equality. The issue of the Teachers' Academy became entagled in the larger question of equitable treatment within confessionally mixed schools, especially for girls within the Trier administrative district, and parity between sectarian, i.e., either Evangelical or Roman Catholic, institutions.

The government's plan to create another nondenominational Teachers' Academy collided with Roman Catholic demands for a sectarian institute. Ideally, interconfessional schools were institutions in which the chief Christian creeds were to coexist on equal terms. But Roman Catholics claimed that such parity did not exist in practice. In support of this charge, Roman Catholics argued that it was "so much sand in the eye" to maintain that the majority of students and faculty in the local Teachers' Academy were Roman Catholic. Five-sixths of the student body belonged to the Roman creed as did eight of the eleven teachers. But, it was argued, the Protestants, though in a minority, taught the chief courses—history, for example—where the teacher's religious viewpoint played a critical role.[57] Reinforcing dissatisfaction was the belief that certain textbooks in general use made deprecatory remarks about the Roman faith.[58] "Parity" in such interdenominational schools, Roman Catholics concluded, "meant . . . Protestant."[59]

If the addition of another nondenominational Academy was resisted because of practical disparities, real or imagined, the Roman Catholics used this issue to vent their hostilities concerning a related educational grievance. With particular reference to a confessionally mixed girls' school attached to the Academy for practice teaching, they claimed that in comparison to the Evangelicals, Roman Catholics had disproportionately fewer denominational schools. De-

manding the creation of sectarian schools in place of the extension
of nondenominational institutions, the local Centrist press reminded
its readers that in all Prussia there were 172 secondary girls' schools:
114 Evangelical, fifty-four nondenominational but only four Roman Catholic. Without parity in numbers of confessionally segre-
gated schools, the press could only conclude that "in Prussia Catholics are second-class citizens."[60]

Countering these charges, the government alleged that the academic attainments of students from confessionally mixed schools
were higher than those of pupils from denominational schools. In
cases where young girls transferred from the confessional school to
the nondenominational institution in the Trier diocese, the trans-
ferees were, without being given an examination, automatically
placed one year behind the other students, a procedure resented
because it suggested inferiority.[61] Korum demanded proof of this
educational lag to be established in open competition, the examination to be judged by a neutral commission.[62] Undercutting this
stance, however, was the bishop's effort to explain these educational discrepancies, which he suggested had nothing to do with the institution or its teaching staff, but rather with "disparity" in the allocation of funds.[63] Korum also claimed discrimination in the award
of career positions, arguing that employment opportunities were
better for graduates from a nondenominational school. "Is it any
wonder," he concluded, "if the upper classes of nondenominational
schools display more talent than the Catholic institutions?"[64] The
better students, out of a concern for their career prospects, had to
attend non-Catholic educational facilities.

The controversy attained serious proportions when in February
1903 the Roman clergy threatened with ecclesiastical penalities
parents who permitted their daughters to attend the nondenominational academy and girls' school.[65] Liberals and anticlerics launched
a vitriolic campaign publicizing the backward and obscurantist action of the Roman church, ridiculing the hierarchy, and hinting at
legal sanctions, especially the implementation against the local
clergy of the Pulpit Decree of 1871, a device by which the priesthood could be muzzled on political matters.[66] By March, following
an announcement from the pulpit voiding the previous edict, concessions from the government in the way of removing objectionable
texts, and the appointment of a teacher of religion in the new
school, the crisis passed.[67]

This acrimonious conflict left behind a legacy of suspicion and
ill will which poisoned the "Parity Question" for a long time. Not

only was there a grievance concerning what was deemed an insufficient number of denominational schools, but there was widespread
resentment about alleged discrimination toward graduates of Roman Catholic schools in the way of employment.[68]

Nurturing such suspicions was still another educational dispute.
Scarcely had the controversy over the Trier school incident subsided
when the tense religious situation was punctuated by yet a new crisis: the so-called "academic" Kulturkampf.[69] This conflict, caused
by the suppression and prohibition of certain Roman Catholic student organizations at institutions of higher learning in Germany,
also aggravated the "Parity Question."

In 1904 there were in the institutions of higher learning in Germany a total of about 784 corporations or fraternities. Of these,
some ninety-eight—about one-eighth of the total—were Roman Catholic associations. Their very existence, to say nothing of expansion,
was viewed as an unwarranted intrusion into what was considered
an exclusively Protestant domain.[70] Meinecke viewed with disdain
the "rising ultramontane flood" at the University of Strassburg.
Since the autumn of 1904, he observed, four new Roman Catholic
student fraternities had been founded. And the number of Roman
Catholic students was growing tremendously.[71] True, the relative
numbers of Catholic students still lagged behind other denominational groups. But the recent expansion of their sectarian student
associations served to harden anti-Catholic animus.[72]

The quarrel was foreshadowed in December 1900 when a request
for the establishment of a Roman Catholic student association (the
"Cheruscia") at the Technical College in the predominantly Protestant city of Brunswick was denied by the school's rector and senate
on the grounds of its confessional character.[73] But nearly four years
passed before such fraternities became a serious controversy. In
March 1904, the University of Jena forbade all color-bearing fraternities that were related to religious groups. This triggered similar
action at other institutions. Technical schools in Aachen, Berlin-
Charlottenburg, and Karlsruhe were the scenes of demonstrations
against sectarian student associations, some of which had been a
part of the academic scene for decades.[74]

The most serious of these demonstrations occurred at the Technical College in Hanover during June and July 1904. When the administration refused to accede to demands for the abolition of religious associations, the situation became sufficiently ugly that it
was necessary to close the school for one semester in 1905 and to
discipline some of the anti-Catholic agitators.[75]

The "academic" Kulturkampf came up for discussion in the Prussian House of Deputies in February.[76] Addressing the assembly, Konrad von Studt, the Minister of Culture, declared that he had no intention of suppressing these confessional associations. But, he added gratuitously, "in themselves confessional organizations in the colleges remain an unpleasant phenomenon," the reasons for which he did not wish to elaborate upon. In any case, he admitted, there was no legal means by which such associations could be proscribed.[77]

The importance of the "academic" Kulturkampf was not so much that Roman Catholic student associations survived this onslaught. Its significance, rather, was that it gave witness to the extent that adherence to the Roman creed was a social liability in Wilhelmine Germany. Membership in Roman Catholic organizations jeopardized one's prospects in the way of a governmental career. This was no small matter in view of the efforts on the part of the Roman Catholic educated elite to secure equality of treatment in the allocation of governmental posts during the post-Kulturkampf era.

* * *

While this litany of grievances does not claim to be exhaustive, it does indicate that during the quarter century before the First World War, the Roman Catholic population of Germany continued to chafe under a number of disabilities, some legal, some informal, but all stubbornly maintained. The frustration and exasperation associated with the campaign to dismantle the remaining vestiges of such legislation, together with the Roman Catholics' inability to neutralize confessional antagonism, had an informative effect on the Centrum party, and influenced its subsequent internal strife.

3: AN ALLIANCE OF KNIGHTS AND SAINTS

*Wir müssen mit dem Zentrum paktieren. Dann
sind wir egal raus.*

von Molchow[1]

The Centrum's enemies—from Bismarck on—did all in their power
to stamp the party with a confessional label. Whatever substance the
charge had (and there were Centrists who denied the party's Roman
Catholic character), the persistence of that accusation jeopardized
the party's effectiveness in working its legislation through the Prussian Landtag and the Reichstag. Recent parliamentary setbacks—the
repeated failure to obtain a Toleration Bill, for example, and the
Centrum's inability to abolish the remaining paragraphs of the Jesuit
Law—confirmed this belief.

Under these circumstances the Centrum began shortly after the
turn of the century to reexamine its strategy. That reevaluation
gradually matured by early 1906 into an intention to erase the party's sectarian image. Lofty principle had to be reconciled with political reality. If Roman Catholics were to attain parity in Wilhelmine
society, the Centrum had to allay traditional Protestant fears concerning the party's connections with Rome. Convinced that the
"Parity Question" made it necessary to abandon the religious image,
a sizable and influential segment of the party's leadership disingen-
uously initiated and ceaselessly maintained the argument that the
Centrum was not, nor had it ever been, a confessional or exclusively
Roman Catholic organization.

This view received its theoretical exposition in an article bearing
the provocative title "We Must Get Out of the Tower!" in the pages
of the *Historisch-politische Blätter*, the most prestigious organ of
political Catholicism.[2] Written by Julius Bachem, scion of a prominent Cologne publishing family,[3] this essay urged the Centrists to
refute all claims that their party was a sectarian organization. Em-

33

ploying the metaphor of the tower (the Centrum's emblem being
the silhouette of a fortified citadel), Bachem urged his coreligionists
in the party to leave the isolation represented by that tower and
join forces with Conservative Evangelicals. Bachem was sanguine of
the prospects for such cooperation. Despite religious differences,
the Centrum and Conservative parties shared a number of interests
and pursued similar political and social goals.[4] But because Protestants were understandably sensitive to charges of aiding and abet-
ting ultramontanism, Bachem believed the Centrum's Roman Catholic character alienated the sympathies of otherwise well-disposed
Protestant Conservatives and precluded close political collaboration
with them. He expected a political and secular image, however, to
neutralize Conservative fears, facilitate cooperation between the
two parties, and promote Roman Catholic interests. However much
the formation of this Black-Blue bloc (or as it was derisively called
by its enemies, an "Alliance of Knights and Saints") and the acquisition of political power was stressed by Bachem, this goal was not
so much sought for its own sake as for the means by which to
achieve parity in German society. Bachem's program regarding the
settlement of the "Parity Question," moreover, was made possible
only by a special parliamentary situation and specific regional circumstances within Prussia.

* * *

   This and subsequent writings quickly established Bachem as the
chief spokesman for the secular viewpoint within the party. Although occasionally discussed in previous years, the question of
practicality at the expense of a rigorous sectarian ideology was first
raised to the level of a serious political issue by Bachem in 1906.
More than by any other single event, the ensuing controversy—
known in party history as the *Zentrumsstreit*, or "Centrum conflict"—was precipitated by the appearance of his article.
   But Bachem did not intend, as his detractors within the party
maintained, to transform the Centrum into an interconfessional
political organization.[5] Therefore, his proposals in 1906, as later,
were tactical. Reproaching his critics in 1913, Bachem published a
polemical tract in which he argued that his policy required no
change at all in the Centrum. The party, he adroitly insisted, had
always been a political organization. There was no reason to change
the party platform. Pervading the whole tract was a reluctance to at-
tribute any kind of confessional nature to the Centrum for fear it

would jeopardize its political activities.[6] The essence of his policy
was a program to dispel Conservative fears concerning ultramontanism by which the Centrum could advance step by step along the
road to full and complete parity for Roman Catholics. While not actually making the Centrum's support contingent upon aid in the
"Parity Question," Bachem was prepared to compromise with the
existing system in the belief that this would lead to a relaxation of
the social hostility toward his coreligionists. He believed that with
patience and indulgence the Conservatives could be won over to
grant parity. To win the support of the Conservatives, however, the
party had to find the courage to emancipate itself from a sectarian
phraseology.

Much the same kind of argument can be found in the writings of
Julius Bachem's supporters. In a long disquisition about the "Centrum conflict," Carl Bachem (Julius' younger cousin),[7] endeavored
to demonstrate the practicality of a nonsectarian platform. After
denying in the grotesque rhetorical hyperbole so characteristic of
the *Zentrumsstreit* that his cousin pursued a "Protestant tendency,"
Carl Bachem simply maintained that in light of the Prussian constitution, a confessional party was incongruous.[8] In this work, as in
all the writings of the Bachem faction during the "Centrum conflict," the basic theme was that the Centrum party was a political
organization with membership open to individuals of all religious
persuasions, a definition which implied equality between the Christian creeds. This position was always justified on practical, political
grounds. It was the result of necessary expedient rather than desirable principle. Only this stance could satisfactorily end the "Parity
Question."

The movement which bore Bachem's project forward drew its
force from circles far wider than Bachem and his closest friends;
it reflected the genuine aspirations of the Roman Catholic *Mittelstand.* Yet some Centrists wanted to go even further. Moving beyond Julius Bachem's conclusions, and employing a style much less
circumspect than that used by the eminent Cologne publisher, was
the Strassburg professor Martin Spahn. He maintained that the
Centrum's religio-political mission ended with the termination of
the Kulturkampf. Claiming that a sectarian political mission was
anachronistic in Wilhelmine Germany, Spahn urged the party to become more than a mere simulacrum of a "political" party. He argued that the Centrum must seek a genuine parliamentary accommodation with Evangelicals of similar social and political views.
This program, he said, in keeping with the concern of the Roman

Catholic middle classes for the "Parity Question," would facilitate
the integration of his coreligionists into the political, socio-
economic, and cultural life of the German nation.[9] Precisely how
far Spahn himself was willing to go in this accommodation is not
clear.[10] But it appears that such an alliance with the Conservatives
was in his mind more than a *mariage de convenance* based on coincidence of interests. Spahn subsequently joined the German Nationalist People's party and eventually became a National Socialist.

Inextricably related to these efforts to secularize the party's
image, therefore, was the proposal that the Centrum collaborate
with Protestant Conservatives. Between January 1907 and the summer of 1909, however, such a suggestion was academic. The Conservatives were allied to the National Liberals and the Progressives
in the so-called Bülow bloc. Beneath a cloak of agreement and cooperation, this bloc was divided by fundamental contrasts so deep-
seated as to preclude a constructive and lasting arrangement. The
collapse of the Bülow bloc in 1909 offered Bachem's project the
prospect of success. But to take advantage of this situation, it was
imperative, declared the prominent Rhenish Centrist Karl Trimborn,
to clarify "beyond the shadow of a doubt the relationship of the
party to the Evangelical portion of the population."[11] The opportunity offered by the new situation did not go unutilized. In a session of the Prussian State Committee of the Centrum (sitting joint-
ly in Berlin with the Reichstag deputies from South Germany), the
deputies, following an extensive debate, "reaffirmed" the definition
of the Centrum as a political rather than a confessional party.[12]
Shrewdly taking advantage of the fact that the Bülow bloc had dissolved during the summer, the Centrists scheduled this session for
28 November—just two days before the Reichstag reconvened. By
officially declaring the party's political character at that particular
moment the Centrum was obviously seeking to facilitate an accommodation of some kind with the Conservatives—then cut adrift from
its partners in the bloc, the National Liberals and the Progressives—
when the Reichstag reassembled two days later. Such a declaration
sought to dispel that vague penumbra of ultramontanism which
surrounded the Centrum, impeding close cooperation with the
Conservative party.

These explanations and assurances did not fail of their purpose.
With the collapse of the Bülow bloc Bachem's plan was implemented
by the party and a tenuous and fragile alliance was reached with the
Conservatives that lasted into the First World War.

A similar consideration impelled the Centrist leadership to issue

another declaration affirming the party's political character the following year. On 24 October 1910 the Centrum once again took
pains to reassure the Conservatives and affirmed the political definition of the party.[13] Then, as before in November 1909, the Centrist leadership's reasoning was redolent of confessional fears and
their desire to attain parity in Wilhelmine society. Anxious lest
either the Church of Rome or the Centrum's internal squabbling
imperil the alliance with the Conservatives in the Black-Blue bloc,
the Centrum moved to silence internal dissenters and mollify their
parliamentary partners who undoubtedly felt uneasy in such a political coalition. This was all the more important, as the publisher
of the *Kölnische Volkszeitung* Franz X. Bachem noted, because of
impending Reichstag elections.[14] The party leaders, therefore,
emphasized once again the political nature of the Centrum. They
hoped to neutralize the charges of sympathy with ultramontanism
levelled against their ally and maintain cordial relations with the
Conservatives. Bachem insisted on abiding by the policy of full
cooperation with the government and the Conservative party as the
best hope for improving the Roman Catholic position in the long
run.

That the maintenance of the Conservative ties was a primary objective of Bachem and his friends can be seen in their actions and
the theme of their speeches during the spring of 1911. In a series
of dinners to commemorate the fortieth anniversary of the party,
Carl Bachem and Count Hertling exploited the occasion to lavish
praise on the Centrum's loyalty to the government. With an eye to
the goodwill of the Conservative party, they maintained in their
speeches that "conservatism" was the Centrum's hallmark.[15] These
unctuous pronouncements, reiterated later in pamphlet form, were
contrived to preserve the "Alliance of Knights and Saints."

If these efforts to efface the confessional character of the Centrum party symbolized the sallying forth from the fortress tower,
then the achievement of the Black-Blue bloc in 1909 was the real-
ization of the second of Julius Bachem's proposals—the joining of
forces with those Evangelicals, who, despite religious differences,
pursued similar political and social goals. In various articles and
public pronouncements, Julius Bachem urged his party to permit
Evangelical candidates to stand for election in certain safe Centrist
constituencies. Such a policy, he argued, would make a mockery
of the confessional charges levelled at the Centrum, while simultaneously holding out the prospect of broadening the base of the
party's electorate.[16] The Centrum party, with a steady bloc of

nearly 100 votes at its disposal, and occupying the strategic central
position in the national parliament, had since 1871 been a significant factor in the Reichstag. But it was clear that the base of the
party was too narrow for the Centrists to long maintain their pivotal position in the Reichstag. Since 1877 there was a perceptible
if ununiform decline in the number of Centrists participating in the
general elections. This trend was only temporarily reversed in 1919–
1920 owing to the fears of a new Kulturkampf.[17] The party was
stagnant. Under the circumstances, Julius Bachem, with the con-
currence of many Centrists, concluded that the moment had come
to discard the sectarian label, attract non-Catholic voters, and make
the party more attractive as a political ally.

Admittedly, it was an illusion to maintain, as Julius Bachem appeared to do, that a carefully cultivated political image for the Cen-
trum would result in an influx of Evangelicals into the party's ranks.
The number of Protestants voting for Centrist candidates never exceeded two percent.[18] In the state parliaments—Baden, Bavaria,
Hesse, Prussia, and Württemberg, for instance—there was not a single
Protestant sitting amongst the Centrist benches, not even as a
Hospitant, i.e., a "guest."[19] As late as 1912 there was in the Reichstag only one non-Catholic Centrist. Other groups also found the
Centrum party uncongenial. A Jewish candidate did not stand for
election on the Centrist platform until 1930.[20] Clearly, the Centrum
would always remain a minority party.

And yet the large-scale influx of Protestants into the Centrum's
ranks was never Julius Bachem's primary objective. Close reading of
his statements and those of his supporters revealed that proposals
to run Evangelical candidates for Centrist seats was viewed as but a
means to an end—the neutralization of the party's sectarian image
and a symbolic gesture of equality between the two creeds. Assum-
ing the pose of a "political" party, implying parity between the
religions, would expedite agreements with Protestant Conservatives
in the parliaments and facilitate electoral alliances with them at the
constituency level during a political campaign. The tenor of Julius
Bachem's remarks was that his proposal was little more than a political stratagem to free the Centrum from those restrictions imposed
by a confessional label, thereby increasing the party's influence and
power so as to make progress in the "Parity Question."

Not surprisingly, following the Reichstag elections of 1912,
Julius Bachem and his party associates claimed their case proven
by the event. Karl Hoeber, the chief editor of the Bachem family's
Kölnische Volkszeitung, insisted that the electoral arrangements

which preserved the Black-Blue bloc, averting what could have been
a political rout, demonstrated the practicality of Julius Bachem's
proposals made six years before.[21]

Interpreting Julius Bachem's proposals in a literal sense, the opposition to the Cologne faction, as the Bachem group was called in
the "Centrum conflict," replied that such arrangements were merely
tactical in nature.[22] But this was exactly what the Cologne faction
was seeking—tactical advantage. Given the inherent limitations of the
Centrum party, the only means by which its objectives (parity for
example) could be attained was in alliance with another political
party such as the Conservative. Julius Bachem deftly exploited Conservative fears regarding socialism. Conservative elements, however
abhorrent they found Rome, were still more unwilling to see a socialist victory. Not for nothing, then, was Julius Bachem alarmed lest
the persistence of internal Centrist squabbling alienate those Evangelicals and Conservatives who otherwise might be well-disposed toward
the Centrum. [23] "The so-called 'Cologne faction,'" Carl Bachem
stressed, "keeps ever before its eyes the politics of reality, of what is
possible of being attained under the existing circumstances." What
is more, he added, "the course of events has proven us right."[24] Tactical advantage, political realism, and pragmatism—all for the purpose
of achieving a position of equality in Wilhelmine society—provided
the underpinning of the Cologne group's policy; ideological considerations played a minor role if at all.

* * *

If the cohesion of the Black-Blue bloc was a primary concern for
the Cologne wing of the Centrum party so that equality could be
achieved for Roman Catholics, nowhere was the necessity for such
an alliance and the need for parity more obvious than in western
Prussia where it expressed the will and promoted the interests of the
Mittelstand. Stretching more than 1,000 kilometers from Memel in
the East to the Maas river in the West, Prussia was socially, regionally,
and politically a diverse territory. The western parts of the Hohenzollern kingdom, comprising the provinces of the Rhineland and Westphalia, were heavily industrialized in comparison with the predominantly agricultural East. This area, united by the Rhine river and its
tributaries, extended from the Bavarian Pfalz in the South to the
Dutch border in the vicinity of the Lower Rhine in the North. In addition to Cologne, a major communications center on the Rhine, this
region included the Ruhr industrial basin. The population of these

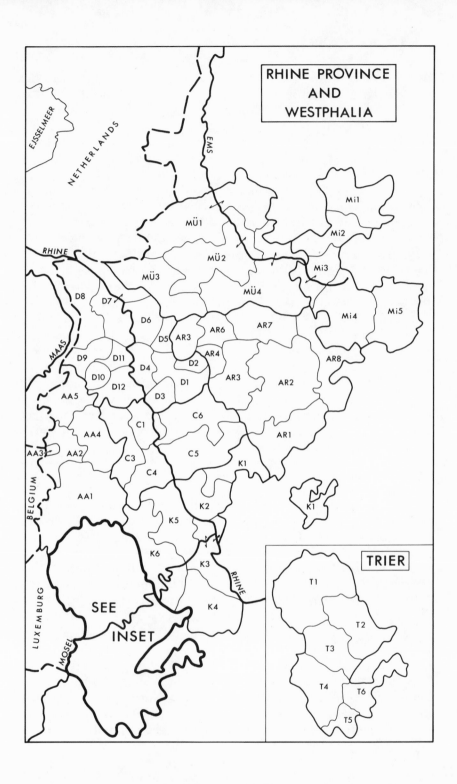

RHINE PROVINCE
AND
WESTPHALIA

TRIER

SEE INSET

LEGEND

Westphalia

Administrative District
Münster (MÜ)

Symbol	Constituency
MÜ 1	Tecklenburg-Steinfurt-Ahaus
MÜ 2	Münster-Koesfeld
MÜ 3	Borken-Recklinghausen
MÜ 4	Lüdinghausen-Beckum-Warendorf

Minden (Mi)

Symbol	Constituency
Mi 1	Minden-Lübbecke
Mi 2	Herford-Halle
Mi 3	Bielefeld-Wiedenbrück
Mi 4	Paderborn-Büren
Mi 5	Warburg-Höxter

Administrative District
Arnsberg (AR)

Symbol	Constituency
AR 1	Wittgenstein-Siegen
AR 2	Olpe-Meschede-Arnsberg
AR 3	Altena-Iserlohn
AR 4	Hagen
AR 5	Bochum-Gelsenkirchen-Hattingen
AR 6	Dortmund
AR 7	Hamm-Soest
AR 8	Lippstadt-Brilon

Rhine Province

Cologne (C)

Symbol	Constituency
C 1	Stadt Köln
C 2	Landkreis Köln
C 3	Bergheim-Euskirchen
C 4	Rheinbach-Bonn
C 5	Siegkreis-Waldbroel
C 6	Mülheim-Wipperfürth-Gummersbach

Koblenz (K) [Coblenz]

Symbol	Constituency
K 1	Wetzlar-Altenkirchen
K 2	Neuwied
K 3	Coblenz-St. Goar
K 4	Kreuznach-Simmern
K 5	Mayen-Ahrweiler
K 6	Adenau-Kochem-Zell

Trier (T)

Symbol	Constituency
T 1	Daun-Prüm-Bitburg
T 2	Wittlich-Berncastel
T 3	Trier
T 4	Saarburg-Merzig-Saarlouis
T 5	Saarbrücken
T 6	Ottweiler-St. Wendel

Düsseldorf (D)

Symbol	Constituency
D 1	Lennep-Mettmann
D 2	Städte Elberfeld-Barmen
D 3	Solingen
D 4	Düsseldorf
D 5	Essen
D 6	Mülheim a.d. Ruhr-Stadt Duisburg
D 7	Mörs-Rees
D 8	Kleve-Geldern
D 9	Kempen
D 10	Gladbach
D 11	Crefeld
D 12	Neuss-Grevenbroich

Aachen (AA)

Symbol	Constituency
AA 1	Schleiden-Malmedy-Montjoie
AA 2	Eupen-Aachen Land-Burtscheid
AA 3	Stadt Aachen
AA 4	Düren-Jülich
AA 5	Geilenkirchen-Heinsberg-Erkelenz

two provinces, especially in the economically more advanced districts to the North and East of Cologne, also contained a large and significant Roman Catholic middle class. It was no accident therefore that the first major pronouncement by the party leadership affirming the political as opposed to the confessional nature of the Centrum should be made by the Rhenish Centrist organization. Assembling in Cologne in September 1909, the Rhenish Centrists, with but four dissenting votes, resolved that the political and nonconfessional character of the party should be maintained.[25] Their decision reflected the "Parity Question's" peculiar situation in the district. That situation which conditioned Centrum tactics was defined by the dissimilar socio-political circumstances of the Roman Catholic community and the nature of its political competition.

In the absence of uniform conditions, the Cologne faction's perception of the "Parity Question" and the tactical means best suited to achieve a position equipollent in society was determined by specific regional circumstances. What distinguished the Roman Catholic population of western Prussia from their coreligionists in the rest of Prussia or Germany was the different class structure, the special socio-political problems they faced, and a more sympathetic episcopate.

Unlike other areas of Prussia, the western provinces underwent more rapid socio-economic change, a development that did not leave the Roman Catholic community unaffected. In the wake of rapid economic progress the class structure in the Rhineland and Westphalia was transformed so that the *Mittelstand* became the most influential group, eclipsing the more numerous peasantry and the traditional aristocratic social elite.

Given the peculiar social relationships in Prussia's western provinces, it was not surprising that the area should become the nucleus for those Centrist efforts to resolve the "Parity Question" by means of deleting the party's religious identity and collaborating with the Conservatives. This region possessed a sizable and influential Roman Catholic middle class desirous of political power and status, indications of their distress regarding parity in German society. Businessmen, lawyers, and civil servants comprised the leadership of the local party organization. The business interest was represented by the publisher Julius Bachem and several prominent journalists. One of the leading figures in this group was Hermann Cardauns.[26] Holding a doctorate in history, he was a distinguished member of the Görres Society and until 1907 the editor of the Bachem family's *Kölnische Volkszeitung*. Other journalists were Karl Hoeber, Car-

dauns' successor on the *Kölnische Volkszeitung*'s staff, and Lambert
Lensing, the editor of the Centrist Dortmund *Tremonia*. Still other
businessmen were officials of the Augustinus Union,[27] an organization concerned with the coordination of journalistic activities.
Among the latter group, the most important individual was Eduard
Hüsgen, the editor of the *Düsseldorfer Volksblatt*, but best known
for his biography of the great Centrist leader Ludwig Windthorst.[28]

This *Mittelstand* was important in politics too. No less than one-
half of the Centrist deputies to the Reichstag from this region were
either lawyers or civil servants.[29] Among them were some of the
most distinguished names in the party. Peter Spahn, a judge who
assumed the leadership of the Centrum party in the Reichstag in
1912, represented a Rhenish constituency.[30] His son, the professor
in Strassburg, also had a brief parliamentary career representing a
district in western Prussia.[31] The representative from Cologne in
the Reichstag was until 1912 the lawyer Karl Trimborn. He was
also the chairman of the Centrum's provincial committee in the
Rhineland.[32] Even Carl Bachem, a member of the publishing family and lawyer by training, was for many years a member of the
Prussian Landtag.

If the *Mittelstand* comprised the most important social group
within the Rhenish Centrum, it was because there was little competition for party leadership. But this was not always the case.
Between the Kulturkampf and the beginning of the new century
agrarian interests within the Centrum assumed great importance.
Having their beginnings in Westphalia in 1862 and the Rhineland
in 1881, Peasant Associations proliferated in the nineties in response to a deteriorating agricultural situation.[33] With the sharp
fall in agricultural prices which occurred in the nineties, together
with the trade agreements for lower tariffs concluded with Austria-
Hungary, Rumania, and Russia, whatever concord existed between
the Centrum and its agricultural quasi-affiliates broke down mark-
ing the beginning of more than a decade of strife between the Centrist leadership and the agrarian wing of the party.[34] Realizing that
they could not win the entire party to their viewpoint, they sought
at least some degree of "parity" for their agrarian program within
the general framework of Centrum policy. They publicized the
notion that the party was a sectarian political organization, an underlying unity, which nevertheless was marked with differences of
opinion in economic matters. Only in questions pertaining to religion and the church was voting discipline to be maintained; in all
other issues the Centrist was to be free to vote as his own interests

dictated.[35] In 1893 the Westphalian Peasant Association demanded
it be given four constituencies for the forthcoming Reichstag election, a demand repeated five years later by its Rhenish counterpart.[36] Both these demands for internal "parity" were rebuffed by
the Centrum. Such requests, the party leadership explained, constituted a bad precedent in view of the various social groups which
comprised the Centrum organization.[37] Peasant complaints were
only muted by the agricultural protection afforded by the Bülow
Tariff of 1902.[38] Preceding the passage of these trade restrictions
were the deaths in 1895 and 1896 of two prominent aristocratic
leaders of these Peasant Associations, an event which also diminished the acerbity of the internal conflict.[39] With the new century
the local peasantry became quiescent. Their passive attitude enhanced the *Mittelstand*'s influence in Centrist affairs, permitting
them a greater tactical latitude in the solution of the "Parity Question."

In addition to the docility of the peasantry in western Prussia,
the tactical autonomy of middle-class Centrist politicians in the
provincial party organization was due to the self-imposed isolation
of the Roman Catholic aristocracy. Following the dissolution of
the Reichstag in December 1906, thirty-nine Rhenish "Catholic
notables," chiefly members of the nobility, published a manifesto
in Düsseldorf denouncing the Centrum party for what it considered
its antinational stance over the colonial question.[40] The most important aristocrats among the group were Count Beissel von Gym-
mich, Count Wilhelm Hoensbroech-Haag, the cousin of the ex-
Jesuit and notorious anti-Catholic polemicist, two barons from the
von Loë family, Prince Salm-Reifferscheidt, and Count Alfred
Wolff-Metternich. Although the chief figure was Hoensbroech-
Haag, one of the guiding hands was that of Baron von Schorlemer-
Lieser, the first Roman Catholic *Oberpräsident* of the Prussian
Rhine Province. Referring to themselves as "National Catholics,"
they ran their own list of candidates against the official Centrist
list in the elections of 1907. After organizing on a permanent basis
under the name "German Alliance," they never acquired more than
minimal influence before dissolving in 1922.[41]

Not only was the perception of the "Parity Question" and the
means for its solution determined by the specific interests of the
Mittelstand in western Prussia, but provincial conditions delineated
the nature and character of the Centrum's policy. Foremost among
these local circumstances was the socio-political heterogeneity of
the area and the role of the church episcopate.

Western Prussia was an internally dissimilar region, lacking religious and political homogeneity. Nonetheless, the Rhineland and Westphalia together composed the most important source of strength for the Centrum party. Even with the six constituencies of Trier excluded (for reasons which will be explained in Chapter IV), these two areas disposed of forty-six seats in the Reichstag. Thirty-one of these mandates were captured by the Centrum in the general elections of 1907. Because many of these electoral districts were confessionally mixed—in some voting precincts the percentage of Roman Catholics barely exceeded fifty percent (see Appendix I) —pluralities were often so narrow that the margin of success depended on attracting a broader electorate or an accommodation with other political parties and groups. A policy which stressed the nonsectarian aspects of the Centrum, as espoused by the Bachems and the Cologne faction, served to assuage traditional Protestant Conservative fears regarding the Centrum's ties to Rome and to facilitate electoral collaboration against the Social Democrats. With that object in mind, Carl Bachem in 1913 bitterly complained that the Centrum's obtuse and intransigent dissidents, opposed to the Cologne wing's nonconfessional stand, were a source of embarrassment for the Conservative party,[42] lest its cooperation with the Centrists be interpreted as sympathy for ultramontanism.

The combined factors of Social Democratic rivalry and the desire to allay Protestant-Conservative suspicions concerning political collaboration were not alone in creating the Cologne faction's program and encouraging it to spurn the ultramontanist appelation. Facilitating that policy's genesis was the social situation in western Prussia. Its tactics were forced upon it by its composition and its environment. Nowhere in Prussia had class differences become so sharp as a consequence of industrialization. The Centrum party, moreover, found itself in the advantageous position whereby it could exploit these differences without concern for repercussions within its own ranks. Scarcely one-fifth of German industrial capital was in Roman Catholic hands.[43] With the exception of August Thyssen and Peter Klöchner, both Centrists,[44] most Rhenish and Westphalian industrialists were Evangelical National Liberals or Free Conservatives and enemies of the Centrum party. There was no reason for the Centrum to treat these people with indulgence. Unlike other areas in Germany where both workers and industrialists had to coexist within the Centrum, there was no necessity in the West to blur class differences with reference to religion.

These efforts denying the Centrum's role as the political exten-

sion of the Roman church were not only the result of the Cologne
faction's ambition to solve the "Parity Question" by means of a
rapprochement with the Conservative party and local socio-political
conditions in western Prussia. Equally important was the benevolent
attitude adopted by the episcopate in the Rhineland and Westphalia.

Cologne, widely known as the "German Rome," was the most
important bishopric in western Prussia if not in all Germany. During
the "Centrum conflict" the archbishopric was held by two incumbents. The most important of these occupants was Antonius Fischer.[45] He was appointed to the see of Cologne in 1902. A man of
modest attainments, Fischer did not possess vision or imagination.
He had little decision of will—a characteristic which allegedly
prompted Pius X's jibe: "Fischer is weak and permits himself all
too often to be carried away emotionally by opposing currents."[46]
For all his faults and weaknesses, the archbishop (cardinal since
1903) was a kind and mild-mannered prelate. He increasingly fell
under the influence of the more liberal Christian party in Belgium,
a country with which he had close ties.[47] Fischer also had a certain
sober, matter-of-fact way of judging political affairs. This led him
to adopt a neutral (even patronizing) attitude toward Centrist efforts to expunge the party's sectarian identity. Without far-flung
aspirations of his own, Fischer's grip on the "German Rome" nonetheless gave him sufficient prestige in German ecclesiastical circles
to afford the Bachem group in his archdiocese a degree of protection and a wider latitude of action.

Following Fischer's death in July 1912, Felix von Hartmann, a
Wesphalian aristocrat and former Bishop of Münster, was translated
to Cologne. Although differing markedly from Fischer in both tem-
perament and political inclinations, Hartmann nonetheless found it
necessary to pursue essentially the same policies as his predecessor.
Hartmann criticized the "left wing" of the Centrum party and expressed the hope "that he would not be viewed as a 'Cologner.' "
He also gave assurances that he "turned down every invitation from
[Julius] Bachem"—that "misfortune for the Catholic cause." At
one point, he even contemplated the suppression of the *Kölnische
Volkszeitung*, or, failing that, the organization of a rival newspaper. [48] Although the Cologne faction caused Hartmann anxiety, he
struggled to suppress inner misgivings and limited himself to complaints. He took no action.

The existence of a highly successful Centrist political machine in
his archdiocese no doubt contributed to Hartmann's irresolute behavior toward the Cologne faction and forced him to maintain some

semblance of amicability. At the same time, however, Hartmann's attitude can be traced to his difficulties with Cardinal Kopp in Breslau. [49] These difficulties with Kopp increased during 1913 as it became clear that the aging, cantankerous, and irrepressible Prince-Bishop was reluctant to tolerate any kind of opposition or competition. Kopp was not guided solely by the lofty idea of the doctrinal purity of his faith; he was driven also by vanity and personal considerations, especially the instinct for self-protection and aggrandizement. Following his translation to Breslau in 1887, Kopp became the most powerful and influential religious leader in Wilhelmine Germany. [50] His wealth, political offices, and personal contacts with Bülow and the imperial court itself,[51] bestowed on Kopp the undisputed leading role among the Prussian episcopate, a position mirrored in the half-admiring, half-contemptuous title: "State Bishop."[52]

Kopp's ambitions had never been confined to the boundaries of his see. Anxious "to strengthen his own position" in Berlin as "State Bishop," and to have in his hands all the connections between the Curia and the German episcopate, Kopp viewed with suspicion other members of the German hierarchy. He especially disliked Cardinal Fischer and his successor in Cologne, Hartmann.[53] With Fischer's death, Kopp remained as the only German cardinal. While Kopp did not occupy what was clearly the most important of Germany's episcopal seats—the "German Rome"—he was by virtue of the red hat he received in 1893 the most important churchman in the country. When in the spring of 1913 the Prussian government sought to obtain in Rome a cardinalate for the new Archbishop in Cologne,[54] Kopp prevented Hartmann from receiving that dignity,[55] denying him ecclesiastical "parity," and revealing his anxiety to preserve this *de facto* position as Primate of Germany. As it happened, it was not until May 1914—two months after Kopp's death —that Hartmann secured the purple. Cognizant of such inordinate ambition and alive to Kopp's animosity toward him, ordinary prudence dictated that Hartmann temporize within his own ecclesiastical province. Although not in total agreement with those policies advocated by the Cologne wing of the Centrum party, a conciliatory attitude was necessary if Hartmann wanted allies in his effort to maintain some modicum of episcopal independence or "parity" in the face of Kopp's depredations.

* * *

Before Julius Bachem's article, a revision of the Centrum's sectarian image had been but a vague idea, cautiously expressed by a few Centrists. After the appearance of the essay, the Cologne faction was a movement with a purpose and direction. But the persistent and truculent "Parity Question" in Wilhelmine Germany did not yield to such easy solutions as those espoused by the Cologne wing. This tactical alternative was vitiated by an insoluble contradiction within political Catholicism. Unlike any other German party, the Centrum was composed of socially disparate elements and interests held together with only the utmost difficulty by a common religious faith. Any transformation of the Centrum from religious interest group to political party was self-defeating. By relinquishing its confessional identity the party compromised its internal unity, converting the Centrists into a patchwork of unmanageable discordant elements, necessitating once again the adhesive of confessional cement. Seeking to negotiate an end to the "Parity Question" by means of negotiations from a position of strength, another wing of the party during its internal "Centrum conflict" cultivated a siege mentality designed to secure solidarity and submission among German Roman Catholics within the confines of a beleaguered citadel. Expressing alarm when the Bundesrat refused in 1912 to repeal the remaining sections of the Jesuit Law, a newspaper opposed to the Bachem faction wrote: "This is a state of war; any day can see us called to arms. An electoral campaign can break out, the likes of which, in spite of all our experiences, we have never seen before. In the Centrum Tower, however, the German Catholics will fortify themselves and repulse all attacks.—Into the Tower!"[56]

4: THE POLITICS OF SECTARIANISM

Catholic voters come to our party on account of their ideology. Just once allow the clergy to remain neutral and the Centrum will be shattered.
                                        Franz Bitter[1]

A siege mentality did not need artificial stimulation. Anti-Catholic animosity, increasing with the advent of the new century, forced German Roman Catholics on the defensive. Testifying to this aggravated confessional climate were the "Strassburg affair," the Trier school incident, the "academic" Kulturkampf, and the furor over the partial repeal of the Jesuit Law. These issues were both cause and symptom of the problem. But sectarian animosities also stemmed from two other developments: increased social mobility and the unusual influence exerted by the Centrum party in national affairs.

A major cause for Protestant complaint was the appearance in large numbers of Roman Catholics in regions which until the end of the nineteenth century were uniformly Evangelical in religious character. Available statistics for the provinces of Brandenburg and Pomerania in Prussia give some idea of the scope of the problem. Between 1900 and 1905 the number of Roman Catholics in Berlin, Brandenburg, and Pomerania grew by nearly 107,000. Expressed in other terms for the period 1897 to 1902, the number of Roman Catholics increased by 50 percent in the German capital, 20 percent in Brandenburg, and (owing to the rising demand for agricultural labor) 40 percent in Pomerania. Overall, the Roman Catholic population increased at the rate of 30 percent in comparison to 7½ for the Protestants. This growth stirred the traditional Protestant animus against the Roman creed.[2] Fearful lest Protestant dominance be eroded, Evangelical circles warned against flight from the land and the importing of labor recruited in Roman Catholic regions.[3]

They also protested the establishment of parishes and religious foundations by the Roman church to minister to the needs of the new confessional element in the population.[4]

Other developments, too, aggravated anti-Catholic sentiments in Wilhelmine Germany. Since 1895 the Centrum party occupied the pivotal [*ausschlaggebende*] position within the Reichstag's constellation of parties. That a confessional minority should exert such influence over the destiny of the Protestant German Empire was an offense to Evangelical sensibilities and grist for anti-Catholic propaganda mills. Roman Catholic boasts that the "Centrum was Trumps," that their leader Ernst Lieber was a veritable "Reich Regent," or Count Franz von Ballestrem's (a Centrist and President of the Reichstag) claim that *the Centrum was the axis about which everything revolved,*" scarcely served to relieve Protestant suspicions.[5] When in 1906, following Centrist revelations concerning the government's scandalous actions in suppressing a rebellion in German Southwest Africa,[6] the Centrum used its position and influence within parliament to defeat a supplementary colonial budget (for the defense force in Southwest Africa), religious hatred peaked. Angered by these actions, and feeling itself importuned by the Centrum's incessant demands regarding the "Parity Question," the government dissolved the Reichstag in December, called for new elections the following month, and skillfully exploited the anti-Catholic issue in order to escape dependence on the Centrum party.

Vehement anti-Catholicism marked the ensuing electoral campaign. The focal point for this hostility was the Centrum party. "Who could have thought," wrote Maximilian Harden, "that the Centrum was so much hated."[7] An officially sanctioned attack was mounted against the Centrum which eclipsed even the simultaneous campaign against the Social Democrats. The Centrum was criticized not on political grounds, observed the Protestant Count Arthur Posadowsky-Wehner. It became the target of "Catholic-baiting," he said, and was stigmatized for its confessional character. The National Liberals spoke of the Centrum's "humiliating yoke" and sought to impugn the loyalty of Roman Catholics to their country. Similarly, the Progressives referred to a "clerical yoke," denounced the Centrum's alleged subservience to the Roman Curia, and made ultramontanism the central issue of their campaign. They reserved special criticism for confessional schools, separate religious instructions in nonsectarian educational institutions, and Centrist proposals to readmit into Germany exiled Roman Catholic religious orders. Joining in this attack was the Evangelical League. What was at stake, the League's polemicists declared, was nothing less than the "indepen-

Auf zum Wahlkampf!

Auf diese Weise wird der Turm schwerlich zum Wanken gebracht werden.

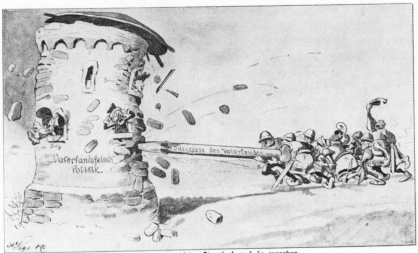

Der einzig richtige Sturmbock muß so aussehen.

Off to the Elections!
By these measures the tower can hardly be toppled.
The only right kind of battering ram has to look like this.

An electoral cartoon which appeared shortly before the Reichstag elections of 1907. It calls on the various parties to abandon interest-group politics and band together on behalf of the Fatherland against the antipatriotic Centrists, Poles, and Social Democrats who are ensconced in the Centrum's tower.

dence of the German state, rooted in the Reformation."[8] Not only
did the liberal parties and the Evangelical League exploit sectarian
hatreds to weaken and isolate the Centrum, but other, minor anti-
Catholic groups coalesced into the Imperial Anti-Ultramontane
Union for the express purpose of attacking the Centrum party as
a religious interest group.[9] By themselves, these splinter groups
would have remained relatively insignificant. But when fused together in a common anti-Catholic front, they constituted a formidable threat to Roman Catholic pretensions and a powerful engine
for anti-Catholic hysteria.

The Centrum party, under the circumstances, forgot its internal
differences and closed ranks. This solidarity permitted the Centrists
to obtain the second largest number of Reichstag seats in their history—105. But in spite of this accretion of strength, there was a
qualitative change in the character of the Centrist position in the
Reichstag. The party lost its preeminent place in parliamentary
affairs when the government fostered a new combination of parties
—the Conservative, National Liberal, and Progressive—in the Bülow
bloc.[10] Confirming the belief that the Centrum could expand its
strength if the confessional bond were stressed, the so-called Hottentot elections of January 1907 led ultimately to the formation
of a group antithetic to Julius Bachem and his associates. Between
1907 and 1914 these "sectarian" and "secular" factions formulated
their ideas and amplified their programs at party congresses, secret
conclaves, and in the press. Both factions were at one in motives
and aims—parity—but not in methods and means. While both sought
to establish a state of confessional equipoise within Wilhelmine society, Bachem's opponents sought to lift the question from the level
of expediency to that of high principle. This sectarian viewpoint mirrored the attitude of the Vatican and reflected special regional conditions and interests within the Centrum party.

The Roman church was seriously challenged in the nineteenth
century by such forces and ideas as liberalism, materialism, and
socialism. Fearful of the threat implicit in these movements, the
Church of Rome retreated toward a more rigorous interpretation
of dogma and a heightened emphasis on ecclesiastical authority in
an attempt to seek security for its spiritual ideals. Italy's seizure of
the papal states in 1860 and the occupation of Rome ten years later
was also not without its effect on the Vatican. Bereft of his territorial sovereignty, the pope placed special emphasis on his spiritual
function. Symptomatic of this trend was the Syllabus of Errors
issued in 1864 and the promulgation of the doctrine of Papal In-

fallibility in 1870. As such, the church's spiritual mission took precedence over temporal affairs.

Although this point of view persisted in the official attitude of the church down to the First World War it did not develop unchallenged. The two gravest challenges to this religious orthodoxy were Modernism and Reform Catholicism.

While never representing what might be called a coherent body of theological thought, Modernism is a collective term used to describe those various strands of theological argument which emerged during the waning years of the nineteenth century. Modernism sought a transmutation of doctrine in an effort to "update" the church, to bring its views and teachings into line with the realities of the modern world. It represented not just a current of thought contrary to the general trend of dogmatic development prevailing in the Roman church at that time, but it also typified attempts to attain "parity" between doctrinal matters and the secular world.

Modernism, however, never became as virulent in Germany as elsewhere. Admitted Modernists in Germany such as the theologians Joseph Schnitzer and Thaddäus Engert were not thinkers of stature or marked originality. More important was Reform Catholicism, a trend not substantially different from the liberal Roman Catholic movements of the nineteenth century. Having few of the characteristic features of Modernism, particularly its abstract theological formulation, Reform Catholicism was more practical, concerning itself with resisting political ultramontanism and advocating political and social reform.[11] The chief proponents of this viewpoint in Germany were Albert Ehrhard and Hermann Schell.[12]

Although implicit in Reform Catholicism—as in Modernism— the idea of establishing "parity" between spiritual matters and material values was adumbrated in Ehrhard's writings. His *Catholicism and the Twentieth Century*, published in 1902,[13] maintained that unless his faith adapted itself to the modern world, it "would become a religion only for the uneducated and the weak."[14] He recommended furthermore that the "laity should interest themselves more intensively in ecclesiastical tasks," stressing the cultural importance of individualism, subjectivism, nationalism, and laicism.[15] Ehrhard's program, decried by his critics as a "false policy of concessions,"[16] nonetheless provided the theoretical underpinning for Julius Bachem and Martin Spahn.

Even more important for the genesis of Reform Catholicism were

the writings of Schell.[17] From 1884 until his death in 1906, Schell
was a professor of apologetics in the Bavarian University of Würzburg. He achieved notoriety when in 1896, upon his election as Rector of the university, he delivered an inaugural address which infuri-
ated many of his coreligionists. Seeking to reconcile his religious
faith with the inferior status of his fellow Roman Catholics in Wilhelmine society, Schell was compelled to distinguish between Catholicism on the one hand and the "Roman or Latin" tradition on
the other, characterizing the former as the "principle of progress."[18]

Much of Schell's attention, as we have already seen, was given to
the "Parity Question." To remedy this inequality Schell espoused a
religious program which encouraged the German church to resist so-
called Roman influences, which were responsible for the backward-
ness of his coreligionists. Like Ehrhard, he advocated the wider participation of the laity in ecclesiastical affairs and the training of
future church personnel, not in the seminaries where they were in-
sulated from all contact with the secular world, but in the universities.[19] This idea foreshadowed one of the chief arguments in defense
of the government's Strassburg project a few years later.

Schell's Reform Catholic approach and remedies were practical
and pragmatic,[20] a characteristic which they shared with the Cologne
faction during the "Centrum conflict." Basically anti-Curial, Schell
was concerned with resisting political ultramontanism and assimilat-
ing his coreligionists into the mainstream of German society.

Both Modernism and Reform Catholicism were fiercely challenged
from Rome. The Curia viewed such ideas with undisguised alarm.
Seeking to curb these "pernicious" doctrines, the Church of Rome
retaliated with ecclesiastical censure and political pressure.

The Modernist controversy assumed serious proportions when in
1903 Pope Leo XIII died at the age of ninety-three. His successor—
Pius X—was Joseph Cardinal Sarto, the Archbishop of Venice. The
choice of the name Pius was itself an ill omen, because such a name
harkened back to the blatantly obscurantist policies of Pius IX.[21]
Far more rigid, doctrinaire, uncompromising, and conservative in his
approach to questions of dogma and religion than his immediate
predecessor, Pius X intensified the church's efforts to extirpate Modernism.

Following official condemnation, the movement rapidly died out.
Modernism was in part condemned by the decree *Lamentabili* of
July 1907, the encyclical *Pascendi dominici gregis* of September of
the same year which denounced the movement in its totality, and
the Oath against Modernism which was enforced after 1910.

Reform Catholicism, however, was not so easily suppressed. Led by the Bishop of Trier, the Prussian episcopate made accusations against Schell which eventually brought him into conflict with the Roman Curia. Rome condemned his ideas in 1898, placing on the Index of prohibited books not only his inaugural lecture, but also two of his earlier works. [22] Forced to recant in the spring of the following year, Schell found only temporary respite from ecclesiastical pressure. A second attack against his writings, occasioned no doubt by the numerous lectures which Schell delivered before overflowing houses in major German cities and by the reawakened suspicions of Bishop Korum, followed in 1904–1905.[23]

Even with his untimely death a year later, the "Schell case," as it came to be known, refused to subside. Serving to keep the Reform Catholic issue alive was the formation, shortly after Schell's death, of a committee with the avowed intention of raising funds for the construction of a memorial for the theologian.[24] The controversy also led in 1906 to the creation of an Anti-Index League in the Westphalian city of Münster. Rumors that prominent Centrists belonged to this organization contributed to its influence and aggravated the debate over Schell.[25]

* * *

Bachem's proposals of 1906 elicited critical reproaches from Rome and the Centrum party's clerical wing. "In addition to Modernism," Chancellor Bethmann Hollweg was told by the Prussian envoy to the Holy See, "the entire Cologne faction" and its "Bachemism" was viewed as an "abomination" by the Curia.[26] Churchmen in Rome, who were not much inclined to accept political advice from lay Centrist leaders in Germany, had only contempt for Bachem's line of thought. Such thought filled them with profound foreboding. The Bachem wing of the Centrum, emphasizing as it did its sectarian neutrality and the need for collaboration with Evangelical Conservatives, appeared as the political extension of Modernism and Reform Catholicism in the eyes of the Vatican. Unlike other countries (notably England), where the church was mainly concerned with theological questions related to Modernism, the Curia's focus of attention in Germany was the Centrum party and its affiliated organizations.

Sharing this view was the Berlin faction within the Centrum's ranks. What appeared reasonable and logical to Julius Bachem seemed like errant fantasy to this group. The "Berliners" were skeptical of the party's ability to secure, by parliamentary methods, any appreciable improvement in the position of Roman Catholics in Wilhelmine

Germany. They deplored any alignment with Protestant Conservatives. A coalition with the Conservatives, ran the basic complaint of
these dissidents, was fraught with uncertainties. It led to the Centrum's subservience to the Conservative party, endangered Roman
Catholic unity, and compromised the church's political aims. It was
not that the Berlin group was "liberal." On the contrary, it was
as opposed to liberalism and socialism as were the "Cologners." The
Berlin faction's approach was legalistic. Its technique was to exert
the utmost pressure on the Imperial government to secure categori-
cal guarantees which would safeguard Roman Catholic interests
against any change in parliament or shift in public opinion. Furthermore, the understanding with the Conservative party depended on
the Centrum's secularization. This process, the "Berliners" concluded,
could only weaken the Centrum party and cut it off from the church's
support. And according to the Berlin faction, a settlement to the
"Parity Question" could only be achieved from a position of strength
in alliance with the Roman church. In its own way, then, the Berlin faction was no less practical than the Cologne group. Like the
Cologne faction, the "Berliners" sought to establish a state of confessional equipoise within German society. But they resented all attempts to neutralize the Centrum's sectarian identity. Although frequently obscured by passionate ideological rhetoric, this sectarian position was the result of very real fears concerning the ability of the
Roman Catholic community and the Centrum to survive without a
close relationship to the church and to specific regional conditions in
Prussia.

The Berlin wing feared it was the Cologne faction's aim "to free
the public life of Catholic Germany from the influence of the episcopate and orthodoxy" so as "to weld together the Catholic people with
the Protestants into a large Christian social bloc in all areas of public
life and spiritual activity."[27] This point was made with wearisome
iteration. Exasperated beyond measure, the "Berliners" expressed
alarm about the "de-Catholicization" of the Centrum party's platform, the secularization of its organization, and the laicization of its
leadership.

Indicative of this concern were the pronouncements of the Berlin
faction throughout the "Centrum conflict." If the "Cologners" based
their political definition of the party on practical grounds, the Berlin
wing stressed the primacy of ethical considerations.[28] Moral and spiritual values played an important role in the doctrine of this group.
Seeking to integrate politics with the premises of their faith, the
"Berliners" explicitly rejected attempts to divorce Roman Catholic

principles altogether from politics, or to separate private from public morality. They attempted to divine a political policy from spiritual precepts.

The Berlin faction agreed that the Centrum was a political party, an organization having its field of activity in the Landtag and in the Reichstag. But, the "Berliners" added, such a party must be guided by the precepts of the Roman Catholic church. In all their political writings the Berlin group tediously expatiated on the argument that all Centrists agreed that the party was a political organization, but emphasized that the Centrum had the political task of representing Roman Catholic interests in Germany. They also repeatedly charged that the Cologne faction represented "the tendency to set aside the Catholic basis of the most important organization of German Catholicism in order to substitute a so-called nondenominational Christian basis" as the party's guiding philosophy.[29] Like the Curia, then, the Berlin wing of the party was alarmed lest temporal affairs take precedence over the church's spiritual mission. They urged instead a policy of strict attention to church interests.

Behind the Berlin faction's rhetoric and recondite argument, obsessed as it was with the question of the definition of the Centrum, another dimension of the "Parity Question" could be discerned. Bachem's proposal, like those of Ehrhard and Schell, implied an equality between the Roman Catholic laity and the clergy. By way of contrast, a definition for the party such as that given by the Berlin faction, emphasizing spiritual values and stressing the great dangers of moral complacency, required that the influence of the pulpit had to increase in the Centrum party.[30]

The process of "de-confessionalization" involved not only the despiritualization of the Centrum's political ideology. A necessary concomitant of that development was the secularization of the party's organizational framework.

During the Kulturkampf the Centrum's organizational system was informal and diffuse. A *Wählerpartei* rather than a *Mitgliederpartei*, that is to say, a party of voters rather than actual subscribing members, the Centrum was scarcely more than a confraternity of like-minded deputies in the Reichstag and in the state parliaments. There existed none of that clearly defined organizational framework which the modern mind associates with the ideal party structure. There was no element of continuity between sessions of the Reichstag and the state diets. Nor was there an organizational framework which spread itself out over the country as a whole, thereby making possible systematic political agitation. This absence of a party machine

left a gap which was filled by a different organization—the church.
To an appreciable extent the Centrum relied upon the church apparatus and laymens' organizations under clerical sponsorship for
its very existence.[31]

This situation could not long endure. Important changes in party
organization and electoral campaigning were necessitated not only
by the waning of the Kulturkampf, but by large-scale socio-political
developments. The last decade of the nineteenth century witnessed
the emergence of the masses into party politics.[32] No longer were
the lower classes, as in the preceding period, politically amorphous.
They, too, as the Centrum discovered, were seeking "parity" for
their viewpoints.[33] Industrialization, together with the effects of the
Great Depression of 1873–1896, increased social and economic conflicts for which remedies were sought in the political sphere. Increased political involvement, along with the emergence of the
masses, compelled the Centrum to develop a structural organization
which could politicize and maintain the allegiance of these masses.[34]
Gradually a program of administrative reform took shape, designed
to free the party from reliance on the clergy and the church and to
place party affairs on a more durable foundation. Its keynote was
the development of an organizational framework, the use of lay
leaders, and centralization.

A major step in this direction was the creation in 1890 of the
Volksverein für das katholische Deutschland.[35] Although such an
organization did not represent a complete break with a religious
identity—mirrored in the denominational reference in its name—it
nonetheless was a departure from previous practice. It represented
the establishment of an autonomous organizational structure, separate and distinct from the church, achieving at last "parity" with
that institution. The *Volksverein* was and remained an appendage
of the Centrum given the tasks of strengthening and tightening party organization. It assumed the task of campaign agitation and political education within the party, and maintained and cultivated
the ties between the Centrist electorate, especially the workers
and the urban middle classes, and the party. This service was indispensable since it neutralized the great economic and social tensions within the Centrist rank and file.[36]

As an auxiliary institution of the Centrum party rather than the
church, the *Volksverein* was primarily concerned with secular issues.
This division of labor, reflecting "parity" between secular and religious considerations, revealed itself in the *Volksverein's* structural
pattern. Its territorial divisions were not coextensive with ecclesi-

astical districts and dioceses, but were based on political considerations. [37] This independence from ecclesiastical organization was enhanced because the *Volksverein* collected a modest financial contribution from its membership. [38] While the secularization of the Centrum's organizational framework did not occur uniformly throughout Germany, by 1914 its membership had swollen to over 800,000, the vast majority being concentrated in the area between the Elbe and Main rivers, essentially the western half of Prussia. Despite all efforts the *Volksverein* was unable to appreciably extend itself beyond this geographic area, [39] a region dominated by the Centrum party's Cologne wing.

This spectacular growth, even if confined geographically, dismayed the hierarchy who allegedly viewed the entire "Centrum conflict" as a "question of power for the Catholic episcopal authority in Germany." [40] Giving evidence that this secularization of the Centrum's organizational framework was a source of grave concern were the activities of the party's Berlin wing, the German episcopate, and the Roman Curia.

A clerical spokesman for the Berlin faction, Karl Marie Kaufmann noted that the *Volksverein* had in recent years made tremendous strides in terms of growth and the acquisition of influence independent of the church. By 1908, he said, it comprised a huge membership and disposed of an income in excess of a half million marks. Apart from this growth and wealth, the *Volksverein* exerted direct influence over five journals, sent its news releases to several newspapers throughout Germany, and in the course of a single year distributed something like 30 million leaflets. In view of this inordinate influence, Kaufmann argued that the time had come to ascertain the *Volksverein's* position within the ecclesiastical framework and the authority to which it must subordinate itself. Lest the *Volksverein* be misused, Kaufmann concluded, it must be closely supervised by the episcopate. Cleverly avoiding any reference to the *Volksverein* as a party or political organization, he defined it instead as an interdiocesan organization. Described as such, the *Volksverein* fell under the purview of the church. [41] Kaufmann clearly postulated a basic premise of the Berlin group during the "Centrum conflict." The concern for the preservation of religious orthodoxy, especially in the face of Modernism and Reform Catholicism, required not equality between party and church, but the subordination of the former to the latter.

Ever since the "Hottentot" elections, when the Centrum party was relegated to the margin of political events, the "Centrum con-

flict" had subsided. But "complaints about inferiority and disparity," even though "little could be accomplished" at the time, were
discussed by leading Centrists such as Hertling, Count Hans von
Praschma, Adolf Gröber, Peter Spahn, and Aloys Fritzen.[42] When,
however, in October 1908 Bülow addressed the Reichstag inform-
ing its members of his intention to reform the Reich's finances by
imposing an inheritance tax, he resuscitated the flagging "Centrum
conflict." Because of the precarious nature of the Bülow bloc, a
coalition which sought to pair "the liberal with the conservative
spirit," the Chancellor's pronouncement threatened to disrupt the
bloc's cohesion. Presenting as it did the opportunity for the Centrum to escape its political isolation, the imminent dissolution of
the Bülow bloc revived the "Centrum conflict."

Shortly after Bülow's speech, the latent factionalism within the
Centrum party, obscured by a superficial harmony during 1907 and
1908, was disrupted by a spasmodic exchange of polemics within
the Roman Catholic press.[43] Many Centrists were sympathetic to
the notion of a confessional party without, however, having any
clearly defined program. It was to fill this need that early in 1909
a first step was taken to clarify their position and organize these
interests.

Edmund Schopen, a priest in Oberhausen (Rhineland), invited a
number of the party's dissidents to crystalize their views in a con-
fidential conference scheduled in Cologne. This meeting became
known as the Easter Tuesday Conference because its deliberations
took place on Easter Tuesday, 13 April 1909.[44]

Shrouded in secrecy,[45] the conference discussed the relationship
between the *Volksverein* and the church hierarchy. Calling for increased episcopal control over the *Volksverein*, the Easter Tuesday
Conference deplored "the fact that the headquarters of the *Volksverein* in München-Gladbach . . . refused . . . the demand of the entire episcopate to exercise a codetermining influence on the policies of the directorate." This situation, the conference said, gave
"rise to serious thoughts about the independent position of the
Volksverein." The most urgent matter, the participants concluded,
was the preservation of ecclesiastical authority over the Centrum
party.[46] For these people, the "Parity Question" stood for the
attainment of a position equipollent in German society; it did not
refer to equality or "parity" between Centrum and church in political matters.

In addition to the Easter Tuesday Conference, the Berlin faction
held a public conclave some months later in August 1909. Meeting

in Coblenz, this gathering also discussed the question of the exact relationship between the Centrum party and the Roman church on the one level and the *Volksverein* and the episcopate on the other. Emblematic of this concern for the preservation of ecclesiastical control over the Centrum party was the conspicuous participation of clerics. Of the 400 to 500 people attending these discussions, most were clerics and adherents of the principles laid down by the Easter Tuesday Conference the previous April.[47] Although "the Coblenz conference . . . turned out completely satisfactorily for nobody,"[48] it delineated the basic differences between the two factions in the "Centrum conflict," making it quite clear that the "Berliners" feared the erosion of church control over the party's activities.

That fear was especially prevalent within the episcopate. "What's the Centrum to us?" Korum once asked. The Centrists, he replied to his own question, "are our [the episcopate's] defenders in Berlin." Since this was their mission, "they should devote themselves to the church's interests and serve with complete trustworthiness . . . ."[49] Statements such as this, demanding the party's submission to the dictates of churchmen, gave substance to warnings allegedly given Bülow that Korum was "overly zealous."[50] This surfeit of zeal led the Bishop of Trier to resist Modernism, Reform Catholicism, and the Centrum's secularization.

The secularization of the Centrum party was also a source of anxiety for Cardinal Kopp. His major objective was to protect eastern Germany against "contamination" from the West.[51] He denounced Ernst Lieber, the Centrist leader from Nassau, as a "democrat." The Centrum, moreover, was becoming "too mighty," no longer responsive to church hierarchy and more and more preoccupied with the secular dimensions of the "Parity Question." The clearest indication of this change in priorities, complained Kopp, was the Centrum's behavior in passing the Naval Bill of 1898. Ignoring the church's interest in the repeal of the Jesuit Law, the Centrists were primarily interested in winning a preeminent position for themselves in the Reichstag.[52]

Because of Kopp's dread for secular "contamination" from western Prussia, he refused to permit political organizations such as the *Volksverein* any freedom of action in his Breslau diocese. Declaring himself opposed to all attempts "to defend and to recommend . . . the *Volksverein*" and "the centralizing efforts of München-Gladbach," the seat of the *Volksverein's* administration, he laid down certain conditions. Before permitting this Centrist organization to

function in his diocese, Kopp demanded more personal control over
its activities than that exercised by the episcopate in the West because he was unwilling to surrender any of his jurisdictional rights
within the Breslau diocese.[53] Political agitation and organization
were to remain in his hands, subordinate to the hierarchy's interests.

It was not only Kopp and Korum who challenged the Centrum's
secularization. The Curia also viewed such a trend with grave suspicion and serious misgivings. A response made by the Vatican to a
speech delivered by Theodor Wacker, a priest and Landtag deputy
from Baden, reveals the hierarchy's worries about the maintenance
of ecclesiastical authority in the Centrum party. As the main speaker
at a Centrist conclave in the iron and steel city of Essen in February
1914, Wacker delivered an address entitled "The Centrum and
Church Authority."[54] Echoing Julius Bachem's opinions, Wacker
argued that any effort such as that represented by the Berlin faction,
which stressed the sectarian nature of the Centrum party, only
served to increase the Centrum's political difficulties. In his native
Baden the Centrum faced the bitter animosity of the National Liberals and the Social Democrats, two groups that poured scorn on
the "priest-ridden" Centrum.[55] Speaking as a practical politician,
not as a priest or theologian, Wacker asserted that the hierarchy had
no voice in the party's affairs.

Wacker's address upset the princes of the church. They retorted
by placing the published version of his speech on the Index of forbidden books in June 1914, an action which was interpreted as a
"blow aimed at the Centrum."[56] Only the widespread secularization of the Centrum could have prompted the Curia to react in
such a harsh fashion.

More than "de-spiritualization" and secularization, the process
of the Centrum's de-confessionalization required the laicization of
its bureaucracy. Ever since its founding the Centrum party had been
heavily reliant upon the clergy for its very existence. This dependence was due to a number of circumstances. With its strength concentrated largely in rural areas, the party encountered difficulty
in providing adequate local leadership. In these areas where capable
functionaries were difficult to recruit, the clergy replaced the electoral machine. His religious office, the object of deference and respect, bestowed upon the cleric an influence which transcended
purely ecclesiastical questions. In such a man the Centrum was in
possession of an organizer and agitator in the smallest of villages.
The parish priest was thus a local leader and the party could ill afford to ignore him.[57]

Financial considerations also dictated the Centrum's reliance upon clerical leadership. The Centrum party was not a wealthy organization. Its federated structure and the lack of centralization made the regular collection of dues difficult. Patronage within the party was nonexistent. Nor was there, given the nature of the Imperial bureaucracy, patronage in the governmental service. Inducements and rewards, therefore, were not available for that laborious day-to-day organizational and administrative work within the party. Until the Centrum could offer this incentive or pecuniary inducement (a goal not realized before the appearance of the Weimar Republic, and then only partially), the party was compelled by dint of necessity to use clerical personnel rather than laymen as its functionaries.[58] Under the circumstances the clergy predominated in at least the lower levels of the Centrist hierarchy.

Reliance on the clergy had certain consequences. As long as the Centrum wished to retain this assistance, it had to emphasize its confessional basis.[59] While this kind of arrangement was not wholly unexpected during the Kulturkampf, it became increasingly anachronistic by the turn of the century in those areas where there emerged a self-confident Roman Catholic *Mittelstand*. During the Wilhelmine era, therefore, a noticeable development was the laicization of the Centrum's bureaucracy and parliamentary leadership. This displacement of the clerical element in party organization was not complete before the First World War. Initially, the creation of the *Volksverein* brought not increased numbers of laymen into positions of influence and responsibility, but additional clerics. In the opinion of one observer, admittedly hostile, the bulk of the chairmen and speakers at *Volksverein* gatherings were Roman Catholic clergy.[60] The predominance of clerics in the *Volksverein's* highest administrative positions also attests to an important clerical role. As late as 1914, the *Volksverein's* Central Office (*Zentralstelle*) was composed of three directors who were ecclesiastics, their nine clerical assistants, and eleven laymen. With the exception of Franz Brandts, a textile manufacturer who served as Chairman of the Executive Committee from 1890 until his death in 1914, his successor Trimborn, and Emil Ritter, many of the chief functions continued under clerical control. Playing a more important role than these three laymen were the priests Franz Hitze, August Pieper, and Heinrich Brauns.[61] Although laicization was therefore far from complete, the cleric was being challenged within the Centrum party by the emergence of the laity as an interest group with concerns separate and distinct from the Roman church itself. "Parity" between these two social groups was not fully achieved, but it was being demanded. While this new arrangement permitted the clergy to continue for some years to participate in the major policy decisions, it nevertheless marked the beginning of their decline. After the creation of a separate party organization the clergy did not long remain a preponderant factor in the Centrum.

Even though the *Volksverein's* staff was still largely in the hands of the clergy, the situation was nonetheless a source of anxiety. These functionaries and agitators, said their critics, were ecclesiastics who were motivated less by theological concepts and canon law than by a kind of broad socio-political approach. Instead of shaping their policies around the tenets of the church, the *Volksverein's* clergy plunged ahead on the Centrum's program unmindful of the teachings and guidelines laid down by the hierarchy. A kind of bureaucratic attitude, as Kopp bitterly noted, began to pervade the Centrum party.[62]

Though the clergy remained important in the Centrum party, their grip was relaxing and their influence was shrinking. This laicization was most perceptible in the party's parliamentary leadership at both the national and state level.

Clerical influence slowly but perceptibly waned in the Centrum's Reichstag delegation.[63] From a high of eighteen in the election of 1903 their numbers continued to decline. In 1907 thirteen were elected. This fell to eleven in the general elections of 1912. A similar trend can be perceived in terms of percentages. In 1903 clerics constituted 15.3 percent of the Centrum's Reichstag candidates and 20 percent of its deputies. By 1912, nine years later, these figures were 8.5 and 10.9 percent respectively.[64] Even in decline, however, the clergy as a social group still constituted an important force in the Centrum's Reichstag delegation in Wilhelmine Germany.

De-clericalization made its greatest strides in Prussia.[65] Whereas the bulk of the Centrum's clerical delegates to the Reichstag came from southern Germany (Bavaria in particular), only four of the eleven clerics in the XIIIth Reichstag, for instance, represented Prussian constituencies.[66] Whatever foothold churchmen maintained in the Reichstag, their numbers declined even more sharply in the Prussian Landtag. Clergy were conspicuously absent. Whereas twelve of the 97 Centrists elected to the Prussian lower house in 1903 were clerics, that figure was reduced to nine out of 104 in the Landtag of 1908. Among the other German states, only Baden witnessed a reduction in the numbers of clergy sitting in the local diet.

"In this systematic de-clericalization of the party organization," Count Hans Georg von Oppersdorff, a prominent Silesian Roman Catholic declared in 1913, was to be found "the simple explanation for the decreasing intercession of the Centrum for the religio-political demands of the Catholic people." "With the exclusion of the 'clerical' element the old Catholic Centrum has disappeared and in its place has stepped a new interconfessional, democratic, nationalistic party that possesses naturally little zeal and understanding for specific Catholic claims." The "common sense" of the Cologne faction, he continued, could not determine the morality of an issue. That, Oppersdorff concluded, "requires the *grace* and the *direction of the church* . . . ."[67] This theme repeatedly emerged in the Berlin wing's Silesian meetings held in Ratibor and Breslau and in the polemics of that faction's adherents.

In an effort to restore ecclesiastical influence in the Centrum party a large number of priests held a clerical caucus in Ratibor in 1911. Protesting what they considered their shabby treatment by the local Centrist leadership, thirty-five clerics sent off a petition stating that they "as the born leaders of the Catholic people" want a "powerful and *truly Catholic* Centrum without the admixture of 'Cologne,' without any hazy interconfessionalism."[68] Obviously, these clerics resented their exclusion from positions of leadership within the party.

The anguish expressed in this statement was reinforced in September by a conference in Ratibor which was attended by prominent laymen and large numbers of clergy from all parts of Silesia. From this meeting a new religio-political movement was formed. Calling itself "Catholic Action," the movement stood on a program identical with the views of the Easter Tuesday Conference. Recognizing the Centrum as a political party, Catholic Action insisted nonetheless that as a political organization it represented all Germans on the basis of Roman Catholic principles. While such a definition was designed to reverse the de-clericalization of the Centrum, Catholic Action underscored its intentions with the declaration that in all its activities the Centrum party must work in close conjunction with the church hierarchy. Bent on painting as black a picture as possible, hinting in fact that the Roman church stood on the threshold of a major schism, one priest relentlessly castigated the Centrum party and complained about its collaboration with other confessional groups.[69] Pervading all his remarks was the fear that ecclesiastical influence was waning in the Centrum.

Similar fears were betrayed by the Silesian clergy several days

later. Alarmed by such dissident behavior on the part of its clergy,
the Silesian Centrum party called for a special meeting of the leadership in Breslau. At this assembly the priests demanded, among other
things, that the party declare as its own the platform of Catholic
Action and a reaffirmation of the Centrum's adherence to Article
17 of its organizational statutes which stipulated that only a prac-
ticing Roman Catholic could stand for election on the Centrist
ticket. Not only was this an expression of the clergy's anxiety for
their continued influence in the party, but the stress placed on Article 17 was designed to obtain candidates who were thought to be
tractable to clerical pressures. While these demands were rendered
innocuous by various amendments,[70] the whole affair was indicative of clerical fears for their authority in the party and, indirectly,
with the German Roman Catholic population. "Parity" between
cleric and layman, in their eyes, was anathema.

In addition to the anxieties revealed by the Silesian clergy regarding the laicization of the Centrum's leadership, the fear of diminished clerical influence was expressed in the "Centrum conflict's" polemical writings. Aware that the Ratibor and Breslau con-
ferences in themselves would not be entirely effective in stemming
the party's de-clericalization, the Berlin faction resorted to polemics
for the purpose of reaching and influencing a wider audience. The
most significant of these polemical efforts were those of Edmund
Schopen, Hermann Roeren, and Franz Bitter.

During the summer of 1910 there appeared a new tract of shrill
and offensive character. No author was indicated on the title page,
but it soon became known that it was Schopen, the moving force
behind the Easter Tuesday Conference the year before. The pamphlet was a bitter diatribe against the idea of a nonsectarian Centrum.
By a detailed analysis of the Bachem wing's program, Schopen
sought to impugn its loyalty to the church. Infintely more aggres-
sive and doctrinaire than any of his associates, he claimed that the
Bachem-led Cologne faction was the culmination of nearly a decade's efforts to secularize the Centrum party. While using the customary arguments and well-worn phrases of the party's Berlin wing,
Schopen nonetheless saw that an important underlying factor in the
Cologne faction's program was the overriding concern of the Roman
Catholic *Mittelstand* in western Prussia to achieve parity in Wilhelmine society. But, argued Schopen, the benefits conferred were
meager when set against the cost; the success of the middle classes
would be paid for by the church and ultimately the party itself.
The Cologne program, he admitted, might lead to some semblance

of religious peace in Germany. But at the same time, justifying the clerical position, Schopen feared that any downgrading of sectarian identity had as its corollary the de-clericalization of the party and led inevitably to religious indifference and loss of faith.[71] In addition to possible defections from the church, Schopen more realistically argued that the political bond alone was insufficient to hold the Centrum's disparate social groups together in one party. If the views of the Cologne wing prevailed, he warned, the Centrum party would inevitably disintegrate. That the Bachems and their supporters did not perceive this contradiction was all the more surprising, he concluded, precisely because they perceived the party and its organization as an end in itself rather than as the political extension of the Roman church.

For the Cologne faction, Schopen said, the interests of the party transcended all other considerations. The Cologners unflinchingly sacrificed ecclesiastical interests for the Centrum's benefit. This opportunism, argued Schopen, induced the "Cologners"—the lay, middle-class leadership in the party—to diminish the clergy's influence in Centrist affairs. Believing themselves less encumbered by dogmatic considerations than the priesthood, and for that reason more flexible and compromising in political situations, the lay leadership, according to Schopen, systematically excluded the clergy from the Centrum's affairs.[72] He accused the Cologne wing of trying, by fighting shy of the sectarian appellation, to undermine the authority of the church hierarchy. Schopen claimed that the clergy were the real leaders of the Roman Catholic people and the Centrum party, an argument which denied "parity" between the lay leadership and the priesthood and the Centrum's political objectives and the interests of the Roman church.

Similar opinions were expressed by the Reichstag deputies Roeren and Bitter. Roeren, the Cologne faction's most persevering protagonist, argued that the Cologners' policies, if consistently pursued, would destroy the one bond, a shared religious belief, that held the Centrum's various social elements together.[73] Any effort to tone down the party's affinity with the Church of Rome, moreover, would in his opinion alienate the clergy upon whom the Centrum was so dependent. Bitter, too, in a speech delivered in 1910, expressed much the same belief. "Catholic voters," he declared with fervent emphasis, "come to our party on account of their ideology." That being the case, Bitter warned, "just once allow the clergy to remain neutral in an electoral campaign and the Centrum will be shattered."[74] Both Roeren and Bitter were convinced that the con-

fessional bond was essential to the party's solidarity, and the continued presence of the clerical element was the best guarantor of
that ideology. In their opinion, only a united party, led by the
church, could achieve progress in the "Parity Question."

The arid rhetoric and sterile debate of the *Zentrumsstreit* tended
to obscure the real source of discord. At first approach these trends
among the party theoreticians would appear to be rooted in purely
ideological factors unconnected with any aspect of the social and
political reality. Such a view is, however, superficial. The mechanism of conflict rested on real differences of ideas, interests, and
social composition. It was not so much an ideological dispute then
which provided the underlying cause of the quarrel, as it was regional differentiation.

* * *

Bachem's program, in Roeren and Bitter's opinion, precluded
such unity because the absence of a religious bond either exacerbated or set in train ethnic and class animosities to which the party
nearly succumbed. Nowhere was this point made more clear than
in Upper Silesia and in the Saar. The nature and character of the
social situation in these areas was the clearest demonstration to
the Berlin faction that a political label had only negligible utility
for the Centrum. It also bore witness to the fact that the Berlin
program was based on specific regional interests and experience.

Comprising the southeastern extremity of Prussia, Upper Silesia
was wedged between Russian Poland and the Austrian provinces of
Galicia and Moravia. The area, particularly the region lying east of
the Oder river, was an important mining and metallurgical center.
For administrative purposes, Upper Silesia, with its local governmental seat situated in the town of Oppeln, was divided into twelve
districts. Although the population was almost entirely Roman Catholic, it was ethnically a mixture of Germans and Poles. These differences were of no consequence as long as the religious issue remained
in the foreground as it did during the Kulturkampf. But during the
Wilhelmine era that bond was weakening. This process deprived the
Centrum of its inner coherence and ushered in a period of internal
strife and division between the two nationalities. "We may be Catholics," roared a character in a German novel published in 1904,
"but that doesn't make us Polacks!" [75] Even as early as 1886, as
the end of the church-state conflict became imminent, the Poles

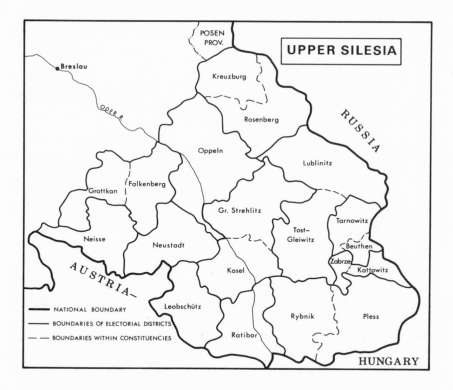

became "greatly excited" over these ethnic differences. The feeling was widespread within the Polish community "that if Bismark [sic] makes peace with the *German* Catholics" it is "only in order to be able to trample down the Poles to his heart's desire."[76] Not without reason, the Poles also feared that with the termination of the Kulturkampf the Centrum party, dominated as it was by German Roman Catholics, would retreat from its position of opposition toward the government in Berlin.

Subsequent events confirmed Polish fears. Even with the end of the Kulturkampf and the temporary relaxation of anti-Polish measures during the Caprivi administration (1890–1894), the Poles remained one of Wilhelmine Germany's oppressed minorities. Finding itself in the vortex of a nationality struggle, the Prussian Polish community was victimized by discriminatory legislation which attempted to obliterate their cultural heritage. Subjected to the anti-Polish campaign waged by the H–K–T Society, virtually unrepresented in the civil service, commerce, and industry, deprived even of the public use of their language, the Poles found themselves at a disadvantage in everyday life.[77] Whatever the importance of

these injustices, however, the foremost cause of discord within the
Centrum was discrimination by German Roman Catholics against
their Polish coreligionists.

The Centrum's German leadership chose to ignore Polish complaints. They attributed the party's difficulties with its Polish con-
stituents to the absence of "a thoroughgoing political organization"
with "a strong economic underpinning." However, Felix Porsch,
one of Silesia's leading Centrists,[78] was forced to admit that "when-
ever possible the Polish side has resisted and still resists the spread
of German organizations into Upper Silesia." Institutions like the
Volksverein could have provided the Centrum with that necessary
political infrastructure. The "main cause for this deficiency,"
Porsch added, was found in "linguistic differences" between the
two ethnic groups.[79]

And yet the Centrum was particularly insensitive to these linguistic differences. For years there was no Centrist press in the
Polish language.[80] Nor did the Poles occupy a prominent place
within the local party. Ever since 1894, Porsch declared, the party's
organizational statutes prescribed that "at least one" Pole must be
represented among any list of Centrist candidates.[81] That concession, together with assurances that "in the selection of candidates
for parliamentary mandates consideration is being shown" to "the
wishes of the Polish population in linguistic relations," represented
a token gesture and fell short of placating Polish sensitivities. But
even this concession was virtually nullified by Porsch's qualification
—echoing the government's excuses for the disproportionately small
number of Roman Catholics in the state service—that these efforts
were "not always easy because the selection of such suitable candidates is small." What is essential, he continued, is not "that the deputy can speak to the electorate, but that he can speak and work in
parliament."[82] Betraying a greater concern for the Centrum's interests than for Polish needs, this requirement precluded an equitable representation of the Polish minority within the Centrum
party's leadership.

Even those Poles who held Centrist parliamentary mandates from
Upper Silesia were not always acceptable to their Polish constit-
uents. Some of these deputies lost their ethnic affinity with the
Polish community. Paul Letocha, a parliamentary representative
of Polish extraction, is a case in point. Paying tribute to Letocha's
ability to straddle ethnic differences, Windthorst, the great Centrist
leader, claimed in 1886 that his colleague was no longer certain if
his children were German or Polish.[83] Having been at least partially

assimilated into the German community, such a candidate was obviously viewed with suspicion by the Poles.

Conflict, however, was "not merely the difference of language, but also of property." Whereas "the Polish-speaking population of Upper Silesia belonged to the lower estates, to the worker and peasant estates," [84] much of the Silesian industrial capital was concentrated in the hands of wealthy Roman Catholic German magnates—the *Hüttenpartei* or industrial wing of the Centrum party. Count Franz von Ballestrem provides the best example. His extensive landed possessions (in excess of 6,500 hectares), together with his industries which employed more than 5,500 workers, made Ballestrem one of the wealthiest men in Germany. Ballestrem was also a prominent Centrist. He represented a Silesian constituency for the party in the Reichstag from 1872 to 1893 and from 1898 until December 1906. During that second phase of his Reichstag career, Ballestrem was also President of the Reichstag. Furthermore, between 1891 and 1903 he sat in the Prussian lower house. And from 1903 until his death in 1910 he was a member of the Prussian House of Lords. The count, therefore, was a significant economic and political factor in Silesian affairs.[85]

"Polish radicalism" which was so disruptive of the Centrum's unity during the first decade of the twentieth century was "traced back to the wretched"—and unequal—"conditions that exist" in the Upper Silesian industrial belt, an area comprising the towns Königshütte, Tarnowitz, Zabrze, and Kattowitz. This region was not only the center of Polish nationalist activity, but was also the site of Ballestrem's industrial complex. The situation was thus made for class (and ethnic) conflict. Upper Silesian industrialists like Ballestrem were "of the view that no trade union" was "the best trade union." Ballestrem and other aristocratic mine owners did not flinch from using police against working-class organizations. Their aim was to place the workers into the "strait jacket" of "harmless" sectarian labor unions.[86] (For the differences between the various labor organizations, see Chapters V and VI).

Ballestrem's policies, in general, were twofold. First, he frustrated trade-union development, ascribing such activities to Marxists. During periodic visits to his industrial works, he was accustomed to assemble his employees and workers and to warn them against the "seductive" socialist and liberal ideologies. The count urged instead the harmonious collaboration between estates and interests groups. Having once supported Bismarck's anti-Socialist legislation, during the "silent" Kulturkampf he advocated the repeal

of the Jesuit Law on the grounds that this religious order was the
most formidable opponent of socialism. [87] His solicitude for religious matters was related to his second policy. Ballestrem's emphasis on religious solidarity was calculated to unite contradictory
elements within the Silesian population (industrialists, aristocrats,
and Polish laborers) together by means of a religious bond. But
he wanted to maintain the old hierarchical social framework. Because of Ballestrem's inability to accommodate his Polish Roman
Catholic workers as coequals within the confessional community
the Poles denounced this prominent Centrist leader as the "German
crusader on Polish soil." [88]

Ethnic and social discontent among the Poles was translated into
political opposition against the Centrum party in the national elections. [89] Although at least eleven of the twelve Upper Silesian constituencies, according to the Evangelical League, "were colorfast
black,"[90] that advantage was diminished by ethnic differences
among the electorate (see Appendix II). In 1903 Polish Roman
Catholics put up their own candidates in seven of these constituencies, garnering a total of 44,175 ballots and "winning the bulk
of the Polish working class."[91] Even in Oppeln 6 (Kattowitz-
Zabrze), a constituency which until then had been "safe" or
"bombproof" as the German term goes, the Poles defeated the
Centrist incumbent (it was Letocha) who had held this seat without interruption for twenty years. [92] This trend continued in subsequent elections. A Polish candidate won against a Centrist in the
by-election for Oppeln 5 (Beuthen-Tarnowitz) held in November
1906. Following the Reichstag elections of 1907 the Poles retained
these two seats and sent three additional delegates to Berlin.[93] The
Poles also retained their grip on Oppeln 7 (Pless-Rybnik) in still
another by-election held in December 1907. Within the span of
four years, therefore, the Centrum suffered seven electoral defeats
and lost five constituencies out of twelve to the Poles.[94] These
losses were the consequence of the Centrum's dissolving confessional image.

These events demonstrated that the Centrum could exist in
Upper Silesia only as a sectarian party. By relinquishing its confessional identity, the party compromised its internal unity and con-
verted the Centrists into a patchwork of unmanageable discordant
elements, necessitating once again the adhesive of confessional
cement.[95] Although Polish defections from the Centrum were
apparent before 1906, Bachem's proposals of that year clearly
aggravated the situation. It was no coincidence that in April 1906—

precisely one month after Bachem urged his party to comport itself as a "secular" political organization—and again in October 1908
as the impending collapse of the Bülow bloc intensified debate over
the Centrum's stance, that the Silesian Centrists implicitly rejected
this program. They reaffirmed Article 17 of the Silesian party's
organizational statutes making it mandatory for all candidates to be
members in good standing of the Roman faith. [96] Not only did the
Silesian Centrum underscore its religious character, but it created
an atmosphere of ideological siege calculated to form a congruence
of interest between Roman Catholic Germans and Poles. Opposing
Berlin's attempts to Germanize the eastern provinces, the Upper
Silesian Centrum courted Polish favor and warned German Roman
Catholics that "Germanization" of the Poles meant "Protestantiza-
tion," the correlate of which was a shrinking perimeter of defense
for Roman Catholic interests.

The chief spokesman for this viewpoint was the parliamentary
deputy Roeren. [97] He argued that the Poles deserved *"complete
constitutional equality* with" Prussians "of German nationality."
Any systematic program of *"de-nationalization"* which refused
"by means of intelligent and equal [*paritätische*] treatment" to
win the Polish-speaking population of the Prussian state, but which
"considered the Poles as a politically attached *foreign nation* which
should be suppressed and rendered harmless," had serious implications for German Roman Catholics. Claiming that the government's
policy had grave implications for the "Parity Question," Roeren
warned his coreligionists that any defeat suffered by the Poles in
the East would be felt in religio-political issues throughout the entire nation. Prussia's policy, he said, was to divide and conquer.
Precisely in those areas where the Poles were subjected to the most
governmental pressure, Roeren argued, occurred the worst viola-
tions to the concept of confessional parity. A "Germanization"
policy, therefore, not only denied "parity" between German and
Pole, but it also weakened the overall position of the Roman Catholic population regarding the sectarian "Parity Question" within
German society. By interpreting all attempts to suppress the Poles
as an assault on the Church of Rome,[98] Roeren sought to transform
the ethnic and social issues peculiar to eastern Prussia into a religious problem—the "Parity Question"—thereby winning the allegiance of Polish-speaking Roman Catholics and preserving party
unity.

In addition to ethnic and class problems faced by the Centrum
party in Upper Silesia, there was still another reason why the local

party stressed its sectarian nature. Because the Polish leadership was
mostly clerical in social composition, and because the Centrum itself depended on political agitation carried out by the priesthood,[99]
the emphasis on the Centrum's religious identity was designed to
retain the loyalty of the Polish clergy. Polish clerics were defecting
from the Centrist ranks in significant numbers. In the Reichstag
elections of 1907, for example, fourteen Upper Silesian priests actively supported Polish nationalists against the Centrum.[100]

Other local circumstances also permitted the Upper Silesian Centrum to accentuate its Roman Catholic image. In the absence of a
powerful Social Democratic or liberal opposition in Upper Silesia
there was no urgent political necessity to adopt a secular stance to
facilitate an alliance with the Conservatives as suggested by Julius
Bachem. On the contrary, a program which professed the Centrum's
sectarian character served to blur, if not to completely bridge, the
ethnic divisions between Pole and German and the class animosity
between labor and industrial capital within the regional Roman Catholic community. That this policy was not entirely ineffective can be
seen in the Polish willingness to collaborate with the Centrum in
1908 and the decline of the Polish nationalist vote in the general
elections of 1912. Although the Centrum regained only one of the
five constituencies lost to the Poles in 1907, the Polish vote fell
from more than 115,000 in 1907 to about 93,000.[101]

If local conditions and regional interests determined the Centrum
party's preference in Upper Silesia for a sectarian label, similar interests in the Saar led the party to also adopt a religious image.
Foremost among such factors were social peculiarities, ideological
considerations, and political self-interest.

The Saar, like the Ruhr and Upper Silesia, was one of Imperial
Germany's major industrial centers. Situated in Prussia's southwestern corner, adjacent to Alsace-Lorraine and the Bavarian province
of Pfalz, the Saar was an integral part of the Trier administrative
district. That region, with its governmental center in the ancient
episcopal city of Trier on the Mosel river, was composed of six constituencies, three of which were located in the Saar industrial basin.

As in Silesia, the Centrum's program in the Trier area was influenced to an unusual degree by the episcopate. While few doubted
that Korum, the incumbent of the episcopal seat in Trier from 1881
to 1921, sought "to imprint the Centrum with a specifically confessional character,"[102] that influence was circumscribed by internal
divisions within the local ecclesiastical organization. Trier's cathedral chapter, for instance, comprised two chief dignitaries—the pro-

vost and the dean. In addition, there were eight chaplains and four honorary members. With the exception of the provost who was always selected by the Emperor, the chaplains were appointed by either Wilhelm II or Bishop Korum according to whether the vacancy occurred with a death of the incumbent during an even or uneven numbered month. Given this unusual arrangement, Korum designated representatives of the Berlin faction. Wilhelm II, when exercizing his option, chose supporters sympathetic with the idea of interfaith cooperation in social and political issues. This scheme, understandably, inhibited but did not neutralize Korum's influence over Centrist policy.[103]

In addition to Korum's influence, the Trier Centrum's adhesion to the Berlin faction was dictated by the region's religious uniformity. All six constituencies were Roman Catholic in confessional composition, with percentages ranging from 59 to 99 percent (see Appendix III). Such a situation had political consequences. In those areas like Trier 4 (Saarburg-Merzig-Saarlouis), which was 96 percent Roman Catholic, the sectarian label was a source of strength for the Centrum. Having stressed the confessional tie, Roeren, the Centrist incumbent of Trier 4 and a major spokesman for the Berlin faction, produced stunning electoral victories in this constituency. During the electoral contest of 1903, he based his campaign on the "religious" obligation both to participate in the elections and to vote for the Centrum because it represented a public manifestation of support for the Roman church. His plea, it was said, substantially increased the turnout.[104] Similar entreaties produced equal success in the national elections held in 1907 and 1912. Such results were all the more remarkable in 1907 because Roeren entangled himself in the thorny colonial issue and was the object of severe criticism.[105] His plurality, nonetheless, was in excess of 24,000 votes.[106] Again in 1912 Roeren enjoyed a comparable electoral victory. Roeren's electoral experiences convinced him and the local Centrist leadership that the party's confessional image was a source of political strength.[107]

This continued identification of the Centrum with the Roman Catholic church can also be traced to the preponderance of what were called "peasant-workers" in the population. Within the Saar the majority of workers were not concentrated in cities, but lived in rural communities or even in isolated homes and farms in the countryside. Many industrial laborers and miners continued to work on the land in their spare time. This circumstance, reinforced for years by a stern patriarchal system, slowed the development of a class consciousness. Where there was little industry, the peasantry were under clerical control and remained docile.[108] Under these cir- cumstances the Social Democrats and National Liberals (except in Trier 5 [Saarbrücken]) found it exceedingly difficult to obtain a foothold.[109]

However important these social factors were in the maintenance of a docile attitude within the local Roman Catholic community in the Trier administrative district, isolated instances of dissent mani- fested themselves in the last few years before the First World War. The center of this dissatisfaction was originally the Saarbrücken constituency where an urban environment combined with an ex- tremely active National Liberal political opposition vitiated the effectiveness of the Centrum's sectarian appeal.[110] By 1913 this internal opposition even affected Trier 4 (Roeren's old constit- uency) when a schism developed between local and district party committees. In May, just prior to the Prussian Landtag elections, a delegation of workers met with representatives from the Rhenish Centrum. They discussed a new organizational statute permitting the working classes both seats and votes in party organizations and committees at the local and district level. When Klisserath, a priest from Saarburg, resigned as leader of the electoral committee, his successor was a layman. For the first time since the party's begin- nings a cleric did not hold this local post.[111]

Although these events demonstrated an emerging self-awareness on the part of the Roman Catholic laity in the Saar (demanding as it were "parity" between layman and cleric), the clerical element still predominated in politics. Contrasting southwestern Prussia with the rest of the Rhineland, Trimborn observed that if the Centrum "held an assembly in Cologne or Düsseldorf," two cities located in the northern Rhineland, "about 150 delegates would be laymen, about 30 to 40 clerics." If the meeting were in Coblenz, a much smaller town situated farther south at the confluence of the Mosel and Rhine rivers, one could expect to encounter "80 clergymen and approximately 70 lay people." A gathering in Trier or Saarbrücken, Trimborn went on, produced "about 120 ecclesiastics" and "about 30 to 50 laity."[112] Because the regional Centrum party in the Trier administrative district was deficient in suitable lay leaders, the clergy held their supremacy by default. Apart from Heinrich Marie Krueckemeyer, a publicist for the Berlin faction and since 1904 the director of the Centrist *Saarbrücker Volkszeitung*, and the parlia- mentary deputy Roeren, there were no well-known lay party leaders in Trier or the Saar. This dearth of lay political leadership was so

serious that all too often suitable candidates for the local constituencies were not found among the Trier administrative district's
population. Candidates for the local Centrum party were imported
from adjoining areas in the Rhineland. Such was the case in Trier 5
(Saarbrücken) and Trier 6 (Ottweiler-St. Wendel). Even Roeren, a
judiciary official in Cologne, was a "foreign" candidate. Throughout the Wilhelmine era, therefore, it remained "a peculiarity of the
Saar territory that the clergy were the leaders in political life."[113]

Given these peculiar conditions and circumstances, the majority
of Centrist leaders and Roman churchmen in the Trier district concluded that a settlement of the "Parity Question" depended on a
position of strength based on religious solidarity. The sectarian argument was thus a tactical formulation. Recent events—the "Trier
school conflict" to cite a significant case—seemingly corroborated
this viewpoint.[114] Three large-scale demonstrations in February
1903 in Trier, March 1903 in Kreuznach, and May 1904 in Coblenz,
all in support of Bishop Korum's stand, were impressive manifesta-
tions of Roman Catholic loyalty when their church appeared to be
in danger.

Viewed from an external vantage point, these regional victories
were only achieved at high political cost. If the task of harmonizing
divergent social and class interests in Upper Silesia was simplified by
the confessional appeal, and if the Centrum's electoral successes in
the Trier administrative district owed much to the sectarian label,
the Berlin faction's religious stance isolated the Centrum in Prussia
as a whole. The inability to resolve this contradiction led to inter-
minable dispute.

* * *

Preoccupation with the "Centrum conflict" diverted the Centrists from their primary task—a satisfactory resolving of the "Parity Question." Although once a supporter of the confessional wing,
by 1912 the rising young Centrist Matthias Erzberger changed his
mind.[115] Seeing himself in the position of mediator in this trouble-
some affair, he declared the party had "other things to do, larger
questions to solve," and "higher tasks to fulfill." The most important of these was to bring "the silent Kulturkampf to a swift end
and to attain an equality of status recognized by the state all along
the line." Such a "command of the hour," he continued, "demands
the solidarity and unity" of all Centrists. "The silent Kulturkampf

can only be ended and full Catholic emancipation achieved, if this unity and solidarity continues and grows even closer." [116]

That unity was difficult to achieve. Not only was the Centrum party sharply divided on how best to settle the "Parity Question," but at the same time the Roman Catholic community was torn apart by a "parity question" within its own ranks. The Roman Catholic working classes demanded the removal of class inequities and claimed "parity" with their coreligionists.

5: NEITHER "MASTERY FROM ABOVE"
NOR "CLASS STRUGGLE FROM BELOW"

The reactionary German Catholics are rather well
organized. But all their work is a feeble imitation
of the work of the German Social-Democrats.

V. I. Lenin[1]

Complicating both the "Centrum conflict" and the "Parity Question" was the intrusion of another problem into the Roman Catholic
community. The familiar pattern of religious discrimination in Wilhelmine Germany repeated itself in class discrimination. German
workers chafed under legal restrictions, political disabilities, and social inequalities which reinforced their subordinate position within
Wilhelmine society. This discrimination also had as its counterpart
within the Roman Catholic community an all-pervasive condescend-
ing attitude regarding the working classes and their aspirations. Given
the social composition of the Centrum's leadership that situation
was not unexpected. From its very beginnings the Centrum's leadership was recruited from the ranks of the preindustrial segment of the
Mittelstand (lawyers, state officials, and academics, for example)
and agricultural elements. Neither of these groups, whether laymen
or clergy, was really capable of understanding the problems of labor
in an industrialized society. The Roman Catholic working classes
were for that reason a group apart from their coreligionists. Increasingly aware of their secondary status within both the state and the
confessional community (a "parity question" writ small, as it were),
and inspired by an emerging class consciousness, large numbers of
Roman Catholic workers demanded equality of treatment from
German society and from their coreligionists.

The history of Wilhelmine Germany is replete with unsuccessful
attempts to achieve social and political reform. Participating in this
movement were large numbers of Roman Catholic workers. The
chief interests of their leaders during the Wilhelmine period were

social and not political. They wanted to translate evangelical precepts of love and brotherhood into secular terms of social justice and fraternity. Unlike other reforming, even revolutionary, groups and critics of the existing political system, these workers did not demand basic and fundamental changes within the nation's socio-political framework. They intended, rather, to incorporate themselves peacefully on terms of equality into that system. Under these conditions, such "parity" required equality of rights and of opportunity.

* * *

Equality of rights, as expressed in the complaints of the Roman Catholic proletariat, was construed primarily in a social rather than a political sense. Such compromise as envisaged (and as the government later sanctioned) stopped short at a point which would necessitate the political integration of the workers, on the basis of full equality of rights, into the German political framework. Labor's remonstrances avoided political criticism, focusing instead on appalling living arrangements and gruelling working conditions.[2] Thus the emphasis was on social "parity" rather than politics, and even where a political claim was placed in the forefront—as in the demand for parliamentary representation—it was not so much for its own sake, but rather as a means for realizing the overriding purpose of integration as equals into German society. Testifying to the narrowness of this sense of equality were the complaints from Roman Catholic workers about their humiliations and their disavowals of any claim to special privileges or considerations.

Workers' complaints were redolent of this desire for a position equipollent in society. It was altogether "unworthy," said Gutsche, a laborer from Saarbrücken, that German workers should be given "colorful uniforms, ham sandwiches, free beer, 20-mark pieces, or even cheap potatoes from time to time as a substitute for a legal coalition right." The former concessions were palliatives, incapable of correcting fundamental "disparities" within Wilhelmine society. If the working classes were to remain within the framework of bourgeois society, other social groups had to demonstrate a greater willingness to cooperate with the interests and efforts of the proletariat. Society was obligated, said the former transport laborer Johann Giesberts, to improve "the lot of the worker so that he enjoys life," becomes "conscious that he is a human being having equality of rights," and loses "the impression that he belongs to those who are separated and excluded from society." "We don't want," Giesberts asserted on behalf of the non-socialist working classes, "assimilation as a humani-

tarian gift" grudgingly conceded "from above, but association on
the free, voluntary, and convinced recognition of our equally entitled
position in public and civil life."[3]

The emphasis was hence on equality. Opposed, they said, as much
to "mastery from above" as the " 'class struggle' from below," Roman Catholic workers affirmed their belief in the "orderly and harmonious collaboration of all classes" and insisted that they be recognized as equals by the rest of society. Unlike the Social Democrats,
who, it was said, sought "not a just compromise between the individual estates," but relentless and remorseless conflict, "a struggle
to the finish" ending in "the proclamation of the rule of a single
class," the Roman Catholic workers disavowed the class struggle.[4]
"By no means did we demand a labor movement," the *Volksverein*
secretary August Pieper later reflected, "so that the former worker
remained no longer a worker."[5] Loyal to Emperor and Empire, their
spokesman said, "we demand our place in the existing order." That
"place in the sun" nonetheless was "within the life of the state."[6]

* * *

Important though the affirmation of equality of rights was, many
Roman Catholic workers concluded that reform, winning recognition
for labor, and the attainment of "parity" with other classes and
estates could not come about simply through the "conversion" of
employers or even because of state initiative.[7] Rather than anticipate
a "Damascus" of that kind, workers had to help themselves. This
required equality of opportunity. To help itself Roman Catholic labor
required the right of association, political representation, and trade
unions.

The successful fusion of the working classes into German society
necessitated equality between labor and management. Confining
their efforts to the "protection of worker interests as opposed to employers in the formation and development of labor conditions and
associated concerns," Roman Catholic workers sought "parity" between workers and employers. They specifically demanded the "right
of free association, worker chambers," and "the elimination of multi-
farious class justice." Existing legislation regarding the right of association, they said, left much to be desired. Affronting their sense of
dignity and fair play was the existence of a situation where virtually
all other occupational groups possessed representative chambers while
labor's demands for similar organizations went unheeded. If "parity"
between labor and management was to be realized, however, such

chambers were necessary to redress the balance of socio-economic power. But employers "endeavored to suppress labor organizations by means of their own legally recognized associations" in an effort to stem the workers' drive for equality of rights.[8]

In addition to the right of association (not attained until 1908) equality of opportunity for the Roman Catholic working classes necessitated the exercise of political power. "We must achieve for ourselves a position in political life," said the construction worker Anton Schmidt in 1906. He stressed the necessity of a "healthy representation of the worker estate within the different parties of Germany" and "the parliaments."[9]

Schmidt enjoined his colleagues to approach those politicians, whatever their party affiliation, "who say that they are favorably inclined toward our movement," demanding from them, "as the largest percentage of their electorate, a corresponding representation in the parliaments." In practice this required support from the Centrum party. But the only working-class member of the Centrum's Reichstag delegation in 1906 was Giesberts. Without colleagues of similar background, however, he was isolated and ineffectual. Roman Catholic workers, therefore, were clearly underrepresented within the Centrum's leadership. Recognizing this situation, Schmidt wanted, as in the case of the agrarians before the turn of the century, the political parties to allocate to the workers on the principle of numerical "parity" several "safe electoral districts . . . not merely in the Reichstag but in the various state parliaments as well!" Reinforcing Schmidt's demand was Stegerwald's claim for proportionate working-class representation on the Centrum's local electoral committees.[10] Roman Catholic labor could solve its own "parity question" if its efforts were not encumbered by discriminatory practices, if it were given the equality of means.

Attesting to their parliamentary success, Stegerwald claimed in 1907, were the seven non- socialist workers in the Reichstag. Six others, he added, belonged to various state parliaments, and about 150 sat in community administrations. In light of this political progress, he optimistically drew the conclusion that the "incorporation of the wage-earning estate into bourgeois society was therefore visibly taking place."[11] It demonstrated to his satisfaction that with equality of means and opportunity the Roman Catholic working classes could be absorbed into Wilhelmine society.

Equality of opportunity for the integration of the Roman Catholic working classes into Germany's social fabric was also dependent on the existence of an effective trade-union movement. For

this intention the Christian Trade Unions were the most important
and useful. Although technically nonpartisan and nondenominational, these Christian unions were associated with both the Centrum party and the Church of Rome. Union membership was almost entirely coextensive with Centrist and church affiliation. The
primary objective of the Christian Trade Unions was the attainment
of "parity" for their adherents within the existing social framework.
In June 1912, for instance, the unions' Executive Committee
claimed for their organizations equality with all other estates in
matters of economic freedom and independence.[12] Nearly six
months later, Stegerwald reiterated the same basic aim. Speaking
in Essen, he said, "our trade-union movement claims without ulterior motive that very same attention and freedom of action as all
similar organizations of the other estates."[13] "The everlasting patronizing of the workers has its limits," he cried in despair.[14] His
fellow workers demanded "the same independence as the hundreds
of influential syndicates and powerful employer organizations, or
thousands of trade and peasant cooperatives, leagues, guilds," and
professional organizations.[15] Obscured but not entirely hidden in
this program was the desire for social integration without full political assimilation.

As their very name suggests, the Christian Trade Unions represented the attempt to achieve a working accommodation between
the chief creeds of Germany. "In these confessionally mixed worker
organizations," it was maintained, "the idea of parity was manifest
as in few other institutions of public life in Germany."[16] Workers,
both Evangelical and Roman Catholic, stood on an equal footing.
While never a large contingent—numbering perhaps 21,500 in 1912[17]
—the Protestant workers in these unions were never a mere "appendage." They were equals, the union leadership never tired of
repeating. In any case, "the importance of Evangelical membership
within the Christian trade-union movement must not be judged by
mere numbers." In a nation, Stegerwald reminded his coreligionists
and compeers, where the governmental bureaucracy was overwhelmingly Evangelical in religious affiliation, as were three-fourths of all
employers, whatever influence Roman Catholic workers had was
the result of interconfessional cooperation.[18] Collaboration in such
economic matters implied successful cooperation between the principal creeds on equal terms within Wilhelmine society.

* * *

This drive for social equality on the part of a sizable segment of
the Roman Catholic working classes represented another more
complex dimension of the "parity" issue in Wilhelmine Germany.
Complicating the problem were the tactics of the workers themselves. Seeking to fuse themselves into society, they threatened to
disrupt the fragile social harmony of the various Roman Catholic
class interests. Any integration of the workers into society had as
its corollary their association on the basis of "parity" within their
confessional community. Inevitably, such a process menaced the
unity, harmony, and traditional relationships between the Roman
Catholic workers and their coreligionists. "Parity" within the German Roman Catholic community threatened to abolish church
domination over the working classes and the privileged or preferen-
tial status of other groups.

This is not to imply that the church displayed no interest in the
problem of the working classes. The church was interested. Among
the most outstanding German ecclesiastical figures who expressed
concern for the welfare of the laboring man in an industrial economy were Bishops Adolf Kolping of Cologne and Wilhelm Emanuel
von Ketteler of Mainz. Even before the revolutions of 1848, Kolping perceived the need for apprentice organizations to protect the
spiritual and material well-being of young workmen. Influenced by
these Kolping Associations, the church in 1880 also established
Worker Benefit Associations for the same purpose. Equally significant were Ketteler's writings. He advocated a broad program of
social reform between the early sixties and his death in 1877 that
provided the foundation for much of the Roman church's program
on behalf of the working classes.[19] By the nineties the Roman
Catholic church had not only a well-developed social ethic but a
wealth of experience in treating social problems. For all its good
intentions, however, the church's program did not entirely satisfy
the worker's needs.

Although sectarian labor organizations had been in existence for
a long time in Germany, it was not until the waning years of the
century that they flourished and experienced substantial growth.
Responsible for the initial lag was the Kulturkampf which diverted
the attention of the Roman Catholic worker from socio-economic
problems to religio-political matters and the defense of his church.
Much of the incentive for social and economic action among church
leaders, furthermore, was eliminated because Bismarck's anti-
Socialist legislation reduced socialist competition. The end of the
Kulturkampf, the expiration of the Socialist Law in 1890, together

with the appearance of the labor encyclical *Rerum Novarum* the following year, encouraged the expansion of labor associations affiliated with the Roman church. Supplementing previous organizations like the Worker Benefit and Kolping Associations were the Catholic Worker Associations which came into being in 1890. Like their predecessors, these Worker Associations viewed the labor problem as essentially a religious and ethical question, not as an economic matter. Conforming to the Roman church's sectarian beliefs and closely connected administratively to that institution, the Worker Associations were led by clerics who in turn were appointed by the local hierarchy.[20] Preoccupied with religious and cultural matters, they were unable to bargain effectively with employers. Because they were not genuine trade unions, Worker Associations were shunned by many Roman Catholic workers.

As dissatisfaction with the Catholic Worker Associations mounted, a group of miners coalesced into a nondenominational Christian Trade Union for the express purpose of improving their economic position.[21] This objective, they believed, could only be attained when their economic needs were granted equal recognition with those of other interests within the Roman Catholic confessional community.

From its origins in Dortmund, a major manufacturing city in Westphalia, the Christian Trade Union movement spread to other areas of the Ruhr industrial district and into the textile regions of the Lower Rhine.[22] The growth and development of the interconfessional trade unions was watched with distrust and hostility both by the Catholic Worker Association leadership and by the overwhelming majority of the German hierarchy. As it became obvious that the Worker Associations were not competitive with the Christian Trade Unions, the church, lest it lose its control over its working classes, constituted a new form of labor organization to supplement, but not to supplant, the Catholic Worker Associations.

Initially discussed in May 1901, these efforts culminated in the formation the following year of what were called *Fachabteilungen* or *Fachvereine*, i.e., Craft Associations. These Craft Associations, organized as their name implies along craft lines, provided a surrogate trade-union formation within the framework of the existing Catholic Worker Associations. Although charged with the task of protecting and forwarding the economic interests of the working classes, the Craft Associations nonetheless were subordinated to the religious and moral program sponsored by the Worker Associations and remained under the influence of employers and clergy.

In their opinion, the Craft Associations conformed to papal and
other ecclesiastical regulations and did not seriously upset the
industrial peace.[23]

* * *

As organizational forms, the Craft Associations and the Christian
Trade Unions stood in sharp contrast. Because the latter unions
demanded "parity" with the church-affiliated Craft Associations,
a bitter labor conflict broke out within the Roman Catholic population. Known as the *Gewerkschaftsstreit* or "trade-union conflict,"
this dispute was intimately related to the question of equality between the Christian Trade Unions and the church-sponsored organizations.

Competition between the two organizational forms was especially acute in the Saar and in Silesia. Craft Associations first made
their appearance in the Saar in 1902 when the Worker Associations
in that area joined their counterparts in North and East Germany to
form the League of Catholic Worker Associations (Berlin), a parent
organization created to supervise the new form of labor association.
These Craft Associations soon encountered competition in 1904 as
the interconfessional unions, spreading southwards, attempted to
extend their activities into this industrial region. With the emergence of the Christian Trade Unions, the relative harmony that
had prevailed between industry and the Worker Associations was
jeopardized. Anxious as they were with the improvement of wages
and working conditions, the Christian Trade Unions sought to in-
tensify the struggle against the employers to achieve equality for
its members.

Not only did the interdenominational unions seek to make gains
in the Saar, but they also attempted to expand into the industrial
regions of eastern Germany. This effort was closely associated with
the election in July 1902 of Stegerwald as Secretary-General of the
Christian Trade Unions.[24] Two years later Stegerwald sought to
increase the size of his organization by making a membership drive
in Silesia.[25] This *Drang nach Osten* was not viewed with equanim-
ity by the leaders of the League of Catholic Worker Associations
(Berlin) and the Prince-Bishop of Breslau. Their fears were rooted
in the well-established belief that the Christian Trade Unions were
growing more rapidly than the Craft Associations. The refusal to
subordinate the Roman Catholic worker's material welfare to his
spiritual well-being and the erosion of church authority by the

demand for "parity" with church-affiliated organizations also accented the anxieties of Kopp and the sectarian labor leaders.

By publicizing the superior benefits claimed for the nondenominational unions over the Craft Associations, the Christian unions won substantial support. From the very beginning the interconfessional unions possessed a larger membership than did the League of Catholic Worker Associations (Berlin). In April 1903 the Christian Trade Unions' total membership was 190,000. By 1914 that figure had swollen to 330,500. The comparable figure for the Worker Associations (Berlin) was about 50,000 in 1903 and 120,000 in 1914.[26] This disparity in growth was all the more significant in that every advantage was given the Craft Associations in the dioceses of Breslau and Trier. Nevertheless, the Worker Associations in the district of Neisse (Upper Silesia), under the very shadow of Breslau, seceded from the Berlin group and affiliated with the Christian Trade Unions. During the same period the mining branch of the interconfessional unions made progress in the Saar at the expense of the Craft Associations.[27]

Owing to this limited membership, the Craft Associations were ineffective in altering wage and working conditions. Worker Associations, the basic unit in this organizational framework, never possessed sufficient numbers to organize adequately effective Craft Associations as subsidiary units. The Worker Association itself possessed only 100 to 150 members, and these were subdivided into the ten or twelve trades most commonly represented among unionized labor, so each Craft Association had only ten to fifteen members. Numerically weak, such organizations possessed no economic power. Even in the event that hundreds of these Craft Associations banded together in common purpose, their connecting links were too loose to unite them sufficiently for any concerted action and effective pressure on their employers. Detracting even further from their effectiveness was the fact that not all members of the Worker Associations held membership in a Craft Association. Because the Worker Associations and the Craft Associations were so decentralized, they could scarcely achieve the influence nor have the economic impact of their much more centralized and numerically larger rival, the Christian Trade Unions. Craft Associations could only aspire to success in those areas where industrialization and class consciousness were not fully developed.[28] As it was so difficult to effectively represent working-class interests the denominational unions languished and declined. But not without a struggle.

Given these advantages over the denominational labor organizations, proponents of church-sponsored unions—known in the "trade-

union conflict" as the Trier faction—resisted the Christian Trade
Unions' demand for "parity." The underlying reason for this opposition was their inability to accommodate as coequals the Roman
Catholic workers within the confessional community. "The founders
and adherents of the Catholic Worker Associations," wrote August
Pieper, "represented the maintenance of the authoritarian-feudal constitution of the old social order which visualized the differentiation
of membership in that order into guardians and wards, ruler and
ruled." Relegated by the Worker Associations to the status of "wards
and ruled" were the "propertyless workers," who were thought unable to liberate themselves from the tutelage of their social superiors.
Because the Christian Trade Unions threatened to diminish the dominion exerted by these classes over labor, old vested interests were
moved to action. They assigned "to the authoritative direction of the
church, the pope, episcopate, clergy, the task of impeding any emergence of the Catholic worker to an equal degree of freedom within
society."[29]

Consistent with this program was the Trier faction's denunciation
as erroneous and pernicious the notion that the working classes had
a voice in their own destiny.[30] Trier's supporters, numerically weak
but vocally strong, preferred that the proletariat remain docile and
subservient to the authority of the church hierarchy. Hermann Paul
Fleischer, a Secretary in the League of Catholic Worker Associations
(Berlin) and an economist by profession,[31] expressed the same idea.
Submitting himself to ecclesiastical authority, he argued that "we
have no right" to modify in any way church directives. "The only
duty incumbent upon us," Fleischer continued, is "to carry out these
directives with unreserved, child-like obedience."[32]

Justifying the existence of nondenominational unions, their Roman Catholic supporters, identified as the München-Gladbach group,
argued that such organizations were more effective economically.
But they also demanded these unions with reference to the "parity"
argument. They claimed equality of rights. Other interest groups,
composed in the main of Roman Catholics, existed independently
of the church. Individual dignity, the München-Gladbach faction
maintained, required that the working classes be permitted to form
independent associations similar to those of these other groups—
the peasantry, for instance. Refusing this claim for "parity," the
Trier group speciously alleged that moral or spiritual dangers were
less evident in a peasant league than in a working-class organization.
Unlike the workers, they replied, the peasantry was innately "conservative" "distrustful of everything new," and immune to

the perils of religious disbelief.[33] That line of reasoning reflected
"Trier's" lack of confidence in the ability of the Roman Catholic
working classes to resist Social Democratic blandishments.[34]

The sectarian union's other arguments were equally ineffective and
ill-chosen. Apart from the insulting imputation that the worker was
emotionally susceptible to ideologies corrosive of his religious faith,
the Trier faction in the "trade-union conflict" claimed his economic
inability to maintain even the barest semblance of independence vitiated the demand by the Roman Catholic worker for "parity" among
his coreligionists. Although the opponents of the München-Gladbach
group acknowledged the affiliation of Roman Catholic industrialists,
manufacturers, and employers with nondenominational business
groups, they insisted that this situation was not comparable to that
of the nonsectarian trade unions. Businessmen, the Trier faction
confidently asserted, in the event of moral conflict between economic associations and their consciences, could withdraw without
incurring any special disadvantage. Should the individual worker's
moral beliefs clash with union policy, however, that worker, with
no power base of his own, "must pay with his entire stake and
with all his hopes" if he resigns from the labor association.[35] Superficial arguments of this kind denied "the entire principle of the
independent worker and trade-union movement."[36] As such, Roman Catholic workers were denied "parity" within their own religious community.

But opposition was grounded on more than the fear that the
worker was susceptible to socialism and unable to take care of his
own interests. Although the Trier faction protested the "levelling
of religious differences" and the appearance of "Social-Democratic
tendencies" within the Christian Trade Unions, the "reason for hostility" was also "found in the fact that the unions" were "not directly and immediately under ecclesiastical direction." If, declared
the Prussian envoy to the Vatican, "in place of Mssrs. Pieper and
other laymen [*sic*], bishops and parish priests took care of the
Volksverein's business" and Rome "had the final, decisive word,"
the "trade-union conflict" would cease. "The position of the interconfessional unions is for Rome," he alleged, "overwhelmingly a
question of power."[37]

This observation was substantiated by the German episcopate's
pronouncements. Denying the demands of the Roman Catholic
working classes for an equal voice with the church in their own affairs, the Bishop of Trier announced that "even if the unions could
claim a purely Catholic membership and but one worker was as-

signed to the leadership, it would be necessary for the church to
protest." He candidly admitted: "Everything depends on the reten-
tion in the hands of the clergy the control over the Catholic workers."
Religion, Korum said, was not merely "an unspecified number of
religious truths," but only the beliefs and teachings of the Roman
church. Its principles must imbue all modern labor organizations
just as they once did the guild system during the Middle Ages.[38]
Inasmuch as churchmen were best able to interpret these principles,
the episcopate's control and influence over the Roman Catholic
workers must be preserved and the workers subordinated to that
control.

Contrary to Korum's wishes, the leadership of the interconfessional trade unions (as in the case of the Centrum party) was heavily laicized.[39] Achieving prominence in the Christian Trade Unions
were such laymen as August Brust, Johannes Becker, Johann Essert,
Carl Matthias Schiffer, Adam Stegerwald, Johann Giesberts, Franz
Hüskes, and even the Protestant Franz Behrens.[40] Almost all came
from the working classes. Whereas Schiffer was a master weaver,
Behrens, Brust, Essert, and Hüskes were miners. Stegerwald was
once a cabinetmaker. Giesberts, a former transport worker, served as
the editor of the interdenominational unions' *Westdeutsche Arbeiter-
Zeitung* and the *Zentralblatt der christlichen Gewerkschaften.* Only
Becker, who later took over the *Zentralblatt*, came from a nonwork-
ing-class background. This de-clericalization of the Christian Trade
Union leadership signified the emancipation of the Roman Catholic
working classes from clerical tutelage and a step toward their social
and economic independence within the Roman Catholic population.

This trend was at cross-purposes with the hierarchy's intentions. A
clerical presence within the trade-union movement was a safeguard
both for the continuation of episcopal control and for the teachings
and the principles of the Roman Catholic faith. [41] It also represented
the subordination of the worker's material welfare to the needs of his
spiritual well-being. In keeping with the church's predilection for
manners and morals, it was stated that the essential factor in the social problem was not difference of wealth or income, but cultural
and intellectual disparity. The "parity question" within the confessional community from this standpoint necessitated the extension of
education among the working classes. Inextricably intertwined in
this cultural and educational process, said the Trier faction, was the
inculcation of religious principles. Religion, in their opinion, must
be restored to its basic position, [42] an implicit denial of "parity" between secular and spiritual needs.

This dual objective—integration of the Roman Catholic working classes both into national society and into the confessional community—testifies to the complications and the contradictions of the "Parity Question" for German Roman Catholicism. While the nature and character of the "trade-union conflict" between the München-Gladbach and Trier factions was intertwined with the aspirations of the Roman Catholic workers and the meaning of "parity," the development and vicissitudes of this intraconfessional dispute affected the vital interests of the German government, the closely related "Centrum conflict," and the "Parity Question" regarding Roman Catholics in German society.

Given the German government's attempt to integrate the working classes socially but not politically into the nation, the Christian Trade Unions were tolerated as a "battering ram" against Social Democracy.[43] Their existence, furthermore, facilitated the Cologne faction's program which sought to efface the Centrum's sectarian image, to cooperate with the government and the parties of the Right, and to attain a position of respect, status, and influence within Wilhelmine society. Once again, as in the tactical dilemma faced by the Centrum, the nondenominational labor union disrupted the internal harmony of the Roman Catholic community. But a strictly confessional worker movement estranged the working classes and drove them into the folds of the Social Democratic party. This too was detrimental to the internal cohesion of the Roman Catholics.

6: POLITICAL ECONOMY CONTRA LABOR ENCYCLICAL

*If a pope induced the hostile King Attila
to yield by means of his high-priestly
authority, why should not a simple chaplain, with the Labor Encyclical in his
hand, repel the antilabor employer . . .?*

Franz von Savigny[1]

It was not only the problem of ends—"parity" for the working
classes—that constituted a divisive issue for German Roman Catholics in the "trade-union conflict." Another cause for discord was the
question of means to attain those ends. This question remained of
importance throughout the Wilhelmine era and led to bitter debate
and intractable conflict.

* * *

There was "in Germany not just one clash, but two; the Centrum
conflict and the trade-union conflict," said Karl Marie Kaufmann.
"Both touch one another in basic particulars while the effects are
to be found in different areas."[2] As in the "Centrum conflict,"
where the party leadership quarreled about competing stratagems,
the Roman Catholic labor leaders faced essentially the same tactical
alternatives. The arguments were dull and repetitive, yet they exerted much influence. Those who espoused the interconfessional
trade unions were economically and politically pragmatic in their
line of reasoning, while the adherents of sectarian labor associations
subordinated practicality (to them it was opportunism) to moral and
doctrinal beliefs.

The methods by which the Christian Trade Unions sought to
achieve "parity" were eminently expedient. Their style was characterized by a more objective attitude and a stronger emphasis on
nontheoretical aspects. Skillfully disassociating themselves from all
doctrinaire political and religious issues, they emphasized a policy

of economic and social improvement for their membership. Unlike
the rigidly doctrinaire Social Democratic party, which they described as "an enemy of religion pursuing utopian goals, rejecting
efforts of small progress, ridiculing pacts with opponents," and "urg-
ing a policy for the future but little practical work for here and now,"
the nonsectarian unions confined their sphere of activity to *practical questions of an economic nature.*"[3] For similar reasons they did
not wish to enmesh themselves in the abstract debate of the "trade-
union conflict," claiming they had "no more time for the mere theoretical defense" of their position because of "more urgent and important things to do in the broad field of practice."[4] Throughout the
"trade-union conflict" the nondenominational unions stressed their
utility and endeavored, they said, to attain only what was socially
feasible within the existing framework of society.[5]

Expediency and concrete results, therefore, were important for
the interconfessional unions. Membership statistics from this point
of view indicated success or failure. These figures, in realistic terms,
verified the effectiveness of nondenominational unions. All too frequently, therefore, the Christian Trade Union leadership twitted the
Trier faction, demanding to know the size of the Catholic Worker
Associations so as to demonstrate the "winning power"[6] of the Craft
Association idea.[7] If for no other reason, the "München-Gladbachers"
decided, the limited membership of the Trier group demonstrated
its economic unfeasibility.

But the resourcefulness of the Christian Trade Unions was proven
by more than München-Gladbach's self-avowals. Also attesting to their
practicality were their tactics. To seriously represent working-class
interests—so as to attain "parity"—it was necessary to use the strike
or threat of a strike in order to apply pressure on the employers.[8]
"Whoever does not make himself felt economically," an exasperated
miner once said, "and move with strength and not shrink back from
the ultimate action"—the strike—"remains a zero." The worker, it
was admitted, might possibly attain his equality through requests,
supplications, and resolutions. But the moment must come when "it
doesn't help to purse the lips, you've got to whistle."[9] Determined
to advance the working-classes' economic rights, the Christian Trade
Unions assumed a realistic position and admitted that the strike was
legitimate in certain socio-economic disputes.

The interconfessional unions were not only reasonable in this economic sense. They also demonstrated an astuteness and practicality
in politics. Realizing that their economic stance—the strike, for instance—could frustrate the integration of the working classes into

society, the Christian Trade Unions stressed the political utility of their labor movement for Wilhelmine society. At pains to distinguish their program from socialism, the Christian Trade Unionists eschewed all language of the class struggle and emphasized their efforts to solve labor's "parity question." They ascribed the worst social and political motives to the Social Democrats. The socialist unions, claimed the Christian labor leaders, "did not want a legal compromise between the individual estates"; they preferred "a struggle to the knife" and accented "the class struggle" which would eventuate in "the proclamation of the dictatorship of a single social class."[10] By way of contrast, the Christian Trade Unions affirmed their loyalty to the political status quo and stressed their usefulness in stemming the socialist advance. The program of the interconfessional unions represented the quest not for power but "parity." It was bound up with the desire for status and recognition within the existing order.

Nowhere was this political pragmatism of the Christian Trade Unions more apparent than in the Rhineland and in Westphalia. The existence of such unions was dictated by the presence and growth of a large and influential Social Democratic movement. In 1912, of the twenty-nine Rhenish seats for the Reichstag, the Social Democrats held five. And whereas the Centrum party polled 653,000 votes in the general elections that year, the Social Democrats obtained 322,000. Evidence suggests, furthermore, that the socialists were gaining on the Centrists. Between 1907 and 1912 the Centrum increased its vote in Rhenish Prussia by 14,000. But during the same period the Social Democratic party's support increased by 84,000. These gains, to be sure, were not uniform throughout the locality. In the rural areas where the population was predominantly Roman Catholic, the socialist vote was under five percent. Similarly, in small and middle-sized towns such as Siegkreis-Waldbroel and Rheinbach-Bonn, the Social Democratic vote remained negligible.[11] But in the large industrial cities where the Roman Catholic masses were "exposed to the corrosion of urban scepticism and materialism," the Church of Rome found its influence declining.[12]

Alarmed by the defection of the Roman Catholic working classes —in 1913 over 800,000 belonged to Social Democratic organizations[13]—the Centrist leadership reasoned that without a viable labor organization it would "become impossible to maintain" the party's "strong position in Cologne and other large cities of the West."[14] This conclusion was not unwarranted. In 1912, Cologne, a Centrist stronghold for more than forty years, was lost to Social Democracy.[15] Essen was the only large industrial city with a predominantly Roman Catholic population which remained in the Centrum's hands after that general election. Under these political circumstances in western Prussia, it was only prudent to win the Roman Catholic working classes back to the Centrum rather than lose them to the ever-growing strength of the Social Democratic party. Herein was a functional and practical trade-union movement of great value. It was concerned with social as distinct from political reform.

The Centrum party, therefore, fostered the development of the Christian Trade Unions for political objectives. More than anywhere else in Germany, the Centrum in the Ruhr was compelled to turn to the working classes to retain or even to expand its position in the region. Prudent judgment dictated that these unions stress practical matters such as the advancement of economic rights rather than the cultivation of the workers' spiritual life. It was not by chance that the first interconfessional labor organizations emerged in the Rhenish and Westphalian industrial areas immediately after the impressive victories scored there by the Social Democrats in the general elections of 1893.[16] Not only did effective competition from the Social Democrats and the fear of losing its hold over the Roman Catholic working classes compel the Centrum in western Prussia to tolerate the Christian Trade Unions, but the party sought directly to retain the working classes' confidence. During the electoral campaign of 1907, the Centrum, seeking to grant some semblance of "parity" to the workers, nominated no less than eight labor-union secretaries as official Centrist candidates, even withdrawing candidates in Osnabrück and Arnsberg in favor of labor secretaries. A spokesman for the League of Catholic Worker Associations (Berlin) called this action a "cowardly concession" and a "crass surrender" to the fear of socialist competition.[17] Utility rather than sentiment guided the Centrum's actions in western Prussia. Elsewhere, where the socialist threat was minimal, the Centrum party was satisfied with sectarian Craft Associations. Interconfessional unions, the suffragan bishop of Cologne Hermann Joseph Schmitz observed, were justified only "in the Rhine Province" owing to peculiar local conditions, the socialist threat in particular.[18]

This candid emphasis on economic and political ingenuity to achieve equality for the Roman Catholic working classes within German society and the Roman Catholic community was inflexibly resisted by the Trier faction during the "trade-union conflict." And yet in its own way the Trier group (like the Berlin faction)

was itself skillful and pragmatic. The fragile bond between German
manufacturer and Polish laborer, already under strain in Upper
Silesia, would have worsened if it were not for the sectarian union's
"practical" religious appeal. But the Trier faction chose not to base
its case on this line of argument. Ideology was more significant. The
München-Gladbach group's "fundamental error," wrote a critic, was
to believe that economic matters were separable from religio-ethical
considerations.[19] That concept was false, said the Trier faction. In
place of the crass opportunism embodied in economics and politics,
the Catholic Worker Associations of Berlin "restored" the Roman
church's moral teachings and doctrines to the labor question.

Separating the München-Gladbach and Trier factions then, were
"the divergent points of view concerning the question of the com-
petence of church authority for the trade-union organization."[20]
Moral duties, pleaded the adherents of the Craft Associations, can
be expressed only from a sectarian viewpoint. Because of their confessionally mixed membership and their emphasis on economic opportunism, the Christian Trade Unions were deemed unsatisfactory
from the Church of Rome's standpoint as organizations for Roman
Catholic workers. Until the interconfessional unions recognized the
role of ecclesiastical authority insofar as labor activities were related
to religion and morality, there could be no compromise in the
"trade-union conflict." Demanding that the Roman church be permitted to "effectively exercise its teaching and pastoral office," the
Trier faction insisted on the necessity of church authority and
teaching for judgment in those trade-union questions which touch
on religion and morals.[21] Labor-union policy had to be shaped by
the tenets of the Roman church.

Religion, morals, and ethics were more important to the League
of Catholic Worker Associations (Berlin) than economic principles.
According to Pieper, admittedly a hostile witness, Heinrich Fournelle (the Secretary-General of the Berlin league and a cleric) repeatedly said that "for the teaching of the Catholic worker we don't
need the irreligious science of National Economy" because "for us
the catechism suffices . . . ."[22] The Trier faction did not deny the
existence of alienation between labor and employer. But an economic weapon such as the strike was declared "immoral" and its
use was disavowed in keeping with the church's teachings. Better
results, Trier proclaimed, could be achieved if employers were guided
by Christian charity. This notion, amplified by Franz von Savigny,
a retired judge, pious pedant, and lay luminary in the Trier faction,
implied that any work stoppage in the form of a strike designed to

obtain higher wages or to improve working conditions was morally unjustifiable. For the improvement of the social and economic situation, Savigny contemplated only conciliatory negotiations between employer and employees which preserved the economic peace between capital and labor. When such negotiations came to nought, a decision was to be made by compulsory arbitration.[23]

Even more impractical and doctrinaire was Savigny's oft-repeated prescription if workers and employers failed to agree in a labor conflict. "If a pope induced the hostile King Attila to yield by means of his high-priestly authority," he said, referring to the dramatic confrontation between Pope Leo I and the barbarian chieftain portrayed in Raphael's painting, "why should not a simple chaplain, with the Labor Encyclical in his hand, repel the antilabor employer . . . ?" It must be remembered, Savigny added, that "standing behind the Catholic Worker Association movement are more than 200 million Catholics throughout the whole world."[24] No better example illustrates the unbridgeable chasm between the utilitarianism of the interconfessional unions and the inflexible religious dogmatism of the Berlin league regarding the Roman Catholic working classes.

The Trier faction's efforts to avoid or even to suppress social conflict by its doctrinal assertions revealed its inability to integrate on the principle of "parity" the working classes into the Roman Catholic community. Its views were reactionary. "The *wild, free, and competitive economy*," a spokesman declared, "is the evil of evils." Because of this modern economic order and the frenzied pursuit of mammon, "laboring humanity is torn into classes" which "more and more take on the character of castes." Capital and labor coalesced into organizations which, like two hostile armies, converge on a battlefield. Deploring the economic extinction of the artisan and petty shopkeeper, the sectarian labor associations declared "capitalism" as "the enemy" and demanded an end to the growth of corporate conglomerates. The modern factory, their argument ran, did not represent progress. A viable socio-economic order could be created only when labor was freed from the yoke of this "insatiable capitalism" and led back to its "old home of economic and social freedom and independence on the basis of numerous small concerns." Then it would be possible to return to that form of labor association which "in the good old days provided the *happiness* and *satisfaction* of the working people: the old guilds." [25]

This inability to assimilate the Roman Catholic working classes into the confessional community also reflected the outlook of the

Trier faction's preindustrial *Mittelstand* and clerical-peasant leadership. More familiar with a corporate and organic view of society,
they found the organizational framework of a modern industrial
and class society both incomprehensible and frightening. The mis-
take of the München-Gladbach group, they said, was that the trade
union was seen as a "mechanism." By way of contrast, the Craft
Association was an "organism." It was something greater than the
sum of its parts, wherein the universal was harnessed in a moral
union for a common purpose—the regulation of wages and working
conditions.[26]

If the corporate will was something more than the sum of its
parts, then the problem of religious homogeneity and uniformity
of doctrinal belief within the membership became important. The
church's misgivings were grounded in large measure in the belief
that the nondenominational unions were an incongruous alliance
of disparate ideological allegiances. In the case of the interconfessional unions, the Trier faction asserted, it was "*a sophism if one
assumes that a trade union acts according to Christian principles
and can be designated as Christian if its individual members are
Christian in attitude.*" The allegation persisted that along with devout Protestants and Roman Catholics there was within the Christian Trade Union movement a broad spectrum of opinion from
"atheist" to "revolutionary Social Democrat."[27] This too sufficed
to invalidate the "Christian" label in the minds of the sectarian
union's advocates. If moral rectitude was all-important, as the
Trier faction believed, then specifically Roman Catholic doctrines
must inform union policy. In questions of labor contracts, where
moral and ethical ramifications were broad and deep, touching both
public and private law, only the highest moral authority—the church
—was invoked. Recourse to this authority was not possible in a nonsectarian labor organization. "Indifference" or "neutrality" to sectarian affiliation meant that the Church of Rome would not have
the final word.[28]

* * *

This debate over methods was not confined to arid theoretical
discussions, although that aspect was not entirely lacking. Both
sides resorted to polemics, frequently of a petulant and pedantic
character. Between 1900 and 1914 there took place an acrimonious
polemical exchange.[29] Both sides attributed the worst excesses to
the other and displayed lack of restraint in their imprecations. "If

they accuse the 'Berlin group' of fanaticism" in these diatribes, complained Cardinal Kopp, "this charge can with justification be made against the 'Cologne faction.' "[30] Prohibitions on this kind of discussion, such as the injunction of the Bishops' Conference in 1910, proved ineffective.[31] But sometimes it went beyond verbal exchanges. Given the importance of moral and doctrinal issues it was not surprising that the ecclesiastical authorities attempted to suppress the Christian Trade Unions, or at least to render them innocuous. This necessitated, above all on the part of the weaker Trier faction, overt and covert interference.

Overt intervention from the Trier faction during the "trade-union conflict" took several forms. The most important were episcopal directives, threats of suppression, and papal pronouncements.

The first serious ecclesiastical attempt to interfere in the interconfessional unions was made in 1900. Assembling in Fulda in August of that year for their annual conference, the Prussian bishops, at the prodding of the Prince-Bishop of Breslau, were induced to issue a pastoral letter in condemnation of the Christian Trade Unions[32] aimed at bringing the labor movement firmly under the church's moral supervision. Although recognizing the right of workers to organize for the protection of their economic interests, this letter declared that Catholic Worker Associations were already quite adequate for this purpose.

In addition to the action taken by the Prussian episcopate, Thomas Nörber, the Archbishop of Freiburg/Breisgau, also dispatched a circular letter in October 1900 to all his clergy in Baden advising them to refrain from activities connected with the Christian Trade Unions. While it was not his intention to condemn the interconfessional labor movement, he nonetheless wanted to warn them of the moral dangers implicit in a "neutral" religious position. Within a short time the matter was amicably settled between Nörber and the leaders of the interconfessional unions.[33] But the whole affair was another indication of the anxiety among high churchmen and the lengths to which they would go to make their will prevail and insure doctrinal purity.

Not only did the Prussian bishops seek to undermine the Christian Trade Unions by means of their pastoral letter, but they also endeavored to furnish an outline of basic principles which would serve as a guide for labor unions composed of Roman Catholic workers. In late 1910, as rivalry intensified between the Craft Associations and the nondenominational trade unions, a situation aggravated no doubt by the unusually acrimonious nature of the "trade-union conflict" in that year, the Prussian prelates assembled in Fulda in order to impose some kind of settlement on the warring Trier and München-Gladbach

factions. These churchmen, again under the leadership of Cardinal
Kopp of Breslau, formulated five principles which were to guide the
activities of these antipathetic labor associations. Among other
things, these principles demanded that the Christian Trade Unions
scrupulously restrict their activities to purely economic matters (what
constituted an economic matter was to be determined by the hierarchy), enforce simultaneous membership in the League of Catholic
Worker Associations (Berlin), and, above all, submit to the decisions
of all proper ecclesiastical authority in questions pertaining to religious
principles.[34] Designed to emasculate the Christian Trade Union movement and to subordinate it to the church hierarchy, these principles
reaffirmed the supremacy of doctrine over economic opportunism.

Seeking to check the influence of the Christian Trade Unions, the
Trier faction also resorted to intimidating tactics. In March 1902, for
example, the *Trierische Landeszeitung* argued that bishops had not
only the right but, in certain circumstances, the duty to suppress organizations such as the interconfessional trade unions. Although it is
true that this extreme step was never taken, the mere appearance of
such a statement in a newspaper under clerical control was indicative
of the hierarchy's anxiety regarding the secularization of the labor
movement and the laicization of its leadership.[35]

Even less circumspect in his hostility was Cardinal Kopp. In a letter to Pieper, since 1903 a Secretary of the *Volksverein*, Kopp
claimed that only a wave of his hand would suffice to destroy the
interconfessional unions.[36] Given the recent suppression of the interconfessional movement in France, the unions placed much credence
in this threat.[37] Open animosity of this kind was indicative once
again of the German hierarchy's willingness to participate in the
"trade-union conflict" in an attempt to strengthen their influence
and to safeguard the Roman church's moral interests.

If high churchmen in Germany actively supported the Trier faction in the "trade-union conflict" through pastoral letters and even
thinly veiled threats, still another development was the intrusion of
the Vatican's influence. There had long been rumors that a Vatican
pronouncement was imminent, and it was widely supposed that the
interconfessional unions would be suppressed. Anxious to maintain
cordial relations with Germany however, the papacy pursued a tortu-
ous policy regarding the Christian Trade Unions. When finally forced
to act, the pope's statements were an exercise in oratorical tightrope
walking. Seeking to satisfy both the German governments and the
church, the Holy See eventually issued a number of official pronouncements and promulgated an encyclical which impaired the interconfessional labor movement while leaving it essentially intact.

Except for a brief papal note in January 1906 which expressed the hope that the Trier and München-Gladbach factions would soon resolve their differences, the Vatican did not officially intervene in the "trade-union conflict" until some six years later. At Whitsuntide 1912 a Congress of all Christian Trade Unions was held in Frankfurt am Main. Simultaneously, however, the League of Catholic Worker Associations (Berlin) assembled for their own Congress in the German capital. Confronted by the unassailable evidence that the Christian Trade Unions were outstripping the Craft Associations in terms of membership and unable to conceal the limitation of its program, the Trier faction was compelled to adopt new expedients to avert its collapse. It was out of a sense of weakness of their own cause that they turned hopefully toward the Roman church. More than ever before, the Trier group needed the authority of the church hierarchy to support its ideas concerning the role of the working classes. When aid from the German episcopate proved insufficient (or when it was not forthcoming) the Catholic Worker Associations sought to outflank the hierarchy by going directly to the Vatican. The Craft Associations "went over the heads of the German bishops to the head of the Catholic church" in Rome. They "went for broke," as someone expressed it, seeking to save a "lost cause."[38] An obscure priest from Berlin named Beyer was dispatched to Rome by the Berlin Congress where Pius X granted this emissary the rare privilege of a private audience. Yielding to the clamor of the Berlin group, the pope praised the activities of the League of Catholic Worker Associations (Berlin) and expressed the wish that all German workers would adhere to that organization because the Christian Trade Unions held "erroneous principles which" the Holy See could "not recognize." These remarks, indicative of a grave concern for doctrinal and moral considerations, were instantly communicated back to the Berlin Congress. The Congress of Christian Trade Unions meeting in Frankfurt also sent felicitations to Rome. But there was no immediate acknowledgement. Finally, after an ominous delay, a perfunctory reply was received in Frankfurt which, aside from the customary formulae, contained the admonition that all the activities of the Christian Trade Unions must comply with the moral principles laid down in *Rerum Novarum*.[39]

These telegrams caused a stir. The news greatly disheartened the München-Gladbach faction. Their gloom was deepened by fear of suppression. But the League of Catholic Worker Associations (Berlin) exulted over this development because never before had Pius X made such a clear statement in the "trade-union conflict."[40] The language of the denominational unions, clamoring for suppression of their opponents, evoked grave apprehensions among the München-Gladbach faction. These events gave rise to a host of rumors concerning the future of the Christian Trade Unions. According to the most persistent, the pontiff was on the point of banning such organizations. For the Trier group, however, all this proved to be a sterile satisfaction because the pope's words did not amount to a formal condemnation of the Christian Trade Unions.

The sectarian unions obtained merely a nominal victory; in actuality they gained nothing because the status of the trade-union question was left unchanged. A few months later, following the death of Cardinal Fischer, the papacy again intervened in the "trade-union conflict."[41] Early in September 1912 the papacy issued its encyclical *Singulari quadam* which amplified the remarks about the "trade-union conflict" made by the pope at Whitsuntide. Although the Vatican obviously preferred the Catholic Worker Associations and their craft subsidiaries, it declared that Christian Trade Unions could be tolerated where they already existed—an interesting touch of pragmatism—especially in areas of mixed religious affiliation. To be sure, this toleration was conditional upon the fulfillment of certain requirements. Especially significant was the insistence on closer ties with the German episcopate and dual membership for Roman Catholic workers in Catholic Worker Associations. This prerequisite insured that the workers received the moral and spiritual training deemed so necessary by the church.[42] While it is true that the papacy avoided any formal condemnation of the interconfessional trade unions, these organizations were to be tolerated only under the most carefully defined conditions. Such restrictions seriously inhibited their growth and gravely circumscribed their economic effectiveness—two considerations of great importance to the Münchengladbach faction.[43] The Vatican's intervention aggravated the situation without resolving the fundamental problem.

Simultaneous with these developments in the "trade-union conflict," fair means and foul were used by both sides. There was a less systematic, less effective, but no less persistent attempt to undermine the Christian Trade Unions. This covert intervention assumed the form of mischief and calumny.

The "trade-union conflict" was not confined to polemics and episcopal pronouncements. Countless obstacles were placed in the way of union activities. Sometimes, as in Breslau for instance, the interconfessional unions were expelled from their local headquarters or pressure was indirectly applied so that suitable meeting places were unavailable for their activities.[44] Other frustrating obstacles—the prohibition of speakers, for instance—were also encountered. Carl Son-

nenschein, a priest and social reformer, [45] was forbidden by Cardinal
Kopp to address a labor gathering in Berlin. This incident led to fears
that *Singulari quadam* would be strictly interpreted in the Breslau
diocese and that the *Volksverein*, underrepresented as it was, would
"completely disappear there."[46]

Meetings were not only prohibited but also subjected to spasmodic
disruptions and interference. On occasion the meetings and assemblies of opposing groups were broken up and placards and posters
either defaced or torn down.[47] A single incident in the Saar bears witness to this kind of interference. The electoral committee for the constituency of Trier 6 (Ottweiler-St. Wendel) invited Bitter and Roeren
to address the local Centrum party at a rally which took place in
Neunkirchen on 25 July 1909. Ostensibly addressing himself to the
question of financial reform in the Reich, Bitter, the main speaker
of the day, directed his concluding remarks toward the recent exchange of polemics in the press and endeavored to justify his position
in the "Centrum conflict." This meeting was perceived as a threat by
the Christian Trade Unions operating in the Saar, for the Easter Tuesday Conference's animosity toward the interconfessional unions and
the *Volksverein* had recently become known. As a result, the district
leadership of the miner's branch of the interconfessional unions believed that the meeting in Neunkirchen presaged an attack on the
Christian Trade Unions. To frustrate any such plan, therefore, a circular was sent three days before the meeting requesting that a large
delegation of miners attend this Centrist gathering to voice a protest.
Fearing disruptions, Hansen and Dechant, the chairmen of the electoral committee, declared that the "trade-union conflict" was not on
the party's agenda.[48] In any case, the miners did not disrupt this
meeting. But their fears and suspicions, together with their call for
action, were indicative of the passions unleashed by the "trade-union
conflict" and its close relationship with the "Centrum conflict."

Calumny was still another tactic all too frequently employed. A
notorious case which briefly discomfited the Christian Trade Unions,
embarrassed the Cologne faction within the Centrum party, and
estranged Protestant from Roman Catholic was the so-called Trade-
Union Trial in Cologne during December 1913.[49] Following the publication of *Singulari quadam*, Karl Marie Kaufmann, a participant in
the Easter Tuesday Conference, made extraordinary charges against
the interconfessional unions which the Protestant and socialist press
promptly reproduced. He claimed in the pages of his *Cölner Correspondenz* that the leadership of the Christian unions submitted to
Rome and gave the German episcopate a guarantee of unconditional

obedience. This caused a sensation. The *Wartburg*, a Protestant periodical closely associated with the Evangelical League, seized upon this report. Accepting Kaufmann's information, the *Wartburg* claimed that the Craft Associations had emerged victorious over the interconfessional concept advocated by the Münchengladbach group. This theme was then picked up by the Social Democratic press and given wide publicity. Hopeful of making some political capital out of the incident, some twenty socialist newspapers printed articles asserting (though in no way proving) that as a result of a large financial contribution on the part of Rhenish industry to the Roman church, the ecclesiastical authorities suppressed the interconfessional unions. Incensed by such charges which received wide credence and jeopardized their position among the working classes as well as their bargaining power in industry, the Christian Trade Unions brought suit against their calumniators. During the ensuing trial Kaufmann was compelled under oath to admit that his allegations were spurious. The editor of the *Wartburg*, therefore, along with his co-defendents from the Social Democrats and Free Union press, retracted their charges, were given fines, and made to pay all court costs. And finally, particularly wounding, they were forced to publicize the verdict. [50] The whole affair was an ostentatious failure for the Evangelical League, the Social Democrats and the sectarian unions. At the same time, it demonstrated the Trier faction's deep-seated antipathy for the mode of operation preferred by the Christian Trade Unions to achieve "parity" for the Roman Catholic working classes.

* * *

The "trade-union conflict," therefore, represented an internal problem for political Catholicism in Germany. It was a "parity question" within the sectarian community, quite similar in several respects to the Roman Catholic "Parity Question" within Wilhelmine society. If the traditional Protestant elites of Prussia and Germany found it difficult to assimilate as equals the Roman Catholic minority, similarly the upper strata of the Roman Catholic community resisted the integration of their own working-class coreligionists on terms of "parity." On both levels, furthermore, there was a struggle between political pragmatism which sought an accommodation among the sectarian groups in society and the classes within the religious group. At the same time, both in society at large and within the Roman Catholic community, there were those who stubbornly and inflexibly resisted any change. [51] Ideas, slogans, and ideology played their significant role, but in the end the ideological element was subordinated to political and social needs.

7: CHRISTIAN TRADE UNIONS: A NATIONAL NECESSITY

There can exist no doubt that the Christian Trade
Unions form the most effective weapon against
the Social Democratic organizations.

Bethmann Hollweg[1]

"The Curia," said Bethmann Hollweg in 1910, "places so much weight on politics" that "in religious questions we must also think policitally."[2] Aware of their usefulness as disciplinary and welfare agencies, the government valued interconfessional unions as a countervailing political force against Social Democracy. However much the Christian Trade Unions resented this fact and deplored society's insensitivity to labor's "parity question," it was precisely their political utility which shielded them from ecclesiastical censure and ultimate extinction. Despite the bitterness of the attacks, these unions survived. Their success cannot be explained by reference to a single factor. The favorable outcome was due to reasons inherent partly in accident, partly in tactics.

* * *

Fortuitous factors played a role. The "trade-union conflict" had its share of human contingency. With the untimely deaths of Prince-Bishop Kopp and Pope Pius X in 1914, the Trier faction lost its most powerful spokesmen.

Kopp was the most influential German churchman between the end of the Kulturkampf and the First World War. To Kopp's ineffable mortification, however, that influence was on the wane during the final two years of his life. "The Vatican's soil," he admitted despondently, was "like a sand dune." After 1913 the Prince-Bishop left little impression in Rome because "a wave," as he expressed it, erased "every trace" of his "imprint."[3] As though humoring a man at the end of his career, Rome politely listened to his complaints

106

but displayed greater caution in the use of Kopp's frequently prof-fered advice.[4]

There was still another reason for Kopp's inability to have his own way in the "trade-union conflict." The disparity between the ferocity of Kopp's utterances and the tepidity of his deeds was dic-tated by political circumstances. His inability to execute his threat to Pieper in 1910 was conditioned by strained relations between Berlin and the Holy See rising out of certain remarks critical of Protestantism made by Pius X (see p. 132). A massive attack on the interconfessional unions would have aggravated those tensions and led to a severance of diplomatic ties between church and state. Kopp had to be especially careful here. It was the restoration of those ties in 1887 which were responsible for so much of the Prince-Bishop's reputation.[5] Thus practical considerations stayed his hand.

At the age of 76, in the wake of debilitating ailments, the Prince-Bishop of Breslau died in March 1914. Tension subsided following his death and München-Gladbach's tactical position seemed greatly strengthened.[6] With Kopp's passing, the Trier faction lost its most powerful and resourceful patron. Other episcopal critics of the in-terconfessional unions were not as forceful and skillful in the "trade-union conflict" as had been the Prince-Bishop. Korum never be-longed to the same league of political prelates as Kopp. His abilities were inadequate to the tasks he attempted in the "trade-union con-flict." The papacy, moreover, instructed the Bishop of Trier to show restraint in the handling of the Christian Trade Unions so as not to disturb the peace in Germany.[7] And although the vacancy in Bres-lau was not filled by the candidate preferred by the Prussian govern-ment (the appointment going to Adolf Bertram, the former Bishop of Hildesheim),[8] Kopp's successor moved with caution, moderation, and goodwill.[9] Before Bertram's formal installation, and before he could familiarize himself with the local situation and the exact na-ture of the *Richtungsstreit* or "struggle of orientation" (the collec-tive term used for the "Centrum" and "trade-union conflicts") in Silesia, these concerns were eclipsed by larger, national issues such as the outbreak of the First World War.

Coinciding with the international crisis of August 1914 was the death of Pope Pius X. While His Holiness privately admitted his hos-tility toward the Centrum party's "Bachem faction," he (the encyc-lical of 1912 notwithstanding) never took the final step to suppress the Christian Trade Union movement. But that possibility was al-ways present during Pius's pontificate, even though it was claimed he "spoke with moderation and forbearance," in contrast to his previous pronouncements about the trade-union issue, following Kopp's death.[10] Hence the care and assiduity with which all factions in the "trade-union conflict" cultivated the Vatican authorities.[11]

The new pontiff Benedict XV, determined to relax tensions within the Roman church, reversed his predecessor's policy. This desire was a natural corollary to Benedict's diplomatic interests, especially his efforts to use the Vatican's good offices to bring the belligerents of the First World War together in a compromise peace. To effectively concentrate his attention as an intermediary among the Great Powers, it was necessary that the church's internal affairs remain in a state of repose. Therefore, the Holy See no longer pressed its attack against Modernism or Reform Catholicism. Following the publication of *Ubi Arcano*, the pope's circular letter of November 1914, a wide latitude of opinion was permitted in labor questions. Simultaneously, the *Sodalitium Pianum*, the body charged with the task of suppressing Modernism, suspended its operations.[12]

Although significant, these developments were not fully responsible for the survival of the Christian Trade Unions. Part of the explanation must also be sought in divisions among the German church hierarchy. These divisions revealed themselves as early as the pastoral letter of 1900 when several members of the Prussian episcopate refused to support the extreme measures advocated by the Prince-Bishop of Breslau.[13]

His chief opponent within the hierarchy during the "trade-union conflict" was Cardinal Fischer of Cologne. Working for many years as a religious teacher in the industrial city of Essen, Fischer gained a new awareness of the distressing problems faced by Germany's laboring classes and took a sincere and special interest in their material welfare.[14] His contribution of 1,000 marks to the Christian Trade Unions during the Ruhr mine strike of January 1905 was indicative of his beliefs.[15] Neither Kopp nor Korum would have made such a gesture, a fact mirrored during the strike in the ditty

> What do I care about *Rerum Novarum*,
> I snap my fingers at Kopp and Korum!

chanted by the workers.[16] Fischer's name was not omitted simply in the interest of rhyme.

In addition to the Archbishop of Cologne, other churchmen were also sympathetic toward the interconfessional labor movement. The Archbishop of Freiburg, together with the bishops of Hildesheim, Metz, Paderborn, Speyer, and Rothenburg, supported the Christian unions. That support admittedly was not always unconditional. But even prelates like Hartmann and Schmitz in Cologne, who ideally would have preferred sectarian labor organizations, were compelled to support nondenominational unions for tactical reasons.[17]

Because the hierarchy in Germany was not united in its attitude toward the Roman Catholic working classes, the Christian Trade Unions were better able to ward off attacks against them from the ecclesiastical quarter. Without sufficient external support from Germany's high churchmen, the Trier faction's prospects for success in the "trade-union conflict" were poor. Symptomatic of "Trier's" weakness regarding episcopal support was the growing dependence of the sectarian unions on the Holy See for assistance.[18] The Vatican, though not unsympathetic, was unable to intercede without inhibitions on behalf of the Trier group because it feared political repercussions with the German governments in Berlin and Munich.

* * *

Still another reason for the failure of the nondenominational unions to succumb to ecclesiastical pressure was the union leadership's stubborn yet flexible resistance. Galvanized into action by the appearance of *Singulari quadam* in September 1912, Adam Stegerwald protested vigorously against the encyclical and the intention to increase ecclesiastical limitations on the activities of his unions. Feelings ran high among the unions' membership. A variation in the sarcastic ditty about Kopp and Korum quickly made its appearance:

> What do we care about *Singulari quadam*,
> We stand firm and true behind Adam![19]

Stegerwald charged that the encyclical would confine the labor movement in a tactical sense by a "barbed-wire fence."[20] If unable to engage in genuine labor-union activity because of the church's regulations, the workers would lose "parity" with the rest of society. But, he also warned, adherence to the papal instructions would cause massive Protestant defections from the Christian Trade Unions. And that would isolate Roman Catholic workers and jeopardize "parity" between the major religious creeds.

Confronting the threat implicit in *Singulari quadam* and seeking "to avert stagnation and to hinder the slow atrophication of our movement," the interconfessional unions held a special congress in

Essen in late November 1912.[21] This conclave resolved that "nothing will be changed in the character, form of organization, and future activity of the Christian Trade Unions."[22] In keeping with
Stegerwald's intentions, the declaration avoided rupture from Rome
and permitted "the movement" to "retain its backbone and self-
assurance," qualitites without which, it was calculatingly said (for
the benefit of both church and state), no German trade union can
resist the "Social Democratic giant."[23]

But to understand the success of the Christian Trade Unions, it
is necessary to see beyond personalities. Deaths, divisions among
the church hierarchy, even the resolve of men like Stegerwald, all
frustrated efforts to suppress the interconfessional labor movement
based on the "parity" principle. However, these were not the only
decisive factors. Equally significant in averting the proscription of
the Christian Trade Unions was governmental intervention and the
intercession of the Centrum party.

The ecclesiastical pressure generated by the Trier group and the
papacy to suppress the interconfessional unions brought no results.
A critical factor here was the attitude of the German state governments. There were two channels of communication between Germany and the Holy See: the envoys from Berlin and Munich.

It was a peculiarity of German politics that the German Empire
was not officially represented at the Vatican. Diplomatic ties were
maintained by Bavaria and Prussia instead. A papal nuncio was
accredited in Munich, Germany's most Catholic state. The enormous importance of Prussia within the Reich, however, together
with the interdependence of the Prussian and Imperial crowns and
the chancellorship with the minister presidency, bestowed upon the
Prussian representative in Rome a special importance. This fact was
not lost on the leaders of the Christian Trade Unions. As early as
1910 the nondenominational unions sought to enlist the support
of the Prussian state. Pieper suggested that one of the prominent
Evangelicals within the interconfessional labor movement—Behrens,
for example (although Pieper refused to name anyone specifically)
—request Berlin's intercession in Rome to stave off a blow against
the "national" worker movement.[24] During the next few years,
therefore, the Christian Trade Unions solicited governmental help,
professed their "national reliability," and stressed their existence as
a "state necessity." Depicting the electoral growth of Social Democracy for the government's benefit in the most lurid colors, the Christian Trade Unions underscored the irreconcilable interests between
socialism and the German Empire and the inevitability of a mass

strike which would paralyze the nation. The interconfessional unions
eschewed a revolutionary program and portrayed themselves as the
only viable countervailing force to that threat. Stegerwald warned
the government that the Social Democrats could not be overcome
by mere political power! That was demonstrated by the failure of
Bismarck's anti-Socialist legislation. Nor for that matter could the
government by timely concessions and reforms reconcile Social Democracy to the existing state. This socialist threat, he insisted, could
only be turned with the assistance of the clearly-formulated and yet
conciliatory program of a powerful Christian-national labor movement. While acknowledging their own use of the strike, the Christian
unions "viewed the strike exclusively as an economic matter" and
rejected its political use "because in a revolutionary reorganization
of the state" not only were "social values at stake, but ethical, national, and cultural questions." For that reason, the unions repeated,
"an unbridgeable chasm" existed between "Christian-national workers and Social Democracy." Moreover, they said, recent events attested to their "national reliability." Numerous instances were cited.
During the stormy parliamentary debates over tax reform in 1909
Christian labor leaders used their rank-and-file to frustrate anti-
Conservative (and anti-Centrist) socialist agitation. In the Morocco
crisis of 1911, in contrast to the Social Democrats, the interconfessional unions patriotically supported the German government. In
that same year, the Christian Trade Unions also disputed the socialist demand for an additional two million marks for the Reich Insur-
ance Fund, claiming that the German economy, in a time of ruthless
international economic competition, could not bear the strain of
such a financial burden. [25] And finally, in the great Ruhr mine strike
of 1912, the interconfessional unions refused to join the socialist
Free Unions, thereby contributing to the failure of the working-
class objectives and the continuation of the social and political
status quo. [26]

These asseverations were not without their effect. Convinced of
both their loyalty and usefulness the German government treated
the Christian Trade Unions with indulgence throughout the "trade-
union conflict." Much of this policy was shaped by Count Arthur
Posadowsky-Wehner. [27] Reich Secretary of the Interior from 1897
until his dismissal in 1907, Posadowsky used his office and influence
to support religious trade unions. He believed that the Social Democrats could not be combatted through repressive legislation, but
only by an active revitalization of the religious and moral foundations of society. Behind all Posadowsky's reform projects was the

underlying intention that trade-union activities should be channelled
into economic rather than political issues. Economic advantages
were offered in compensation for the sacrifice of political rights.
From Posadowsky's point of view, the Christian Trade Unions were
well suited for this purpose because Christianity represented a sta-
bilizing force in state and society.[28] Like Count Leinsdorf in Robert
Musil's masterpiece, *The Man Without Qualities*, what Posadowsky
"expected of the working class was that, if one merely made concessions to it in questions of material welfare, it should dissociate
itself from unreasonable slogans brought into its midst from outside
and recognize the natural order of things in the world, where everyone had his duties and could flourish in his allotted place."[29]

Following Posadowsky's dismissal in 1907—he was a victim of
the anti-Centrist attitude of the Bülow bloc—the Secretariat of the
Interior was taken over by Bethmann Hollweg. In this capacity, and
especially after 1909 as Minister-President of Prussia and German
Chancellor, Bethmann Hollweg pursued a similar program with even
greater vigor. He, along with Baron Hans von Berlepsch, former Prussian Minister of Trade (the department formally entrusted with labor questions before 1897), openly bestowed governmental approbation on the interconfessional working-class movement by their
public appearances and addresses at annual labor conclaves.[30]

Although Bethmann Hollweg and Clemens von Delbrück, Prussian Minister of the Interior, expressed misgivings about possible
socio-political consequences should Rome implement definitive
measures against the interconfessional unions,[31] no governmental
action was taken until after the publication of *Singulari quadam*.
Even then Berlin cautiously replied to this development with temperate remarks for fear that it would exacerbate the political situation, already tense in Germany owing to another major effort to repeal the remaining clauses of the Jesuit Law.[32] But the passing of
the Jesuit crisis by 1913 made possible Berlin's intervention. Inasmuch as the Reich was not diplomatically represented in the Vatican, however, Bethmann Hollweg interceded through the Prussian
legation.

Expressing himself in favor of the interconfessional labor movement, Bethmann Hollweg said: "There can exist no doubt that the
Christian Trade Unions form the most effective weapon against the
Social Democratic organizations." The Prussian ambassador, he went
on, must make it clear to the Curia "that it has the same interest as
the state in the uninhibited continued existence and strengthening
of the Christian Trade Unions." Unsettled conditions, together with

the church's hectoring attitude and the threat of censure, caused considerable damage and seriously weakened loyal elements in their struggle against socialism. Again stressing political necessity, Bethmann Hollweg asserted his conviction "that in the absence of the trade-union conflict the last Reichstag election [January 1912] would have turned out essentially different." Emphasizing "the seriousness of the situation," he declared "that the struggle against" Social Democracy "can be won only if all Christian elements join together in order to meet the enemy with united strength." Political exigencies required an end to the "trade-union conflict."[33]

A subsequent diplomatic *démarche* presented at the Vatican was even more explicit. It stressed, in the spirit of a serious warning, that under no circumstances could Berlin accept the suppression of the interconfessional unions. Because "the Christian Trade Unions were a bulwark of the loyal parties against Social Democracy," the Prussian note read, neither their destruction nor the interference of the Roman church in German economic affairs was tolerable. In a tone that was "very sharp and angry," Berlin demanded the church terminate the "trade-union conflict." These unions were viewed by Berlin as institutions whose continued existence was considered vital to the state's interests.[34] If the forces in possession of the German government would tolerate no step toward self-government, the working classes had somehow to be reconciled to the autocratic regime. This task was assigned to the nondenominational trade unions.[35] Not only would ecclesiastical censure outrage public opinion and worsen the religious antagonisms in Germany, but the prohibition of the Christian Trade Unions, contrary to the Trier faction's expectations, would result in a massive influx not to the Craft Associations, but to the socialist Free Trade Unions.[36] All attempts to stabilize the social situation would thus be frustrated.

Only the intervention of Berlin kept the Vatican from yielding to the demands of the Trier faction. Mindful of the restraints imposed by Berlin's diplomatic pressure, the Vatican's reply contained such reticences and ambiguities as to permit the continued existence of the interconfessional unions. Seeking to evade complications with the Prussian government, the Cardinal State-Secretary asserted that the Curia did not intend to destroy the Christian Trade Unions. While clinging to the position outlined in *Singulari quadam*, the papal pronouncement represented further equivocation on the unions. The Cardinal State-Secretary said that the church tolerated nonsectarian working-class organizations as long as certain conditions were met. Expressing sympathy with Prussia's political position, especially the intention to erect "a dam against the Social Democratic floodtide," he nonetheless stressed the church's apprehensions about religious purity. But he gave assurances that no steps were to be taken against the nondenominational unions. Otto von Mühlberg, the Prussian envoy, suspected that the Vatican wanted to go no further than what was already contained in the encyclical of 1912. Prussia's warnings averted a crisis, but Mühlberg was admittedly pessimistic about how long peace would endure in the "trade-union conflict." But for the moment the Vatican was persuaded that "in order to save Roman Catholic workers from Social Democracy," Christian Trade Unions "must be tolerated in certain parts of Germany." This opinion confirmed Bishop Michael Faulhaber's impression gained the previous year. Although confessional working-class organizations were preferred, he said, the Christian unions would be tolerated—at least for a while.[37]

If overriding political priorities played a critical role in Prussia's intercession on behalf of the interconfessional unions, similar considerations impelled the Bavarian government to intervene in the "trade-union conflict." In several respects this intervention was coordinated and agreed upon by both Berlin and Munich so that the Holy See was convinced it was confronted by a united Germany regardless of the differences of the religious faiths of its sovereigns. Such action also served as a deterrent to the Vatican. The moving force behind the Bavarian remonstrances was Hertling. Both before and after his appointment in 1912 as the Bavarian chief minister, the count manifested his solicitude for the interests of the Christian unions.[38] As a devout Roman Catholic, Hertling was not insensitive to Rome's doctrinal interests. But like Bethmann Hollweg, the Bavarian Minister-President called the Vatican's attention to the question's political importance and attempted to elicit from the pope a promise not to suppress the interconfessional unions. As early as the appearance of the *Singulari quadam* in 1912 Munich urged the Holy See to keep a sense of proportion in the "trade-union conflict." Hertling reminded the hierarchy of the tense religious atmosphere in Germany and the critical attitude toward the Roman church taken by Bethmann Hollweg and Delbrück. The Bavarian leader maintained this stance throughout the two-year period before the World War.[39] He also facilitated the efforts of prominent personalities, both lay and clerical, from German society to intercede in Rome for the Christian unions. A long procession of notables, including the Duke and Duchess Albrecht von Öttingen, the Bavarian Landtag deputy and priest Carl Walterbach, and the

Prince of Hohenzollern-Sigmaringen, made the trek to Rome in
1913 and 1914 to express their opinions in the "trade-union conflict." The Bishop of Speyer, who was on close terms with the Bavarian chief minister, also visited the Holy See in 1914.[40] They
were all eager to see the papacy treat the Christian Trade Unions
with indulgence. Rome, as a result, informed Munich that it did not
want to aggravate the situation in Germany over the labor question
and expressed a willingness to collaborate with the Bavarian government to ameliorate the situation.[41]

More than any other factor, it was governmental intervention
that prevented the Holy See from condemning the interconfessional
labor movement. But the Centrum party's intercession in Rome also
played a significant (if less important) role. That intercession, however, was slow in coming. "Until now," complained a labor leader in
1912, "one cannot speak of the highest organs of the party and
their intervention" in the "trade-union conflict." Either the storm
over the trade unions was said to be unrelated to party affairs, or—
more frequently—the fear was expressed that meddling would bring
down Rome's wrath on the Centrum itself. That attitude was not
shared by all Centrists. "One must be naive," an official of the
Volksverein said, if one did "not see that the actions against the
trade unions" were "but a link in the chain, an organic component
of a system" with consequences for the Centrum party.[42] But anxious to avoid involvement in the trade-union squabbles, Centrist
leaders—with notable exceptions—seized upon any pretext to remain complacent. As late as 1910, because of assurances from
Rome, Hertling, Porsch, and the elder Spahn convinced themselves
that "for the moment nothing further need be done." While admit-
ting that "the danger, to be sure, was for the moment averted,"
Carl Bachem warned that "at any moment it can flare up again."
With some difficulty, Bachem persuaded his colleagues of the "urgent necessity" to convince Rome of the "trade-union conflict's"
serious political implications. Slowly "the recognition penetrated
that the Centrum party . . . must defend itself" because the labor
question definitely had "a serious political aspect."[43]

If the Centrum displayed a reluctance to adopt a formal position
in the "trade-union conflict" or to actively and openly intervene,
the Cologne faction did indirectly support the nonsectarian labor
organization. As early as 1904 several "Cologners" made a joint
appeal to Raffaele Merry del Val, the Cardinal State-Secretary, in
which they justified the need for nondenominational working-class
organizations in Wilhelmine Germany. Apart from assurances that

such unions were responsible and religiously reliable, these lay lu-
minaries emphasized the increasingly important political function
of such working-class associations. Enumerating these political advantages, the "Cologners" declared that the Christian Trade Unions
were a vital asset in the campaigns against liberalism and socialism,
a moderating influence in economic problems, and a force which
rendered extraordinary support in electoral contests.[44] These
points provided the nucleus of the Centrum's attitude toward the
München-Gladbach faction throughout the labor dispute. On two
occasions at least, October 1908 and July 1912, Carl Bachem also
visited the papal nuncio in Munich and discussed the labor question
in Germany.[45]

    "If the Centrum party takes pride in the fact that it is the only
bourgeois party in the large industrial districts which up to now has
victoriously held those constituencies so hard pressed by the Social
Democrats," prominent Centrists admitted in 1910, it is due to the
loyalty of the Roman Catholic working classes and the *Volksverein*.
Chiefly because of the Christian Trade Unions, Social Democracy
failed to make even greater inroads among the Roman Catholic
electorate. If the Centrum was to remain a viable political institution, the Vatican was told, it could not afford to lose the large cities
and industrial districts of western Prussia and confine its electoral
support to the rural areas. Making the Christian Trade Unions even
more indispensable was the mixed confessional nature in this industrial zone. Given the peculiar confessional nature of western Prussia,
the Curia was informed, and in the face of a powerful Social Democratic organization, political cooperation between Protestantism
and Roman Catholicism was a necessity. It was in the Centrum's
own interest that the Christian Trade Unions not be hindered by
the church authorities.[46] Experience demonstrated, Carl Bachem
rationalized, that they were the only organizations capable of keeping Roman Catholic workers out of Social Democracy's reach. If
such unions were crushed, he said, the loss of the great metropolitan
centers of the West was a certainty. And "over the city of Cologne,"
he noted ruefully, "despite the Centrum party's greatest exertions,
the red flag would wave." Bachem added that should such "electoral losses enfeeble the Centrum, the Roman church's interests in
Germany would be in jeopardy," a warning that was not without
its effect on the Curia. The party's survival—and with it Roman
Catholic interests such as the "Parity Question"—depended on the
Volksverein and the Christian Trade Unions.[47]

    The *Volksverein's* ability to mobilize the Centrum's electorate

in the industrial areas was compromised by the "trade-union conflict." Wherever the Craft Associations were active, as in Saarbrücken, the *Volksverein* encountered electioneering difficulties
because of its close relationship to the interconfessional unions.
Internecine strife among the Roman Catholic working classes paved
the way for Social Democratic advances.[48] Given these conditions,
together with the expectation that general and state (Prussian) elections were pending for late 1911, the Centrum's anxieties concerning the trade-union problem in Germany were explicable.[49]

Except for these indirect efforts on behalf of the Christian Trade
Unions, it was not until February 1914, on the occasion of Wacker's
famous speech, that the Centrum explicitly stated its position regarding the labor problem. In an address that was widely publicized,
Wilhelm Marx, later to become Chancellor of the Weimar Republic,[50]
reminded his Centrist audience "that it was the duty of every single
member of the party to ward off everything likely to hinder the
unity, the cohesiveness, [and] the furthering of the strivings of the
Christian-national workers."[51]   At the same time, Marx's remarks—
the emphasis on Christian and national—represented Centrist obei-
sance to their Evangelical-Conservative partners in the Black-Blue
bloc and the political value of a nonsocialist, antirevolutionary labor movement.

* * *

Whatever their changes of fortune in the "trade-union conflict,"
the Christian Trade Unions continued their coexistence with the
Craft Associations. Governmental support rallied the Centrum's
Cologne faction and weighed the balance against the sectarian
unions. The strength of the denominational organizations ebbed
away, condemning them to virtual economic extinction. When in
December 1912, to cite but one instance, the Catholic Worker Associations (Berlin) rented the brewery hall in Friedrichshain, a
working-class quarter in the German capital, to celebrate the recent
declaration of *Singulari quadam*, the Trier faction was gravely dis-
appointed. Rows of empty seats bore witness to the declining support given the denominational unions. The same hall, noted an observer, which was filled to overflowing just a few weeks before
during a massive Roman Catholic protest against the Jesuit Law, or
even for Kopp's silver jubilee that same year as Prince-Bishop of
Breslau, on this occasion "was almost empty on two sides of the
hall and on the tribune." Of the 1,000 persons attending, most

were women and children. The number of workers present was no
more than four or five hundred. A lifeless atmosphere, listless audience, and sporadic applause characterized the gathering. Even in the
midst of the concluding speeches, the audience began to melt away.
"All in all," it was clear that "with such speeches and assemblies no
labor organization can be given life" nor could the interconfessional
unions "be scotched." [52]

Faced with negligible support for confessional labor associations
and the magnitude of the Social Democratic threat to the Black-
Blue bloc, the Vatican agreed to tolerate the Christian Trade Unions.
Politics triumphed over ideology. The "parity question" in its narrow sense (i.e., the working-class claim for a position of equality in
Wilhelmine society and in the German Roman Catholic community)
was, however, eclipsed by political considerations. More preoccupied
with status and position than with political power to achieve those
objectives, the Christian unions were channelled into economic
rather than political activities. Such policies maintained the political
status quo.

Under the circumstances both government and Centrum party
were able to collaborate. The Centrum's leadership, engrossed with
the Roman Catholic *Mittelstand's* "Parity Question," perceived a
tactical advantage in their support of the Christian Trade Unions.
That working-class movement did not seriously undermine the social and political order. Instead, it facilitated cooperation between
the government, Conservative Evangelicals, and the Centrum party.
These were the prerequisites, in the opinion of the Cologne faction,
for a successful solution to the "Parity Question."

8: THE CENTRUM IS A POLITICAL PARTY

*In the Kulturkampf the formation of the party
in Upper Silesia resulted from religious principles;
in the present according to economic and national
[factors]. From our standpoint that is to be re-
gretted, but not to be hindered.*

                                    Jan Kapitza[1]

As in the case of the "trade-union conflict," the Cologne faction's
success in the "Centrum conflict" was facilitated in part by such
accidental factors as the death of Cardinal Kopp. Without his presence, the dissidents within the Centrum's ranks lost heart in the
contest.[2] But much more important in determining the outcome of
the "Centrum conflict" were disparities in strength and tactics between the two factions.

German Roman Catholics did not constitute a monolithic bloc
in Wilhelmine Germany. Neither concentrated in one area nor evenly distributed throughout Germany, Roman Catholicism reflected
regional and local dissimilarities.[3] The Centrum party too was a
strongly localized political organization. The pattern of its organization in Wilhelmine Germany was a patchwork rather than a sym-
metrical design. In order to assess the relative strengths of the Berlin and Cologne factions, therefore, it is necessary to probe local
interests, specific problems, and the heterogeneity of the Roman
Catholic population in Germany.

Provincial distinctions were reflected in the Centrum party's organization, for the dispersal of the Roman Catholic population was
reflected in the separation of powers within the party. It was a tremendously diverse party, a tangled web of sections, localities, and
groups.[4] Accentuating these distinctions was the Centrum's structure. The national leadership rested in the hands of Reichstag deputies. Political, then, rather than administrative personnel predominated in the party's executive. Systematic conduct of party busi-

ness was difficult. The absence until February 1914 of a centralized
party (and even then organizational unity was incomplete) also fa-
vored the proliferation of other power centers. Divided into various
contingents, founded neither at the same time nor for the same reasons, the Centrum was a mosaic of competing interests.

If the Centrum was more localized in its power centers than other
political parties in Imperial Germany, the Prussian Centrum was the
most decentralized. Beneath the veneer of unity imposed by confessional ties, the party was very local in its affiliations. For all its support from the southern states, the Centrum party was in the first
place the party of Prussia. The majority of Germany's Roman Catholics (11,269,500) were Prussians. Bavaria, Baden, and Württemberg
together had a total Roman Catholic population of about 6,516,000.
Secondly, the Centrum was the party of Prussia's western and southeastern constituencies. Unlike Centrist organizations in other states,
the Prussian party was organized on the basis of regional committees
representing the Rhineland and Silesia, a situation reflecting the
Centrum's strong regional roots and local interests in that state.
With the increased politicization of the masses in Wilhelmine Germany the need for more systematic management made itself felt.
Not until 1907, however, was the decision taken to organize a state
committee for Prussia as a whole. And even then the statutes for
such a central body were not drawn up before March 1908. The
creation of a national coordinating committee for Imperial Germany
experienced similar delays; after having done without for over forty
years, such an institution for the direction of political strategy and
policy was finally created in February 1914.[5] Under the circumstances, the Centrum was fragmentized and localized, with little of
the centralization and tendency toward uniformity too frequently
(and erroneously) associated with Catholicism. Each local party
in Germany and regional Centrist organization in Prussia had to
adjust its activity to narrow and specific political, social, and economic conditions. The Centrum's organizations under such circumstances frequently formed policies and programs independent of
each other. These conditions created a situation which was destined
to create inequalities of strength and influence among the Centrum
party's various segments.

These territorial relationships were important in determining the
strength of the various competing factions within the German Roman Catholic community. Like the Centrum itself, the party's affiliated or quasi-affiliated organizations depended on a provincial base.
Interconfessional unions were located in western Prussia where

membership constituted about two-thirds to three-fourths of the total. The rest of the membership was distributed chiefly among the southern states.[6] Catholic Worker Associations (Berlin) were strongly represented only in Upper Silesia and the Saar which together contained three-fourths of the entire membership.[7]

That regionalism was of consequence in these disputes about the policy by which the "Parity Question" could be settled was mirrored in the names of the factions themselves. Each of these groups —Berlin (or Breslau), Cologne, München-Gladbach, and Trier—derived their identities from Prussian cities and towns. This was also significant. It meant that the "Parity Question," especially insofar as it affected political Catholicism internally, was primarily a Prussian problem. The issue of equality (the "Centrum conflict," or the "trade-union conflict") was not totally absent in those states of South Germany that were predominantly Roman Catholic. But these problems were less acute.

In contrast to Prussia, discrimination was less pervasive in the kingdom of Bavaria where more than seventy percent of the inhabitants were adherents of the Roman creed. Hertling's experience is illustrative of the different situations. Unable to obtain a professorship in the Prussian University of Bonn because of his religious faith, he nonetheless secured an academic position in Munich. And whereas the higher echelons of the civil service were virtually closed to Roman Catholics in Prussia, Hertling was able to become Bavarian Minister-President in 1912.

There was yet another reason why parity was less a factor in Bavarian society. The Bavarian Centrum, formed only in 1887 out of the old particularist Patriot party, was dominated by conservative-clerical and agricultural interests. Georg Heim,[8] a prominent local politician, was known as the "peasant king"—a title emblematic of the social character of Bavarian political Catholicism. Unlike the situation of the Prussian Centrum, the Bavarian Roman Catholic *Mittelstand* played less of a role in their party.

Still another factor depreciated the significance of the Centrum party's own internal "parity question" south of the Main river. Disputes between laymen and clergy were less important because the *Volksverein* (an agency for the Centrum's secularization) played a smaller role outside of western Prussia.[9] The *Volksverein* was virtually unrepresented in Bavaria except in the Bavarian Pfalz on the left bank of the Rhine. In the absence of any significant secularization of the party organization, ecclesiastical institutions and the clerical element continued to be more important in the Wittelsbach

realm than in Prussia. Even interconfessional unions were not a major issue in Bavaria. Such unions, declared a Bavarian dispatch, "have
their location and radius of activity chiefly in North Germany,"
while in the South, because of lagging industrial development, there
exist "only a scattered few." For that reason, the report concluded,
"the Cologne-Breslau quarrel" had "only a theoretical interest for
Bavaria."[10]

The "Parity Question" and political Catholicism's internal problems were more serious in Baden. Located in southwestern Germany,
this Grand Duchy had a population that was more than sixty percent Roman Catholic. It also had a long record of conflict between
church and state. In 1846 and beginning again in 1860 conflict
erupted between a liberal government and the church. Even with
the end of the Kulturkampf, Baden's Roman Catholics, like their
Prussian counterparts, encountered widespread anticlericalism and
vestiges of discriminatory legislation and practices.[11] But these issues were not as disruptive to political Catholicism as in Prussia. To
be sure, the activities of Nörber and Wacker attracted attention.
But Centrist politicians from Baden did not play as important a
role in the "Centrum conflict" as the Prussians. This situation can
be partially explained by local conditions in the Grand Duchy. Although the *Volksverein* had more than 61,800 members (representing 19.2 percent of the male population) in 1914, the intrusion of
this institution did not lead as in Prussia to the secularization of
party structure or the laicization of the Centrum's leadership. As in
Bavaria, and in contrast to Prussia, control of the local Centrum
party remained in clerical hands.[12]

Owing to the spatial dispersion of Roman Catholics and to the
local character of the Centrum party, there were great inequalities
of power and influence between the Berlin and Cologne factions
in the "Centrum conflict." Under ideal conditions, the Silesians
could aspire at most to control fifteen constituencies—the twelve
in Upper Silesia and perhaps Reichenbach-Neurode, Glatz-Habelschwerdt, and Franckenstein-Münsterberg, the three southern constituencies of the Breslau administrative district in Lower Silesia.
These three electoral districts, like the twelve in Upper Silesia, were
predominantly Roman Catholic in religious composition. In practice, however, four to five of the Upper Silesian constituencies were
controlled by Polish nationalists. Under such conditions, the Berlin
faction in the East was able to mobilize only about nine to ten constituencies for its program. With so few constituencies at their disposal, the "Berliners" were scarcely able to impose their sectarian

policy on the entire Centrum party, especially following Kopp's decline in influence and his subsequent death.

Nor was the basic disparity in strength between the "Centrum conflict's" two warring factions redressed with the addition of the Centrum party from the Trier administrative district. With its six seats (the Centrum held five), the Trier-Saar region did not represent a considerable accretion of strength for the Berlin faction. Even a Silesian-Saar axis could scarcely hope to overpower the Centrum's more influential and powerful secular wing and reshape the party's platform according to its likes.

Whereas the Centrum's confessional faction was concentrated in Silesia and the Trier-Saar districts, the secular-political wing was located in the Rhineland and Westphalia. Having acquired thirty-one parliamentary mandates there in the general elections of 1907, this region constituted the Centrum's most important source of political power. This fact bestowed special advantages in the hands of the Cologne faction, giving it a virtually unassailable position in the party's internecine strife.

The disparity in strength between the Berlin and Cologne factions was not only the difference of fifteen or so and thirty-one parliamentary mandates. Other quantitative differences were significant. Because of clerical domination within the Silesian, Trier, and Saar Centrum parties, few lay politicians emerged within those branches of the party. While some laymen from these areas did achieve prominence—Porsch, Ballestrem, and Oppersdorff, to name but three—the leading Centrist figures were from the West—Carl and Julius Bachem, Erzberger, Trimborn, Hertling, Marx, and Peter Spahn. But there was also a qualitative difference. The clerical platform had few defenders of the caliber of the Cologne faction. Composed of astute politicians driven by secular and pragmatic ambitions, the leaders of the Rhenish Centrum were better able to realize their tactical aims regarding the "Parity Question." All this was apparent in the inherent disadvantages of the "Berliners" and the Cologne faction's successful tactics during the "Centrum conflict."

* * *

These disparities in strength, both quantitative and qualitative, were accentuated by the Berlin faction's tactical mistakes. Obsessed as the "Berliners" were with inequalities of civil rights for their coreligionists, they tried to end the "Parity Question" through a defensive posture which emphasized confessional loyalties. A concomitant of this policy was dependence upon the Church of Rome. This reliance was not without its consequences for the "Centrum conflict." It led the Centrum's confessional wing to neglect the developing party apparatus and, closely related, blinded them until it was too late to establish an independent line of communication to the Roman Catholic masses.

Given their antipathy to the Centrum's secularization through the existence of a separate party structure, it was not surprising that the "Berliners" took refuge in the outdated church-related form of organization and failed to gain control over this new apparatus. By relying on the acquisition of episcopal support and the backing of the church, they doomed their cause to failure. That support was of limited value in the political quarrels dividing the Centrum because the church's influence waned in the face of the party's secularization and the laicization of its leadership. Neglect of the party apparatus cost the confessional wing a determining role within the Centrum and, conversely, bestowed ascendancy within the organization upon the Cologne faction. Handicapped by lack of party organization, without a position of power and influence, the "Berliners" were unable to compel the Centrum to adopt their policy for coping with the "Parity Question."

Compounding the confessional wing's difficulties was the growing isolation of its adherents within the party's ranks. Whatever influence the "Berliners" had within the new party organization vanished with Ballestrem's death in 1910 and in the wake of resignations or expulsions from the parliamentary delegation.

Among the advocates of a sectarian label for the Centrum, one of the most outspoken was the Silesian magnate Count Oppersdorff. A close friend of Kopp, landowner, Reichstag deputy, and leader of the local peasantry, this nobleman also had powerful connections with the Polish community and in the Vatican.[13] He was a shallow, outspoken aristocrat who indulged a freedom of expression and action that made him the bane of his party. Oppersdorff's capacity for intrigue earned him the epithet "half-crazy schemer." Described as "pathological" by many Centrists, Oppersdorff was nonetheless a significant adversary of the Cologne faction. His social and political contacts and his journalistic activities (since 1912 he published a magazine which unreservedly supported Kopp) made him a formidable opponent.[14] But the count was not renominated in 1912 as the party's candidate in the constituency of Breslau 12 (Glatz-Habelschwerdt). Rebuffed by his own party, he exploited his Polish connections and instead stood for election as a Centrist in Fraustadt-Lissa, an elec-

toral district in predominantly Polish Posen. Despite Hertling's telegrams to Fraustadt-Lissa which declared the count's candidature as
"not desired," Oppersdorff was elected. But when the new Reichstag convened in Berlin, the count was not accepted as a member of
the Centrum delegation. Rejected and repudiated by the Centrum,
unable to affiliate with any political party, Oppersdorff became a
mere cipher.[15]

In addition to the loss of this Silesian magnate, the sectarian faction within the party suffered diminuation of influence when Bitter
failed to stand for reelection. Either on account of personal disin-
clination or because of opposition from the electoral committee in
Bersenbrück, Bitter was not a candidate for a second term. In the
ensuing elections held in January 1912 his mandate was lost to the
National Liberals. Bitter's disappearance, like Oppersdorff's, meant
that still another voice in support of a policy of confessional strength
to settle the "Parity Question" was heard no longer in the deliberations of the Centrum's new Reichstag delegation.

Even more detrimental to the Berlin faction's cause was the loss
of Roeren, the most indefatigable exponent of the confessional platform.[16] Although reelected by a large plurality in 1912, Roeren's
influence as the sole representative of a strictly confessional program was sharply reduced. His absences from both the Reichstag
and the Prussian Landtag, ostensibly for reasons of ill-health, became more frequent. Complaining of frustrating and humiliating
attacks on his person, Roeren demanded redress from his colleagues
in the Centrist delegation to the Landtag. Porsch, the chairman of
the delegation, assumed that Roeren once again wanted to open the
question of the Centrum's definition. His patience taxed beyond
endurance, Porsch turned on Roeren with sharp and admonitory
gestures. As his bald head became "red as a lobster," Porsch shouted
in a voice quivering with passion: "As long as I sit here as chairman,
I'll never permit that" discussion to take place. Following this outburst, Roeren realized his isolation, slipped quietly from the chambers, and in March 1912 resigned both his Reichstag and Landtag
seats. He was never seen in parliament again.[17] With his departure
there was no one left in either Centrist parliamentary delegation
who had played a prominent role in the Berlin faction's program
to define the Centrum as a Roman Catholic organization.[18]

The disappearance of these three deputies, the most perservering
and articulate spokesmen for the confessional approach to the "Parity Question," was a serious reverse for the Berlin faction in the
"Centrum conflict." Once the "Berliners" were excluded from the

parliamentary delegations, pressure mounted to stifle murmers of
discontent and to compel other dissidents to fall into line with official party policy. The Centrum's attention was first turned against
the Catholic Action group in Silesia. Under Porsch's chairmanship,
two hundred party officials met in Beuthen, Upper Silesia, in September 1912. Claiming that adherence to Catholic Action was incompatible with membership in the Centrum,[19] the Beuthen assembly censured but did not expel the disaffected elements. Nevertheless, such a decision was an obvious attempt to coerce those individuals opposed to the direction of Centrist policy.

The Centrum's attitude toward these dissidents hardened notice-
ably by February 1914. Virtually unopposed because the party's
apparatus was firmly in their hands, the Cologne faction made a new
and explicit declaration and affirmed for the third time on behalf
of the Centrum party its nonsectarian character. In a highly colored
report which attacked the party's confessional wing as discredited
enemies, Marx mocked his opponents and declared that the party's
pronouncement of 8 February marked "the end of the Centrum's
civil war." Those who stood "on the platform of the Reich Committee" and accepted the Centrum's nonsectarian character were Centrists. "Whosoever with full conviction and knowledge" was unable
to "sign and support such a proclamation," Marx warned, did "not
belong to us."[20] Following this declaration, the Centrum's central
committee—established at the same time—demanded that every
Centrist deputy in the Reichstag and the various state parliaments
affix his signature to the document.

In the face of the coercive machinery of the party organization,
the dissidents either capitulated or were expelled. Led by Hubert
Underberg, a member of the Easter Tuesday Conference, Joseph
Werr (Roeren's successor in the Reichstag), and even Bartholomäus
Kossmann, a leader of the Catholic Worker Associations in the
Saar,[21] most "Berliners" silently acquiesced to the formula. But
not everyone signed. Four clerics in Trier (to furnish the most notable case), including a member of Bishop Korum's cathedral chapter and a professor from the local seminary, declined to subscribe
to the formula. Making their views public in March 1914, Chaplain
Stein, Professor Jakob Marx, Joh. Jakob Roschel, and Jakob Treitz
demanded instead that the party pronouncement include support
for Roman Catholic labor associations and make explicit that the
Centrum acted only in accordance with Roman Catholic principles.
Rejecting such a demand, the Centrum, with the assent of the Trier
electoral committee, stripped these clerics of their political positions

within the party the following month. So important had the Centrum's organization become, that Korum was unable to protect his clergy against party disciplinary action.[22]

Because of the confessional wing's weaknesses, expulsions followed. Fleischer, the Secretary of the League of Catholic Worker Associations (Berlin), and the Silesian priest and leader of "Catholic Action," Paul Nieborowski, were repudiated by and expelled from the Centrum party in 1914.[23] The unity which the party executive was unable to secure by consent it sought to impose by discipline and the exercise of power.

By these means the Centrum's leadership, firmly in the hands of the Cologne faction, induced adherence to their views and eradicated the last pockets of opposition from the confessional wing. The "Berliners" were disorganized, confused, and without a foothold in the party's parliamentary organization. Their failure here was also duplicated in the Berlin faction's inability to control the Centrum's ancillary organizations, especially the Augustinus Union, a party affiliate responsible for press activities. As early as August 1909 it became apparent that this influential organ had aligned itself with the Bachem group. Not only was the Augustinus Union's directorate (Hüsgen and Lensing) openly sympathetic with Julius Bachem's program, but they countenanced the *Kölnische Volkszeitung's* press diatribes against the "Berliners."[24] Three years later, in March 1912, the Augustinus Union hampered the Berlin faction's efforts to establish its own press.[25] More successful were the Union's attacks on the Centrum's confessional wing in 1914. When the party enforced assent to the Centrum's nonsectarian nature, the Augustinus Union made the same demand of its membership. Economic reprisals were implemented against those who proved obdurate. Newspapers and periodicals which supported the Berlin group were boycotted and their access to information from the Union's central press bureau was denied. Kaufmann's "Central Information Office for the Catholic Press," for example, was blacklisted.[26]

The inability of the confessional faction to influence a Centrist institution such as the Augustinus Union not only represented its failure to control the Centrum's organization as a whole. Their failure also restricted their ability to influence the Centrist electorate of the need for a sectarian stance to meet the "Parity Question." It was not that they were unaware of the importance of public opinion. Deploring the partisanship of both the Bachem family's *Kölnische Volkszeitung* and the *Germania*,[27] unable to control the Augustinus Union, the adherents of a confessional policy for the Centrum were compelled to develop their own press and information bureau.[28] But their belated start placed them at a severe disadvantage in the procurement of information and the use of publications available to the Cologne faction.

In the absence of a daily newspaper with such wide circulation as the *Kölnische Volkszeitung*, the "Berliners" announced in December 1911 their intention to establish a newspaper to represent and propagate their viewpoint. Known as *Das katholische Deutschland*, its editorial policies were guided by a two-point program calling for the maintenance of the Centrum's sectarian character and closer cooperation between party and church hierarchy.[29]

From the start the confessional wing's newspaper project encountered difficulties which limited the effectiveness of its message. As a weekly publication *Das katholische Deutschland* scarcely had the impact of Bachem's multiedition daily newspaper. The Berlin faction's mouthpiece was also financially unsound. Without sufficient capital, unable to obtain financial subventions, and hobbled by the need to keep the actual price of the paper sufficiently low to enjoy wide circulation, the press had to incorporate to solicit funds. Selling shares at 500 marks each—no small sum in Wilhelmine Germany[30] —indicated that the paper's future prospects were all too bleak. Not only was the venture economically precarious or even unfeasible, but the periodacy of publication insured that the sectarian point of view enjoyed a narrow audience.

Das katholische Deutschland was not the only publication established to inform the Centrist electorate about the sectarian tactics for the "Parity Question's" settlement. The confessional wing founded another weekly periodical in 1912. Calling itself *Klarheit und Wahrheit*, a name derived from the title of an article published by Kopp in 1909, this journal was the Berlin faction's chief organ.[31] But once again, neither in circulation nor frequency of appearance could it compete with the newspapers and periodicals affiliated with the Augustinus Union. The force of press propaganda was thus effectively on the "Cologne" side.

* * *

Expelled from the Centrum's organizations, unable to effectively convince the Centrist electorate of the efficacy of its sectarian program in the "Parity Question," the party's confessional wing was confused, disorganized, and exasperated.[32] Frustrated with this political impotence, the Berlin faction was reduced to sterile polemical activity and a campaign of personal vilification.[33]

Symptomatic of its powerlessness were the confessional wing's strident attacks in 1910 on Martin Spahn. Running for the seat of Minden 5 (Warburg-Höxter), Spahn again found himself in the vortex of another controversy.[34] Lingering doubts about his past connections with anticlericals and suspicions about the extremes he was willing to go to on behalf of the "Parity Question" continued to haunt the professor. Although he provided the local Centrist leadership with orthodox answers about such issues as the Toleration Bill, the Jesuit Law, exceptional laws against the Poles, and constitutional reform in Alsace-Lorraine—the "Parity Question" in some of its endless patterns—not all Spahn's critics were satisfied.[35] Unable to thwart Spahn's candidacy because they had so little influence within the Centrum's apparatus, the "Berliners," led by Erzberger and Oppersdorff, resorted to calumniatory tactics.[36]

When the Strassburg professor rebuffed their demands that he withdraw his candidature, the Berlin faction made Spahn a target of ire and ridicule. By a calculated indiscretion, his enemies leaked the controversy to a liberal newspaper hoping to embarrass the professor, force his resignation, or bring about his electoral defeat. Failing to defeat Spahn in his constituency, his opponents exposed other alleged shortcomings. They could not refrain from emphasizing Spahn's preference for German nationalism rather than confessional unity to achieve parity for his coreligionists within Wilhelmine society.[37] Oppersdorff and Erzberger hoped these exposures would prevent Spahn from taking his Reichstag seat. Reviled in Vatican circles as *"Martin Luther Spahn,"*[38] this academician was victimized by slander and misrepresentation. Only with difficulty did he take his place in the Centrum's Reichstag delegation. He had to undergo a long tedious ordeal of seven heated caucus sessions with his colleagues lasting some forty hours before a vote was taken and he was accepted as a worthy colleague.[39]

This "second Spahn case" and the confessional wing's need to resort to character assassination demonstrated the "Berliners' " inherent weaknesses within the Centrum party. Given such organizational weaknesses, the Berlin faction could only reconcile itself to defeat or use those reprehensible tactics.

Not only was the younger Spahn subjected to this abuse, but similar efforts were made to vilify the entire Cologne faction. Cardinal Kopp regarded these developments in western Prussia with astonishment and anxiety. His waxing animosity toward church, political, and trade-union leaders in the West resulted in a notorious document known as the "contamination of the West" letter. This missive bore witness to the kinds of tactics that became all too common on the

part of the Berlin-Trier axis. Showing little restraint in this letter
and in his subsequent actions, Kopp launched a full-scale defama-
tion campaign against the Centrist and church leadership in the West
with a view to creating difficulties for them in Rome. His doubts
about Cardinal Fischer's orthodoxy proved unfounded, but were
sufficient to warrant investigation by the Curia. This unbridled attack, Fischer supposedly admitted, was another "nail in my cof-
fin."[40] Kopp's strong language betrayed his frustration that his writ
as Prince-Bishop of Breslau did not extend into western Prussia. But
these invidious tactics and vituperative attacks also testified to the
weaknesses of the confessional wing's position within the Centrum
party.

Hartmann, Fischer's successor in Cologne, and the Bishop of
Paderborn, were in January 1914 also the target of similar calum-
nies and innuendoes of the aging and cantankerous Cardinal Kopp.[41]
Like his attacks against Fischer, the main purpose of this slander was
to frighten these prelates and deter them from pursuing their "liberal" programs of toleration toward the Cologne and München-Gladbach factions.

Following the resignations and expulsions from the Centrum in
1912 and 1914 (a development which deprived the confessional wing
of what little influence it had within the party organization), the
"Berliners'" attacks became more shrill. Even Erzberger and Porsch
were reviled in the Berlin faction's polemics. Although Erzberger, as
a one-time collaborator with Oppersdorff and Roeren in 1910, stood
with if not in the confessional camp, by February 1912 he judicious-
ly reversed himself. This political parvenu then criticized his erst-
while allies and drew near the Cologne faction. Erzberger's "trim-
ming" reflected the way the tide was running in the conflict: it revealed that success belonged to the "Cologners." His defection, moreover, aggravated all the more the confessional party's sense of futility
and frustration. Hence the special vehemence with which it in-
veighed against Erzberger. He was, the Berlin faction claimed in November 1912, a rank opportunist, "initially a friend, then an opponent of Bachem, next a friend of Roeren, then once again Bachem's
friend, then a foe of Spahn and Oppersdorff's friend, and at the
moment was again to be found on the side of 'Cologne.' "[42]

If Erzberger's defection implied their impending defeat, Porsch,
as a Centrist functionary, represented the party apparatus that hampered the adoption of the confessional wing's program. Porsch, like
Erzberger, was treated contemptuously. He was called a "machine
politician" in 1912 who overcame internal opposition through

"steamroller tactics" and a "personality cult." During the following
year Johannes Bell, Eugen Jaeger, Marx, and Trimborn—all Centrist
deputies—were the victims of similar attacks.[43] No longer under the
restraints imposed by party membership and discipline, Oppersdorff
took the lead in these vituperations and resorted to increasingly in-
temperate language in his feud with the party hierarchy. Exasperated
because of his powerlessness within the party, overexcited by Kopp,
and enraged by the Cologne faction's successes, the Silesian magnate's combative spirit drove him to "astonishing indiscretions." He
determined to traduce the western political and ecclesiastical leadership by publicly denouncing to the Curia all his real and imagined
enemies. This led to his close collaboration with Kopp against Hartmann and a temperamental outburst in March 1914 against the
Jesuits. These missteps cost Oppersdorff much sympathy among
churchmen and were long remembered with bitterness by Hartmann
especially.[44] The Archbishop of Cologne was convinced that the
Silesian aristocrat was nothing but "a completely unreliable, char-
acterless, and dangerous man."[45] Oppersdorff's jounalistic attacks
were an unthinkable blunder. Thus Porsch's fears in March 1914
about the count's capacity to work injury on the Cologne faction
proved groundless;[46] Oppersdorff was unbalanced by Kopp's death
and politically impotent.

* * *

Internal policy disputes within the Centrum concerning the most
effective tactic in dealing with the "Parity Question," occupied the
party's attention for over eight years. That wing which advocated an
intransigent pose and the cultivation of a siege mentality based on
confessional solidarity within a "beleaguered tower" were defeated
by a series of accidents and tactical errors. It is probable that none
of these factors alone would have been sufficient to weigh the balance against the Berlin faction; what was decisive was their combination. The Cologne faction was free to transform the Centrum
from a religious interest group into a political party. This transformation was intended to make its legislative proposals (themselves
designed to achieve an equitable position for the Roman Catholic
minority within German society) palatable to other parliamentary
parties and interests. Above all, it became possible for the Centrum
to draw closer to Berlin and the Conservative party.

9: CONCLUSION AND APPRAISAL

*An alliance with the Conservatives promises
no permanence.*

Hubert Underberg[1]

Having become to its satisfaction a secular "political" party, the
Centrum discovered it was no closer to a solution of the "Parity
Question." The high hopes which the Bachem wing attached to the
Black-Blue bloc met on the whole with disappointment. During the
Wilhelmine era the Centrum party fought a long parliamentary bat-
tle, never completely won, to erase the remaining traces of religious
discrimination. It is not surprising that the collapse of the Bülow
bloc and the formation of an "Alliance of Knights and Saints" was
not accompanied by a complete solution of the "Parity Question."
Germany was freed from the direct influence of an anti-Catholic
coalition; but it was not freed from its heritage of religious bigotry.
The Centrum therefore had to struggle to obtain the sole indemnity
its complaisance with the political Right had earned—parity.

Although an alliance between the Centrum and Conservative parties lasted from 1909 until the July crisis of 1917, the existence of
this bloc was dependent upon a very fragile and tenuous community
of interests.[2] That working relationship was an uneasy one, punctuated by crises. On several occasions the alliance was jeopardized.
In his encyclical of May 1910 commemorating the tercentenary of
Saint Robert Borromeo (the Cardinal-Archbishop of Milan and zealous advocate of the Counter Reformation), Pope Pius X made cen-
sorious references to the Reformation which outraged German Protestants. Worsening the confessional situation further was the Anti-
Modernist Oath which the Church of Rome demanded in September
1910 of all Catholic professors and theologians, including those in
German universities. These developments rekindled the flame of religious controversy and impaired the bloc's effectiveness. During the
summer of 1911 the Black-Blue bloc was put to a hard test when

132

Count Hans von Schwerin-Löwitz, a prominent Conservative and President of the Reichstag, referred publicly to the Centrum as "a very unpleasant phenomenon" composed of contradictory social elements held together by a "non-German bond"—"the interests of the Roman Catholic church."[3] Even though the bloc survived these and other squabbles, few tangible results were obtained in the "Parity Question." Between 1909 and 1917 the government and the Conservative party showed little solicitude for Centrist aims related to the parity problem. Indicative of these meager rewards was the Centrist failure in 1912 to repeal the surviving paragraphs of the Jesuit Law. In general, the Conservatives vacillated between opposition to the pretensions of the Roman church and conditional support of the Centrum's claim to a share of the political power.

Only with the First World War and the domestic exigencies of that conflict did the parity issue substantially improve. The remaining clauses of the Jesuit Law (Paragraphs 1 and 3) were finally repealed in April 1917. In that same year, an *annus mirabilis* for Germany's Roman Catholics, Hertling became German Chancellor and Prussian Minister-President. Once denied a professorship at the University of Bonn because of his religious beliefs, Hertling attained the highest positions of the Prussian state and the German Empire on 1 November 1917—virtually the four-hundredth anniversary of the Reformation. This event followed by just a few months the appointments of Peter Spahn as Prussian Minister of Justice and Max Wallraf as Reich Secretary of the Interior.[4] Both the careers and ministerial attainments of these three prominent Roman Catholics were testimonials to that desire on the part of their coreligionists for acceptance and recognition—parity—within Wilhelmine society.

This new recognition accorded Roman Catholics was less the effect of the Bachem program than the consequence of deteriorating political conditions caused by the war. By April 1917 Germany faced a critical military and domestic situation. The first Russian revolution broke out in Petrograd a few weeks before. Berlin was anxious to prevent a similar occurrence in Germany. Furthermore, because of differences over military operations and war policy, Bethmann Hollweg had aroused the hostility of Field Marshal Paul von Hindenburg and General Erich Ludendorff. The Chancellor sought to avoid political disturbances and at the same time bolster his strength in the Reichstag against the military through concessions to the Progressive and Social Democratic parties. He endeavored without complete success to replace the Prussian three-class franchise with universal suffrage. If Bethmann Hollweg attempted

to buy the liberals and socialists with votes, he also tried to win
Centrist support with the repeal of the Jesuit Law. The outcome
was favorable for the Centrum party; repeal of the Jesuit Law was
accomplished in full. But Bethmann Hollweg's instinct for survival
and the government's fear of revolution—not the existence of the
Black-Blue bloc—led to this concession.

The ministerial appointments of the following months were motivated by similar considerations. In fact, these appointments came
after the dissolution of the Black-Blue bloc. That bloc disintegrated
in July 1917 when the Centrum party moved away from its Conservative partners and joined forces with the Progressive and Social
Democratic parties in opposition to Germany's expansionist war
aims. Hertling, Spahn, and Wallraf, all representatives of the Centrum's right wing, were given ministerial portfolios in a belated attempt by Berlin to keep at least a segment of the Centrum behind
the Imperial government.

* * *

The tragedy of the Centrum's predicament was not simply that
the victory of the Cologne wing in the "Centrum conflict" produced no substantive change in the "Parity Question." The supreme
irony was that neither the Berlin nor the Cologne factions could
solve the "Parity Question." Both alternatives were vitiated by an
insoluble contradiction within political Catholicism.

The sectarian stance worked only injury to the real interests of
the church and the Roman Catholic community. Any attempt to
stress religious positions incurred tremendous unpopularity among
the Protestant population. A sectarian nimbus, together with the
permanent numerical inferiority of Roman Catholics in Wilhelmine
Germany, therefore isolated the Centrum and effectively excluded
the possibility for viable political coalitions.

The sectarian label was a liability in that it denoted that the Centrum's strength rested upon a permanent religious minority from
which support was shrinking. Whereas in 1903 68.3 percent of male
Roman Catholics (there was no female suffrage in Wilhelmine Germany) voted for the Centrum party, this figure shrank to 63.8 in
1907 and 54.6 in 1912.[5] And although not as dramatically the
Centrum party also experienced a relative decline if one takes into
account the growth of the population, and with it the electorate.
Out of every 100 votes cast, the Centrum in 1903 received 19.7, in
1907 19.4, and in 1912 16.7.[6] This attrition was especially notice-

able among the working classes. Hartmann, the Archbishop of Cologne, admitted in 1913 that over 800,000 Roman Catholics belonged to Social Democratic organizations.[7]

Any party building its strength on this permanent religious minority condemned itself to impotence, especially if it simply reverted to a policy of strength and studied opposition.[8] Roeren, Oppersdorff, Schopen, and their associates within the confessional camp resorted to a campaign of sterile polemical activity which did much to dramatize their point of view. But this behavior, attracting as it did public interest and evoking enormous controversy between 1909 and 1914, effectively isolated the Centrum from other political groups. The anti-Bachem wing emphasized slogans and ideology which, though in theory tended to unite the party against an external threat, served to divide the parties one from the other. Above all, it engendered an insurmountable mutual distrust between the Centrum and the parties of the Left.

This distrust did not entirely stem from sectarian considerations. The "Berliners," no less than the "Cologners," were conservative in sentiment. However authoritarian, the German Empire corresponded to and satisfied the interests of all factions in the "struggle of orientation." Most Roman Catholics regarded the Empire as a bulwark against those groups, social changes, and ideologies deemed pernicious by their church. That being the case, the Berlin faction could not create a long-lasting coalition with liberals or socialists. In alliance with the church, the "Berliners" hoped to extract concessions from the government. This was done in 1887 to end the Kulturkampf and it was repeated with disastrous results in connection with the Enabling Act and the Concordat in 1933. The Berlin program introduced what was to become the characteristic behavior of German political Catholicism in the final stages of the Weimar Republic. But the Berlin group in Wilhelmine Germany opposed collaboration with the Protestant Conservative party.

The Berlin faction therefore jeopardized the Centrum's understanding with the Conservatives. Any "alliance of the Centrum with the Conservatives" was little more than a chimerical presumption and "promises no permanence," one advocate of the confessional platform stated categorically. "The material interests of the Conservative party will allow them to abandon the Centrum as soon as they no longer need it." An alliance with Protestants was devoid of all value anyway, he added, because *"out of 100 Protestants 99 are no longer Christians."*[9] Such rhetoric, Carl Bachem protested, "repels the Conservatives, even the best-intentioned Conservatives, making it impossible for them to cooperate with the Centrum, and depriving it [the Centrum party] of the possibility to effectively represent the legitimate aims of the Catholic population in parliament,"[10] rendering nugatory all efforts to solve the "Parity Question." Oblivious to political realities, all those who insisted "upon a confessional party," Erzberger also complained, "set back the German Catholics decades into the past" and encouraged "the continuation of the silent Kulturkampf" which denied Roman Catholics equality of civil rights in Wilhelmine Germany.

And yet the solution of the "Parity Question" depended on just such parliamentary arrangements—although not with the Conservative party. The settlement of the "Parity Question" depended on some form of collaboration with reform-minded parties. But apart from its intrinsic conservatism, the Berlin faction's sectarian emphasis made such collaboration impossible because these parties—especially the Progressives and Social Democrats—were anticlerical. Wilhelmine society, although largely secular, was still encumbered by past religious animosities. Under these conditions, the Berlin group's sectarian program intensified confessional antagonisms and reinforced an already dangerous tendency toward political stagnation and immobility based on religious affiliations.

The Cologne platform also revealed the inherent contradictions within German political Catholicism. Beset by contrary councils, the Centrum was mired in disunity and immobility. If the Berlin faction's attempt to solve the "Parity Question" isolated the Centrum, Julius Bachem and his partisans sought to escape from that isolation in alliance with the Conservative party. The "Cologners" thus confronted an invidious choice. As in the case of the Berlin faction, the Bachem group's intrinsic hostility toward those groups and social changes anathematized by the Roman church precluded agreement with the political Left. But any accommodation with the Conservatives meant that the pace and extent of change toward the attainment of parity was predicated on Centrist support for an authoritarian government and opposition to political reform.

The innate conservatism of Bachem and his collaborators, combined with their haste to achieve social and religious parity, insured that democratic political demands would be put aside. A tactical alignment with the Conservative party after 1909 against liberals and the Social Democrats forced the Centrum into a more conservative (even reactionary) stance. Intra-Centrist antagonisms associated with the *Richtungsstreit* also offered the Imperial government and the Conservatives opportunities to wrest political conces-

sions from the Centrum party as a premium for maintaining support
and loyalty toward an ally in their dealings with the anti-Catholic
political Left. Under the Cologne leadership, the Centrum party became more venal. Centrists did not worry themselves if the improvement in the welfare of Roman Catholics was accomplished through
an authoritarian monarchy. With its spokesmen tied by material interests to the status quo, the Bachem wing implicitly endorsed the
policy of reaction.

Unable to transcend these political contradictions and given its
insoluble social incongruities and disharmonious congeries of competing interest groups, the Centrum of necessity subordinated program and ideals to tactical considerations and interests. A creature
of circumstance and opportunity, the Centrum pursued its own interests, unconcerned about the common weal. This policy was inevitably detrimental to the prospects for reform. The Cologne faction was not so much interested in bringing the German Empire into a position in which it could catch up with the other states of
Western Europe, which were far in advance of it politically, as with
the dismantling of the vestigial remains of discriminatory legislation
against Roman Catholics. But the solution of the "Parity Question"
in an alliance with the Conservatives could neither modernize German constitutional life nor democratize Wilhelmine society. In its
efforts to find a settlement to the "Parity Question," the Centrum
thwarted badly needed reforms and upheld the social status quo.

Tax reform was one of the major problems confronting Wilhelmine Germany. The Bismarckian system which left direct taxation
in the hands of the individual states and forced the Imperial government to rely on indirect taxes was by 1909 obsolete and incapable
of meeting the Empire's financial needs. Moreover, the system was
essentially inequitable in that it shifted a disproportionate burden
of the taxes on the lower classes who were least able to pay. Although the Centrum recognized the inadequacies of the system,
it impeded a program of fundamental reform in the system of taxation and confined itself to certain modifications in the existing system of national finance. The party's primary object was to break
the Bülow bloc, appease the Conservatives who opposed any significant reforms, and establish a new voting combination between the
Centrum and Conservative parties for the purpose of settling the
"Parity Question."[11]

If the Centrum stymied tax reform for immediate tactical advantage in 1909, it also helped defeat a badly-needed change in the
Prussian franchise the following year. Since 1850, Prussia relied

on the notorious three-class voting system. The electorate was divided into three classes or categories according to the amount of taxes
paid. One-third of all Landtag members were thereby elected by
three percent of the electorate, an additional third by twelve percent, and the final third by eighty-five percent.[12] Rather than re-
move this flagrant restriction on political equality, the Centrum opposed suffrage reform to appease the Conservatives and preserve the
"Alliance of Knights and Saints."[13]

The Cologne faction also obstructed reform by its support of the
Christian Trade Unions. Preoccupied with the Roman Catholic *Mittelstand*'s "Parity Question," the Bachem group perceived another
tactical advantage in their encouragement of the interconfessional
unions. When the Imperial government refused to extend political
rights to the working classes after the Ruhr mine strike of 1912 and
turned on a more reactionary course, it relied more and more on the
Christian unions to hold labor in check. Ideally, the sectarian unions
of the Trier faction were no more democratic and could well have
served the same intention.[14] But their limited membership made
them less useful for the government's purpose. With its steady if
unspectacular growth, the interconfessional working-class movement
contributed more effectively to the preservation of the political
status quo. From the Cologne faction's standpoint, that movement
located in München-Gladbach simultaneously facilitated collaboration between the Centrum, the Imperial government, and the Evangelical Conservatives. That cooperation was intended to bring about
concessions in the "Parity Question."

If the Centrum party unashamedly pursued the interests of the
Roman Catholic *Mittelstand* at the expense of the German people,
this action was not the result of a deliberate betrayal. It was the consequence of a fear of the limitations of Wilhelmine Germany's parliamentary organizations and the antagonism and bigotry of the political Left. The Centrists were afraid, given their minority status,
that their cultural and political objectives would be frustrated by
an anti-Catholic liberal coalition or a recrudescence of the Bülow
bloc. These fears were not completely unjustified as past and recent
experiences (the Kulturkampf and the "Hottentot" elections) demonstrated. The Cologne faction accordingly concentrated its energies
on keeping Conservative confidence—even if this prevented reform—
with the intent to further the parity issue.

This behavior revealed the self-defeating and contradictory nature
of German political Catholicism. Shared more or less by other social
and political groups—the Social Democratic party (with its conflict

between orthodox Marxism and Revisionism), for example—this dilemma helped bring Wilhelmine German society to an impasse and forced comprehensive constitutional and political reform to a standstill by the eve of the First World War. The "Parity Question," together with the Centrum's predicament regarding a sectarian or secular position, was thus an integral part of the "German Question"— the failure of liberal democracy to take root in Germany. The contradictions inherent in the Centrum's choice between sectarianism and secularism were inimical to the pressing need for Germany's constitutional and parliamentary reform. Such a dilemma only served to accentuate the Wilhelmine Empire's political petrification and social ossification.

ABBREVIATIONS

AAW	Archiwum Archidiecezjalne we Wroclawiu
BHStA, Abt. I	Bayerisches Hauptstaatsarchiv München, Abteilung Allgemeines Staatsarchiv
BHStA, Abt. II	Bayerisches Hauptstaatsarchiv München, Abteilung Geheimes Staatsarchiv
BAT	Bistumsarchiv Trier
BAK	Bundesarchiv Koblenz
FZB	*Frankfurter Zeitgemässe Broschüren*
HpBl	*Historisch-politische Blätter für das katholische Deutschland*
HASK	Historisches Archiv der Stadt Köln
KVZ	*Kölnische Volkszeitung*
PAAA	Politisches Archiv des Auswärtigen Amtes
PJ	*Preussische Jahrbücher*
SVZ	*Schlesische Volkszeitung*
StAK	Staatsarchiv Koblenz
StAMü	Staatsarchiv Münster
StAMö	Stadtarchiv Mönchengladbach
StBMö	Stadtbibliothek Mönchengladbach
SA	Stegerwald-Archiv
SBHA	*Stenographische Berichte über die Verhandlungen des Landtages, Haus der Abgeordneten*
SBR	*Stenographische Berichte über die Verhandlungen des Reichstags*
TLZ	*Trierische Landeszeitung*
WAZ	*Westdeutsche Arbeiter-Zeitung*
ZcGD	*Zentralblatt der christlichen Gewerkschaften Deutschlands*

NOTES

NOTES TO CHAPTER 1

Confession and Community

1. Theodor Fontane, *Der Stechlin* (Berlin, 1898), p. 72.
2. *Protokoll der Verhandlungen des ausserordentl. Kongresses der christl. Gewerkschaften Deutschlands.* Abgehalten am 26. November 1912 in Essen [Ruhr] (Cologne, 1912), p. 14.
3. Quoted in Matthias Erzberger, "Der stille Kulturkampf," FZB, Neue Folge, XXXII, 1 (15 Oct. 1912), 2. The italics are apparently Erzberger's.
4. The basic arguments can be followed in Dahrendorf, *Society and Democracy*, pp. 33–64, and Wolfgang Sauer, "Das Problem des deutschen Nationalstaats," in *Moderne deutsche Sozialgeschichte*, Vol. X: *Neue Wissenschaftliche Bibliothek*, edited by Hans-Ulrich Wehler (Cologne, 1966), pp. 415–428.
5. See Leonard Krieger, *The German Idea of Freedom* (Boston, 1957), pp. 139–173.
6. The case of Ireland confirms this analysis. England, unable to extirpate Roman Catholicism among the Irish, was unable to incorporate that island into the United Kingdom.
7. So divisive was this legacy of Germany's development that Heinrich Ritter von Srbik, the foremost Austrian historian in the interwar period, fashioned a new frame of reference for the study of German history—the *gesamtdeutsch* concept. This was devised to overcome the deep political, cultural, and religious divisions expressed in such contrasts as *Grossdeutsch-Kleindeutsch*, Austria-Prussia, Habsburg-Hohenzollern, South Germany-North Germany, and Catholic-Protestant. See Ronald J. Ross, "Heinrich Ritter von Srbik and '*Gesamtdeutsch*' History," *The Review of Politics*, XXXI, 1 (Jan. 1969), 88–107.
8. Fritz Dickmann, "Das Problem der Gleichberechtigung der Konfessionen im Reich im 16. und 17. Jahrhundert," in *Friedensrecht und Friedenssicherung: Studien zum Friedensproblem in der neueren Geschichte* (Göttingen, 1971), p. 17.
9. Ibid.
10. Ibid., pp. 17 and 23; Fritz Dickmann, *Der Westfälische Frieden*, 2d ed. (Münster, 1965), p. 180.
11. Dickmann, "Das Problem der Gleichberechtigung," p. 30; Dickmann, *Der Westfälische Frieden*, pp. 9 and 495.
12. Mack Walker, *German Home Towns: Community, State, and General Estate, 1648–1871* (Ithaca, 1971), p. 175.

13. For a documentary survey of the religious problem in this state, consult Max Lehmann and Herman Granier, eds., *Preussen und die katholische Kirche seit 1640: Nach den Acten des Geheimen Staatsarchives*, 9 vols. (Leipzig, 1878–1902). These volumes, which appeared in the series *Publikationen aus den K. Preussischen Staatsarchiven*, cover the period down to 1807.

14. Julius Bachem and Karl Bachem, *Die kirchenpolitischen Kämpfe in Preussen gegen die katholische Kirche insbesondere der "grosse Kulturkampf" der Jahre 1871–1887, Sonderabdruck der Artikel aus der dritten Auflage des Staatslexikons der Görres-Gesellschaft* (Freiburg im Breisgau, 1910), p. 4; Ernst Rudolf Huber, "Joseph Görres und die Anfänge des katholischen Integralismus in Deutschland," in *Nationalstaat und Verfassungsstaat: Studien zur Geschichte der modernen Staatsidee* (Stuttgart, 1965), p. 107.

15. This discussion is based on Ernst Rudolf Huber, *Deutsche Verfassungsgeschichte seit 1789*, 4 vols. (Stuttgart, 1957–1969), I, 401, 404, and 406–407.

16. Ibid., I, 51.

17. Ibid., I, 414-415.

18. Franz Schnabel, *Deutsche Geschichte im neunzehnten Jahrhundert*, 8 vols. (Freiburg im Breisgau, 1964–65), VII, 151.

19. Johannes B. Kissling, *Geschichte des Kulturkampfes im Deutschen Reiche*, 3 vols. (Freiburg im Breisgau, 1911–16), I, 72–73.

20. Ibid., 136.

21. Dickmann, "Das Problem der Gleichberechtigung," p. 33; TLZ, XXIX, 19 (24 Jan. 1903), p. 1.

22. The 12-point petition of the Roman Catholics seeking specific social and political reforms to facilitate religious coexistence in Germany is to be found in Ludwig Bergsträsser, *Studien zur Vorgeschichte der Zentrumspartei*, Vol. I: *Beiträge zur Parteigeschichte* (Tübingen, 1910), pp. 166–167. From Coblenz came a petition, interestingly enough, that demanded "equality of rights for all citizens without any distinctions to offices of the state and community." See ibid., p. 168. For details of the Roman Catholic role in Frankfurt, consult Frank Eyck, *The Frankfurt Parliament, 1848–49* (London, 1968), pp. 141–147 and 228–246.

23. Huber, "Görres, " p. 125.

24. Erich Schmidt, *Bismarcks Kampf mit dem politischen Katholizismus*, Teil I: *Pius der IX. und die Zeit der Rüstung, 1848-1870*, 2d ed. (Hamburg, 1942), pp. 84–85.

25. Schnabel, *Deutsche Geschichte*, VII, 145. More recent research suggests that although there was some basis in fact for Roman Catholic grievances, their complaints were somewhat exaggerated. Cf. John R. Gillis, *The Prussian Bureaucracy in Crisis, 1840–1860: Origins of an Administrative Ethos* (Stanford, 1971), pp. 35 and 231, n. 40 and n. 41.

26. Schnabel, *Deutsche Geschichte*, VII, 149.

27. Ibid., VII, 150-151.

28. Schmidt, *Bismarcks Kampf*, p. 88.

29. See Hermann Donner, *Die Katholische Fraktion in Preussen, 1852–1858* (Borna-Leipzig, 1909) and Hermann Wendorf, *Die Fraktion des Zentrums im preussischen Abgeordnetenhause, 1859–1867*, Vol. XL: *Leipziger Historische Abhandlungen* (Leipzig, 1916).

30. Quoted in Bachem and Bachem, *Die kirchenpolitischen Kämpfe,* pp. 30–31; Rudolf Lill, "Die deutschen Katholiken und Bismarcks Reichsgründung," in *Reichsgründung, 1870/71: Tatsachen, Kontroversen, Interpretationen,* edited by Theodor Schieder and Ernst Deuerlein (Stuttgart, 1970), p. 359.

31. Georg Franz-Willing, *Kulturkampf gestern und heute: Eine Säkularbetrachtung, 1871–1971* (Munich, 1971), pp. 19–20.

32. Lill, "Die deutschen Katholiken," p. 346. A fine study of the South German Roman Catholic response to this situation is George G. Windell, *The Catholics and German Unity, 1866–1871* (Minneapolis, 1954). The fear for equality among Prussian Roman Catholics was not occasioned simply by the Hohenzollern kingdom's achieving an unassailable position of hegemony within the North German Confederation. Contributing equally to their dismay was the inclusion of several medium and small-sized states—Brunswick, Mecklenburg, and Schwarzburg-Sondershausen, for instance—renowned for their religious intolerance. This concern was accentuated by Otto von Bismarck's violation of old-established rights and traditions such as the destruction of German unity and the incorporation of the Hanoverian kingdom into Prussia.

33. W. N. Medlicott, *Bismarck and Modern Germany* (New York, 1967), p. 106.

34. See Harald Just, "Wilhelm Busch und die Katholiken: Kulturkampfstimmung im Bismarck-Reich," *Geschichte in Wissenschaft und Unterricht,* XXV (Feb. 1974), 65–78.

35. Windell, *Catholics and Germany Unity,* pp. 235–239.

36. Lill, "Die deutschen Katholiken," p. 363.

37. For details, one can do no better than consult Huber, *Deutsche Verfassungsgeschichte,* II, 185–265, and Heinrich Schrörs, *Die Kölner Wirren: Studien zu ihrer Geschichte* (Berlin, 1927).

38. Schnabel, *Deutsche Geschichte,* VII, 156.

39. Kissling, *Geschichte des Kulturkampfes,* I, 155.

40. Ibid., I, 174.

41. Heinrich von Treitschke, *History of Germany in the Nineteenth Century,* trans. Eden and Cedar Paul, 7 vols. (London, 1915–1919), VII, 156.

42. Franz-Willing, *Kulturkampf,* p. 17.

43. J. Görres, *Athanasius,* 4th ed. (Regensburg, 1838).

44. See Huber, "Görres," p. 123.

45. For details of the settlement, see Rudolf Lill, *Die Beilegung der Kölner Wirren, 1840 bis 1842: Vorwiegend nach Akten des Vatikanischen Geheimarchivs,* Vol. VI: *Studien zur Kölner Kirchengeschichte* (Düsseldorf, 1962).

46. A satisfactory account of the Kulturkampf does not exist. It is therefore necessary to rely on Georges Goyau, *Bismarck et l'Église: Le Culturkampf (1870–1887),* 4 vols. (Paris, 1911–1913); Kissling, *Geschichte des Kulturkampfes;* Erich Schmidt-Volkmar, *Der Kulturkampf in Deutschland, 1871–1890* (Göttingen, 1962); Huber, *Verfassungsgeschichte,* IV, 645–831; Heinrich Bornkamm, "Die Staatsidee im Kulturkampf," *Historische Zeitschrift,* CLXX (1950), 41–72, 273–306; and more specialized monographs such as Josef Becker, *Liberaler Staat und Kirche in der Ära von Reichsgründung und Kulturkampf: Geschichte und Strukturen ihres Verhältnisses in Baden, 1860–1876,* Vol. XIV: *Veröffentlichungen der Kommission für Zeitgeschichte*

(Mainz, 1973); Christoph Weber, *Kirchliche Politik zwischen Rom, Berlin und Trier, 1876-1888: Die Beilegung des preussischen Kulturkampfes*, Vol. VII: *Veröffentlichungen der Kommission für Zeitgeschichte bei der Katholischen Akademie in Bayern* (Mainz, 1970); Stadelhofer, *Der Abbau der Kulturkampfgesetzgebung*; and Franz-Willing, *Kulturkampf*.

47. Wilhelm Mommsen, ed., *Deutsche Parteiprogramm*, Vol. I: *Deutsches Handbuch der Politik*, 2d ed. (Munich, 1964), No. 19, p. 217.

48. Lill, "Die deutschen Katholiken," pp. 352-353.

49. Bornkamm, "Staatsidee," 56-57 and 66.

50. Ibid., 41ff.

51. Ibid., 45-46.

NOTES TO CHAPTER 2

A Silent Kulturkampf

1. Letter to Lujo Brentano, 24 Nov. 1901; Kurt Rossmann, *Wissenschaft, Ethik und Politik: Erörterung des Grundsatzes der Voraussetzungslosigkeit in der Forschung. Mit Erstmaliger Veröffentlichung der Briefe Theodor Mommsens über den "Fall Spahn" und der Korrespondenz zu Mommsens öffentlicher Erklärung über "Universitätsunterricht und Konfession" aus dem Nachlass Lujo Brentanos*, Vol. IV: *Schriften der Wandlung* (Heidelberg, 1949), p. 157.

2. SBHA (2 Mar. 1903), II, 2262.

3. For a discussion of this phenomenon, see Erzberger, "Der stille Kulturkampf," 1-56.

4. A convenient list of the legislation, including the statutes which were abrogated, can be found in Franz-Willing, *Kulturkampf*, pp. 65-66.

5. The latter figure is to be found in the minutes of the State Ministries, 11 Feb. 1903; PAAA, Päpstl. Stuhl 13a No. 1, Bd. 3; the former in Karl Bachem, *Zentrumspartei*, IX, 341.

6. For the exact text of the Jesuit Law, see Ernst Rudolf Huber, ed., *Dokumente zur deutschen Verfassungsgeschichte*, 3 vols. (Stuttgart, 1961–1966), II, No. 248, 363-364. A convenient account of the nature and development of anti-Jesuit legislation can be found in Karl Bachem, *Zentrumspartei*, IX, 265-371, and Bernhard Duhr, *Das Jesuitengesetz: Sein Abbau und seine Aufhebung. Ein Beitrag zur Kulturgeschichte der Neuzeit, Ergänzungshefte zu den Stimmen der Zeit*, Erste Reihe: *Kulturfragen*, 7. Heft (Freiburg im Breisgau, 1919).

7. Repeal depended on tactical considerations. Unsuccessfully arguing for partial repeal in 1903, Chancellor Bernhard von Bülow claimed such a concession was necessary because "the struggle against Social Democracy, especially in the face of impending elections, cannot effectively be carried on if at the time we have the Centrum and the Catholic population as enemies." Minutes of the State Ministries, 11 Feb. 1903; PAAA, Päpstl. Stuhl 13a No. 1, Bd. 3. Although repeal was thwarted by the appearance of the Trier school conflict, the government abrogated Paragraph 2 the following year in exchange for Centrist support for a bill to increase the number of noncommissioned officers in the armed forces. Stadelhofer, *Der Abbau der Kulturkampfgesetzgebung*, p. 286, n. 9. For the effects of the convergence of the Trier school dispute and the at-

tempts to dismantle the Jesuit Law, see Ludwig Freiherr von Pastor, *Tagebücher, Briefe, Erinnerungen, 1854-1928,* edited by Wilhelm Wühr (Heidelberg, 1950), entry of 23 Feb. 1903, p. 402; reports from Hugo von Lerchenfeld, 7 and 8 Mar. 1903; BHStA, Abt. II, Bayer. Gesandtschaft, Berlin No. 1075, Nos. 107 and 108; memoranda, 23 Mar., end of Mar., and 30 Apr. 1903; HASK, *Nachlass* Bachem, Abt. 1006, No. 187; Peter Spahn to Bishop Michael Felix Korum, 27 Mar. 1903; BAT, *Nachlass* Korum, Abt. 108, No. 402.

8. Numerous attempts were made to liquidate the Jesuit Law in its entirety. A particularly major effort was made in 1912-1913, but it too failed. The proscription of the Jesuit order was an issue capable of inflaming deep-seated hatreds, even within court circles. See the *Memoirs of Prince von Bülow,* trans. Geoffrey Dunlop, 4 vols. (Boston, 1931), II, 109 and 282-283. Indicative of the unbridled polemics accompanying the discussion of repeal of the remaining paragraphs of the Jesuit Law were the efforts of *Die Wartburg: Deutsch-evangelische Wochenschrift.* Two special editions—labeled "Jesuiten-Nummer"—were published: XI, 45 (8 Nov. 1912) and XII, 8 (21 Feb. 1913). For a typical article, see the latter issue, especially the essay entitled "Die Jesuiten eine nationale Gefahr," 65-71.

9. SBR (5 Dec. 1900), I, 302, 322-329.

10. Ibid., 302.

11. Ibid., 325-326 and 332-333.

12. For the wording and precise content of the Toleration Bill, see Ludwig Bergsträsser, *Der politische Katholizismus: Dokumente seiner Entwicklung,* 2 vols. (Munich, 1921-1923), II, No. 50, 307-310.

13. For a detailed explanation of the various articles of the draft legislation, together with a reply to charges of "intolerance" levelled against Roman Catholics themselves, see Hermann Roeren, "Der Toleranzantrag des Zentrums," FZB, Neue Folge, XXI, 2 (1902), 1-63.

14. The exact text of these repealed articles can be found in Huber, *Dokumente,* I, 402-403.

15. Revealing the extent of discrimination were the following collections of statistics compiled by Roman Catholic publicists: Julius Bachem, *Die Parität in Preussen: Eine Denkschrift,* 2d ed. (Cologne, 1899), the first edition of which appeared in 1897; Wilhelm Lossen, *Der Anteil der Katholiken am akademischen Lehramte in Preussen: Nach statistischen Untersuchungen* (Cologne, 1901); Hans Rost, *Die wirtschaftliche und kulturelle Lage der deutschen Katholiken* (Cologne, 1911); the same author's *Die Parität und die deutschen Katholiken,* Vol. III: *Zeit- und Streitfragen der Gegenwart* (Cologne, 1914). See also Karl Bachem, *Zentrumspartei,* IX, 65-84 and *Nachlass* Bachem; HASK, Abt. 1006, Nos. 76b, 76c, 85, 92a, 92b, 93, and 94.

16. Hohenlohe, a liberal, demonstrated anticlerical tendencies. Schönstedt, after his marriage to a Protestant, permitted his children to be brought up as Lutherans. See J. C. G. Röhl, "Higher Civil Servants in Germany, 1890-1900," *Journal of Contemporary History,* II, 3 (July 1967), 109-110, which amplifies and corrects material provided by Karl Bachem, *Zentrumspartei,* IX, 67-68.

17. Quoted in Röhl, "Higher Civil Servants," 109-110.

18. Ibid., 110-111; Karl Bachem, *Zentrumspartei,* IX, 68-70.

19. Karl Bachem, *Zentrumspartei,* IX, 70-71.

20. Ibid., 71-72.

21. Ibid., 72.

22. Max Wallraf, *Aus einem rheinischen Leben* (Hamburg, 1926), p. 153.

23. With perhaps some rhetorical exaggeration, Edgar Loening, a professor of civil law in the University of Halle, once said: "Down to the lowest servant only Protestants can be appointed here." Letter to Lujo Brentano, 24 Nov. 1901; Rossmann, *Wissenschaft, Ethik und Politik*, p. 157.

24. Rudolf Morsey, "Zwei Denkschriften zum 'Fall Martin Spahn' (1901): Ein Beitrag zur preussisch-deutschen Wissenschaftspolitik," *Archiv für Kulturgeschichte*, XXXVIII, 2 (1956), 251.

25. Ibid., 248.

26. Count Paul von Hoensbroech, "Der Parität im Preussischen Staate," PJ, LXXVI (June 1894), 314–344. Hoensbroech was a persistent critic of the Roman church and the Centrum party. Even Max Wallraf, however, a Roman Catholic and Prussian bureaucrat, admitted difficulties in finding suitable Roman Catholic candidates. See Wallraf, *Leben*, pp. 152–153.

27. Lossen, *Der Anteil der Katholiken*, pp. 114–115 (these figures exclude the theological faculties); see also P. C. J. Pulzer, *The Rise of Political Anti-Semitism in Germany and Austria* (New York, 1964), p. 12, and Röhl, "Higher Civil Servants," 111. These figures revealed a disparity in academic attainment of only about 3:5 between Roman Catholics and Protestants. Given the confessional proportions of those employed in the Prussian service, it was nevertheless clear that the government's explanation was not entirely convincing.

28. Oskar Schroeder, *Aufbruch und Missverständnis: Zur Geschichte der Reformkatholischen Bewegung* (Graz, 1969), p. 370.

29. See Schell's *Der Katholizismus als Prinzip des Fortschrittes*, 6th ed. (Würzburg, 1897).

30. For a recent and brief account, see Werner Methfessel, "Evangelischer Bund zur Wahrung der deutsch-protestantischen Interessen (EB) seit 1886," in *Die bürgerlichen Parteien in Deutschland: Handbuch der Geschichte der bürgerlichen Parteien und anderer bürgerlicher Interessenorganisationen vom Vormärz bis zum 1945*, edited by Dieter Fricke, 2 vols. (Leipzig, 1968–1970), I, 787–791.

31. See his "Mein Austritt aus der Jesuitenorden," PJ, LXXII, 1 (Apr.–June 1893), 300–327, and *14 Jahre Jesuit: Persönliches und Grundsätzliches*, 2 vols. (Berlin, 1912). Hoensbroech's chief polemical works were: *Der Toleranzantrag des Zentrums im Lichte der Toleranz der römischkatholischen Kirche*, 3d ed. (Berlin, 1904); *Das Papsttum in seiner sozialkulturellen Wirksamkeit*, 2 vols. (Berlin, 1904–1905); and above all, *Rom und das Zentrum: Zugleich eine Darstellung der politischen Machtansprüche durch das Zentrum* (Leipzig, 1910).

32. See Prince Chlodwig zu Hohenlohe-Schillingsfürst, *Denkwurdigkeiten der Reichskanzlerzeit*, edited by Karl Alexander von Müller (Stuttgart, 1931), pp. 38–40.

33. The obstreperous leader of Westphalian Peasant Associations Hoensbroech-Haag was an ex-Centrist parliamentary deputy and, after 1907, chief figure of the "German Union," a National Catholic faction composed mainly of aristocrats who bolted from the Centrum party.

34. Arnold Sachse, *Friedrich Althoff und sein Werk* (Berlin, 1928), pp. 129–131.

35. The government's aims are thoroughly explained in John Eldon Craig, "A Mission for German Learning: The University of Strasbourg and Alsatian Society, 1870–1918" (Ph.D. Dissertation, Stanford University, 1973), Chapter VIII.

36. SBR (6 Mar. 1903), IX, 8444.

37. Ibid., 8450.

38. For both his scholarly and political activities, consult Georg von Hertling, *Erinnerungen aus meinem Leben*, 2 vols. (Kempten, 1920) and the biographical sketch by Rudolf Morsey, "Georg Graf v. Hertling (1843–1919)," in *Zeitgeschichte in Lebensbildern: Aus den deutschen Katholizismus des 20. Jahrhunderts*, edited by Rudolf Morsey (Mainz, 1973), pp. 43–52.

39. Baimher(?) to Hertling, 19 Nov. 1899; BAK, *Nachlass* Hertling, Folio 31.

40. SBR (6 Mar. 1903), IX, 8457.

41. Ibid., 8442.

42. Ibid., 8448.

43. Ibid., 8453.

44. Notes sur la question du Séminaire de Strasbourg (Rome, 7 Feb. 1900); BAK, *Nachlass* Hertling, Folio 34.

45. For details, consult Huber, *Verfassungsgeschichte*, IV, 958–965. But see also Friedrich Meinecke, *Erlebtes, 1862–1919* (Stuttgart, 1964), pp. 155–160. Prominent Centrists were deeply involved in this project. Count Georg von Hertling, for example, served as the government's intermediary in the negotiations with the Vatican. See *Nachlass* Hertling; BAK, Folio 31.

46. Bearing the title "Universitätsunterricht und Konfession," the articles appeared in the *Münchener Neueste Nachrichten* of 15 and 24 November 1901; reprinted in Theodor Mommsen, *Reden und Aufsätze* (Berlin, 1905), pp. 432–436. Ridiculing Mommsen for his melodramatic style and supporting Spahn's appointment was Houston Stuart Chamberlain. See his "Der voraussetzungslose Mommsen," *Die Fackel*, III, 87 (7 Dec. 1901), 1–13. Sympathizing with Chamberlain's criticisms was the German ambassador to Vienna who, apparently because the journal was edited by Karl Kraus, a Jewish (but convert to Roman Catholicism) satirist, believed the only "weakness of the article lay in the fact that it was published in *Die Fackel*." Report to Bülow, 14 Dec. 1901; PAAA, Elsass-Lothringen 3, No. 1, Bd. 5.

47. Letter to Conrad Varrentrapp, 23 Aug. 1901; Friedrich Meinecke, *Ausgewählte Briefwechsel*, edited by Ludwig Dehio and Peter Classen, Vol. VI: *Friedrich Meinecke Werke* (Stuttgart, 1962), p. 25.

48. For details, including reprints of pertinent documents, consult Rossmann, *Wissenschaft, Ethik und Politik*.

49. "Universitätsunterricht," 435. Repeating Mommsen's complaint two years later in the Prussian Landtag, a deputy declared that "the practice of today's parity is in reality the grossest disparity because it no longer envisages the same rights for everyone, no longer the same consideration for all those who are equally qualified, but makes a distinction and calls less qualified individuals of the Catholic religion—for the sole reason because they belong to the Catholic creed—to certain posts within the state and to certain positions within the university." SBHA (2 Mar. 1903), II, 2291.

50. Prominent Roman Catholics were appalled. Ludwig von Pastor, for example, referred to Spahn as the "unmasked traitor of the Catholic cause." Pastor, *Tagebücher*, entry of 8 Oct. 1901, p. 365; Morsey, "Zwei Denkschriften," 255, n. 28.

51. Sachse, *Althoff*, p. 148.

52. "Romisch-katholische Zensur zu Anfang des 20. Jahrhunderts," PJ, CVII, 1 (Jan.–Mar. 1902), 1–9.

53. Sachse, *Althoff,* pp. 148–149.

54. Ibid.

55. Though an extremely partisan account, the basic details are to be found in Jakob Treitz, *Michael Felix Korum: Bischof von Trier, 1840–1921* (Munich, 1925), pp. 125–140.

56. Newspaper clippings, StAK, Abt. 403, No. 15207, Bl. 41 and 45.

57. Bishop Dr. [Michael Felix] Korum, *Unerbauliches aus der Diözese Trier: Darlegung der Verhältnisse höherer Töchterschulen in Trier, St. Johann und Kreuznach, mit Akten belegt* (Trier, 1903), p. 19; TLZ, XXIX, 19 (24 Jan. 1903), p. 1.

58. Korum, *Unerbauliches,* pp. 21–22.

59. Quoted in *Frankfurter Zeitung,* XLVII, 25 (25 Jan. 1903), p. 1.

60. TLZ, XXIX, 38 (17 Feb. 1903), p. 1.

61. Korum, *Unerbauliches,* p. 18.

62. Ibid., p. 19.

63. Ibid., p. 20.

64. Ibid.

65. *Memoirs of Prince von Bülow,* I, 675, Treitz, *Korum,* p. 132; Emil Zenz, *Geschichte der Stadt Trier in der ersten Hälfte des 20. Jahrhundert,* Vol. XII: *Ortschroniken des Trierer Landes* (Trier, 1967), p. 118.

66. Treitz, *Korum,* p. 132.

67. Ibid.; *Memoirs of Prince von Bülow,* I, 675; Zenz, *Geschichte der Stadt Trier,* p. 118; SBHA (2 Mar. 1903), II, 2249–2312; and *Nachlass* Korum; BAT, Abt. 108, No. 402.

68. Such views were expressed in the KVZ, XLIV, 173 (24 Feb. 1903), p. 1 and Korum, *Unerbauliches,* p. 20.

69. See *Nachlass* Bachem; HASK, Abt. 1006, No. 509.

70. Karl Bachem, *Zentrumspartei,* VI, 238. Although Evangelical and a few Jewish student organizations also existed, they did not become the focal point of criticism. References to them, however, were made in the SBHA (23 Feb. 1905), VII, 10416, 10421–10422. As such, it was clear that criticism was directed not at denominational fraternities *per se*—only those that were Roman Catholic.

71. Letter to Varrentrapp, 13 Mar. 1905; Meinecke, *Briefwechsel,* p. 29.

72. Karl Bachem, *Zentrumspartei,* VI, 235; Karl Hoeber, *Der Streit um den Zentrumscharakter,* Vol. I: *Zeit- und Streitfragen der Gegenwart* (Cologne, 1912), p. 9; Sebastian Merkle, "Die katholische Kirche," in *Deutschland unter Kaiser Wilhelm II.,* edited by G. Korte *et al,* Vol. II (Berlin, 1914), 1940–1941.

73. SBR (5 Dec. 1900), I, 325.

74. Karl Bachem, *Zentrumspartei,* VI, 239–240.

75. Ibid., 238–240.

76. SBHA (23 Feb. 1905), VII, 10403–10470.

77. Ibid., 10404.

NOTES TO CHAPTER 3

An Alliance of Knights and Saints

    1. Fontane, *Der Stechlin*, p. 168.
    2. HpBl, 376-386; reprinted in Ludwig Bergsträsser, *Der politische Katholizismus*, II, No. 53, 332-341; Hoeber, *Streit um den Zentrumscharakter*, pp. 16-20; Heinrich Marie Krueckemeyer, *Zentrum und Katholizismus* (Amsterdam, 1913), pp. 25-34; Von einem Geistlichen [Edmund Schopen], *"Köln:" Eine innere Gefahr für den Katholizismus* (Berlin, 1910), pp. 86-96.
    3. A brief but useful biography is Hugo Stehkämper, "Julius Bachem (1845-1918)," in *Zeitgeschichte in Lebensbildern*, pp. 29-42. For the history of this important publishing company, see Karl Bachem, *Josef Bachem, seine Familie und die Firma J.P. Bachem in Köln, die Rheinische und die Deutsche Volkshalle, die Kölnischen Blätter und die Kölnische Volkszeitung: Zugleich ein Versuch der Geschichte der katholischen Presse*, 2 vols. (Cologne, 1912).
    4. Testifying to this ideological congruence between the Centrum and the Conservative parties is a scene in Theodor Fontane's famous social novel *Der Stechlin*, p. 168. When Major Dubslav von Stechlin is defeated by a Social Democrat in a by-election, one of Stechlin's Conservative supporters concludes: "We must come to terms with the Centrum. Then we have made it." Bachem's proposal did not fail to arouse a sympathetic response from Protestant Conservatives who were looking for an ally to stem the advance of the Social Democrats.
    5. For a similar conclusion, see Zeender, "Interconfessional Party," 424-439.
    6. *Das Zentrum, wie es war, ist und bleibt* (Cologne, 1913).
    7. The variant form "Karl" is used only on some of his publications.
    8. *Zentrum, katholische Weltanschauung und praktische Politik: Zugleich eine Antwort auf die jüngste Broschüre von Geheimrat Roeren, "Zentrum und Kölner Richtung"* (Krefeld, 1914).
    9. See his "Zur Vorgeschichte der Zentrumspartei," *Hochland*, VII (July 1911), 415-430.
    10. The *Germania*, a Centrist newspaper in Berlin, was especially fearful of his intentions. See Krueckemeyer, *Zentrum und Katholizismus*, pp. 246-251. For the *Kölnische Volkszeitung's* reservations, see ibid., p. 251.
    11. Karl Trimborn to Carl Bachem, Nov. 1909; HASK, *Nachlass* Bachem, Abt. 1006, No. 285.
    12. Julius Bachem, *Das Zentrum*, pp. 73-74; Hoeber, *Streit um den Zentrumscharakter*, p. 82; Hermann Rehm, *Deutschlands politische Parteien: Ein Grundriss der Parteienlehre und der Wahlsysteme* (Jena, 1912), p. 41; Hermann Roeren, *Zentrum und Kölner Richtung* (Trier, 1913), pp. 12-13 and 114. The declaration promulgated by the party is reprinted in Krueckemeyer, *Zentrum und Katholizismus*, pp. 173-175, and in Bergsträsser, *Der politische Katholizismus*, II, No. 60, 377-379.
    13. Ernst Deuerlein, "Verlauf und Ergebnis des 'Zentrumsstreites' (1906-1909)," *Stimmen der Zeit*, CLVI (May 1955), 122; Hoeber, *Streit um den Zentrumscharakter*, p. 132; Krueckemeyer, *Zentrum und Katholizismus*, p. 232; and Hermann Roeren, *Veränderte Lage des Zentrumsstreites: Entgegnung auf die Kritik meiner Schrift Zentrum und Kölner Richtung* (Trier, 1914), p.

24; for details of the meeting, see Carl Bachem's protocol; HASK, *Nachlass* Bachem, Abt. 1006, No. 296.

14. Franz X. Bachem to August Pieper, 1 Dec. 1910; HASK, *Nachlass* Bachem, Abt. 1006, No. 307.

15. Jean Meerfeld, *Die Deutsche Zentrumspartei*, Vol. III: *Sozialwissenschaftliche Bibliothek* (Berlin, 1918), p. 36.

16. Julius Bachem's speech was subsequently published under the title "Nochmals: Wir müssen aus dem Turm heraus!" in HpBl, CXXXVII (1906), 503–513. Reprinted in Krueckemeyer, *Zentrum und Katholizismus*, pp. 34–44. See also Deuerlein, "Verlauf und Ergebnis," 112–113; and Hoeber, *Streit um den Zentrumscharakter*, pp. 21–22.

17. Hans Rosenberg, *Grosse Depression und Bismarckzeit: Wirtschaftsablauf, Gesellschaft und Politik in Mitteleuropa*, Vol. II: *Veröffentlichung der Historischen Kommission zu Berlin beim Friedrich-Meinecke-Institut der Freien Universität Berlin* (Berlin, 1967), pp. 123–124.

18. Johannes Schauff, *Die deutschen Katholiken und die Zentrumspartei: Eine politisch-statistische Untersuchung der Reichstagswahlen seit 1871* (Cologne, 1928), p. 70.

19. Roeren, *Zentrum und Kölner Richtung*, p. 47.

20. Sigmund Neumann, *Die Deutschen Parteien: Wesen und Wandel nach dem Kriege* (Berlin, 1932), p. 40.

21. *Der Streit um den Zentrumscharakter*. Cf. Heinrich Marie Krueckemeyer, "Der Streit," HpBl, CL (1912), 61–80. In certain constituencies where the Centrum held a relative but not an absolute majority, Centrist candidates stepped down in favor of candidates from other political parties. Centrist votes were then delivered to those individuals in an effort to obstruct the election of a less desirable contestant. Admittedly, this was a tactic which had long been practiced by the Centrum—indeed by all German political parties—long before the appearance of the "tower" article. In 1912 the Centrum systematically supported Conservative candidates in 45 constituencies—though not always with success—in order to prevent the decimation of the Conservative party.

22. Roeren, *Veränderte Lage*, p. 61.

23. Karl Bachem, *Zentrumspartei*, VII, 83; Jürgen Bertram, *Die Wahlen zum Deutschen Reichstag vom Jahre 1912: Parteien und Verbände in der Innenpolitik des Wilhelminischen Reiches*, Vol. XXVIII: *Beiträge zur Geschichte des Parlamentarismus und der politischen Parteien* (Düsseldorf, 1964), p. 13; Zeender, "Interconfessional Party," 427, n. 18.

24. Carl Bachem's notes, 5 Dec. 1910; HASK, *Nachlass* Bachem Abt. 1006, No. 307.

25. Hoeber, *Streit um den Zentrumscharakter*, pp. 82 and 171–172; Heinrich Marie Krueckemeyer, "Köln und Koblenz: Eine Darstellung der Osterdienstags-Konferenz und ihrer Folgeerscheinungen," FZB, Neue Folge, XXIX (1910), 85.

26. For his career as editor-in-chief, see the autobiographical account: Hermann Cardauns, *Aus dem Leben eines deutschen Redakteurs* (Cologne, 1912).

27. The development of this organization is described in Kl. Löffler, *Geschichte der katholischen Presse Deutschlands*, Heft 50: *Soziale Tagesfragen* (M. Gladbach, 1924), and Wilhelm Kisky, *Der Augustinus-Verein zur Pflege der katholischen Presse von 1878 bis 1928* (Düsseldorf, 1928).

28. *Ludwig Windthorst* (Cologne, 1907). Hüsgen used this book as the

vehicle for his thesis, in support of Julius Bachem's position, that the Centrum party from its very inception was a political rather than a confessional organization. This book (and its second edition in 1911) was printed by the Bachem publishing firm.

29. George D. Crothers, *The German Elections of 1907*, Vol. 479: *Studies in History, Economics and Public Law* (New York, 1941), p. 172, n. 202.

30. Brief character sketches of the elder Spahn can be found in Morsey, *Die Deutsche Zentrumspartei*, pp. 559-565, and Helmut Neubach, "Peter Spahn (1846-1925)," in *Zeitgeschichte in Lebensbildern*, pp. 65-80.

31. Some of the vicissitudes of his career can be followed in Martin Spahn, "Selbstbiographie," in *Deutscher Aufstieg: Bilder aus der Vergangenheit und Gegenwart der rechtsstehenden Parteien*, edited by Hans v. Arnim and Georg v. Below (Berlin, 1925), pp. 479-488, and Walter Ferber, "Der Weg Martin Spahns: Zur Ideengeschichte des politischen Rechtskatholizismus," *Hochland*, LXII (May-June 1970), 218-229.

32. For biographical information, consult the older work by Hermann Cardauns, *Karl Trimborn: Nach seinen Briefen und Tagebüchern*, Vol. XXXI: *Eine Sammlung von Zeit- und Lebensbildern* (M. Gladbach, 1922). The most recent sketch is Rudolf Morsey, "Karl Trimborn (1854-1921)," in *Zeitgeschichte in Lebensbildern*, pp. 81-93.

33. Ferdinand Jacobs, *Von Schorlemer zur Grünen Front: Zur Abwertung des berufsständischen und politischen Denkens*, Vol. I: *Schriften zur Landlichen Bildung* (Düsseldorf, 1957), p. 10; Sarah R. Tirrell, *German Agrarian Politics after Bismarck's Fall: The Formation of the Farmers' League*, Vol. 566: *Studies in History, Economics and Public Law* (New York, 1951), pp. 157-158; Müller, "Zentrumspartei und agrarische Bewegung," p. 834.

34. Jacobs, *Schorlemer*, pp. 29-30; Müller, "Zentrumspartei und agrarische Bewegung," p. 840.

35. Karl Bachem, *Zentrumspartei*, V, 352-353.

36. Ibid., 23-24, 291-293; Müller, "Zentrumspartei und agrarische Bewegung," pp. 848-849.

37. Karl Bachem, *Zentrumspartei*, V, 23-24, 291-292.

38. Müller, "Zentrumspartei und agrarische Bewegung," p. 857.

39. Jacobs, *Schorlemer*, p. 32.

40. Karl Bachem, *Zentrumspartei*, VI, 405; Rehm, *Deutschlands politische Parteien*, pp. 50-51; Jacobs, *Schorlemer*, pp. 27 and 34.

41. Jacobs, *Schorlemer*, p. 34.

42. Zeender, "Interconfessional Party," 427.

43. Wilhelm Spael, *Das katholische Deutschland im 20. Jahrhundert: Seine Pionier- und Krisenzeiten, 1890-1945* (Würzburg, 1964), p. 72.

44. Peter Maslowski, *Was ist die Deutsche Zentrumspartei? Klerikalismus und Proletariat* (Berlin, 1925), pp. 38-39. Both Thyssen and Klöchner, moreover, were newcomers to the industrial scene. The former's works were established in 1890, the latter's (on a large scale at least), only in 1900.

45. No scholarly biography of the cardinal exists. But see Johann Schmitz, *Antonius Kardinal Fischer, Erzbischof von Köln: Sein Leben und Wirken* (Cologne, 1915), the eulogistic work of a priest from Düsseldorf-Hamm.

46. Report from Baron Otto von Ritter, 6 Apr. 1910; BHStA, Abt. II, Geheimes Staatsarchiv, MA III 2564 (1910), No. 42.

47. Schmitz, *Kardinal Fischer*, p. 206.

48. Joseph Hansen, *Preussen und Rheinland von 1815 bis 1915: Hundert Jahre politischen Lebens am Rhein* (Bonn, 1918), p. 239; Pastor, *Tagebücher,* entry of 24 May 1914, pp. 597–598; see also the entry for 16 Jan. 1915, p. 615.

49. There exists no full-length biography of Cardinal Kopp. Among the brief character sketches are Hermann Hoffmann, "Georg von Kopp," in *Schlesische Lebensbilder,* Vol. II (Breslau, 1926), 323–332; Franz Schnabel, "Kardinal Kopps Bedeutung für den politischen Katholizismus in Deutschland," in *Abhandlungen und Vorträge, 1914–1965,* edited by Heinrich Lutz (Freiburg, 1970), 1–13; F. Scholz, "Georg Kardinal Kopp, 1881–1887, Bischof von Fulda, 1887 bis 1914 Fürstbischof von Breslau," in *Beiträge zur schlesische Kirchengeschichte: Gedenkschrift für Kurt Engelbert,* edited by Bernhard Stasiewski, Vol. IV: *Forschungen und Quellen zur Kirchen- und Kulturgeschichte Ostdeutschlands* (Cologne, 1969), pp. 511–529; and the perceptive essays by Rudolf Morsey, "Georg Kardinal Kopp (1837–1914)," in *Zeitgeschichte in Lebensbildern,* pp. 13–28, and "Georg Kardinal Kopp, Fürstbischof von Breslau (1887–1914); Kirchenfürst oder 'Staatsbischof'? Ein Beitrag zur Geschichte des Fürstbistums Breslau," *Wichmann-Jahrbuch für Kirchengeschichte im Bistum Berlin,* XXI/XXIII (1967/69), 42–65.

50. Breslau was the single largest see in Germany. Even the German capital, without a bishop of its own until 1929, was under Breslau's ecclesiastical jurisdiction. Once part of the principality of Neisse-Grottkau, the Breslau diocese also possessed estates outside Prussia's frontiers which escaped governmental secularization in 1810. Located in Habsburg territory, these properties were finally lost to Breslau in 1924 when they reverted to Czechoslovakian control.

51. Kopp's wealth was derived from landed estates and on accumulated treasure left behind by his parsimonious predecessor. These sums were considerable. According to Herbert von Bismarck, the Prussian Minister of Culture estimated that in good years the income from the Austrian estates amounted to two million gulden. In 1895, some eight years after this estimate, it was claimed that this income came to a million marks per annum. Such an income was added to an already large treasury. When Prince-Bishop Heinrich Förster died in 1881 he left behind a fortune of six million marks. See Walter Bussmann, ed., *Staatssekretär Graf Herbert von Bismarck: Aus seiner politischen Privatkorrespondenz,* Vol. XLIV: *Deutsche Geschichtsquellen des 19. und 20. Jahrhunderts* (Göttingen, 1964); Herbert von bismarck to Kuno Graf zu Rantzau, 18 July 1887, No. 307, p. 462; Bogdan Graf von Hutten-Czapski, *Sechzig Jahre Politik und Gesellschaft,* 2 vols. (Berlin, 1936), I, 256.

Since 1884 Kopp sat in the Prussian State Council. Two years later he was appointed to the Prussian House of Lords. Because of his Habsburg property, he was also titular Land Captain in Austrian Silesia and presiding officer for the local Landtag. Hoffmann, "Kopp," 330; Hutten-Czapski, *Sechzig Jahre Politik,* I, 256–257; Scholz, "Georg Kardinal Kopp," 518.

In reference to Kopp's contacts with Bülow and the imperial court, see Max Buchner, *Kaiser Wilhelm II.: Seine Weltanschauung und die deutschen Katholiken* (Leipzig, 1929), p. 118; Hutten-Czapski, *Sechzig Jahre Politik,* I, 256 and 395; *Memoirs of Prince von Bülow,* II, 113; Scholz, "Georg Kardinal Kopp," 524; Wilhelm II, *The Kaiser's Memoirs,* trans. Thomas R. Ybarra (New York, 1922), p. 209.

52. Scholz, "Georg Kardinal Kopp," 532. If the Centrists "wanted advice in temporal affairs," Leo XIII once observed, "they could do no better than to defer to the worldly-wise Bishop Kopp of Breslau." Quoted in Karl Bachem, *Zentrumspartei*, VII, 420. Along with a patent of nobility, Kopp also received in 1906 the Order of the Black Eagle, one of Prussia's highest decorations.

53. Ritter to Hertling, 25 July 1914; BHStA, Abt. II, Geheimes Staatsarchiv, MA I 929, Bl. 73; Ernst Deuerlein, "Der Gewerkschaftsstreit," *Theologische Quartalschrift*, CXXXIX (1959), 74 and 76; Jean Meerfeld, *Der Krieg der Frommen: Materialen zum Zentrumsstreit* (Berlin, 1914), pp. 57 and 61.

54. Pastor, *Tagebücher*, entry of 10 May 1913, p. 579.

55. Deuerlein, "Gewerkschaftsstreit," 76.

56. Quoted in dispatch by Wittgenstein to Theobald von Bethmann Hollweg, 7 Dec. 1912; PAAA, Deutschland No. 125, Bd. 4.

NOTES TO CHAPTER 4

The Politics of Sectarianism

1. Meerfeld, *Deutsche Zentrumspartei*, p. 5; Wilhelm Ohr, *Das Zentrum*, Heft 4: *Deutsches Parteiwesen* (Munich, 1911), p. 69.

2. Leo Jablonski, *Geschichte des fürstbischöflichen Delegaturbezirkes Brandenburg und Pommern*, 2 vols. (Breslau, 1929), I, 234–235.

3. Johannes Nichtweiss, *Die ausländischen Saisonsarbeiter in der Landwirtschaft der östlichen und mittleren Gebiete des Deutschen Reiches: Ein Beitrag zur Geschichte der preussisch-deutschen Politik von 1890 bis 1914*, Vol. IV: *Schriftenreihe des Instituts für Allgemeine Geschichte an der Humboldt-Universität Berlin* ([East] Berlin, 1959), p. 186.

4. For pertinent details regarding this agitation, see Jablonski, *Geschichte des fürstbischöflichen Delegaturbezirkes*, I, 232–240.

5. Quoted in *Die Kirchenpolitik der Hohenzollern von einem Deutschen* (Frankfurt a. M., 1906), p. 347.

6. For details, see Matthias Erzberger, *Die Kolonial-Bilanz: Bilder aus der deutschen Kolonialpolitik auf Grund der Verhandlungen des Reichstags im Sessionsabschnitt 1905/06* (Berlin, 1906), and Klaus Epstein, "Erzberger and the German Colonial Scandals, 1905–1910," *The English Historical Review*, LXXXV (Oct. 1959), 637–663.

7. Quoted in Crothers, *The German Elections*, p. 120.

8. Quoted in ibid., pp. 127 and 142–143; Karl Trimborn to Julius Bachem, 8 Jan. 1907; Cardauns, *Karl Trimborn*, p. 112.

9. Crothers, *The German Elections*, pp. 122–128; cf. *Das Tagebuch der Baronin Spitzemberg geb. Freiin v. Varnbüler: Aufzeichnungen aus der Hofgesellschaft des Hohenzollernreiches*, edited by Rudolf Vierhaus, Vol. XLIV: *Deutsche Geschichtsquellen des 19. und 20. Jahrhunderts* (Göttingen, 1960), entry of 14 Dec. 1906, p. 468.

10. This "pairing of the conservative spirit with the liberal spirit" was a most precarious and unstable alliance, an "edifice without a foundation." Despite the fact that the Centrum had actually increased the number of seats held, its position in the Reichstag was significantly altered. The parties of the

old *Kartell*, together with the Progressives, were so strengthened by the defeat of the Social Democrats that they could dispense with the Centrum, whose votes were no longer essential for governmental bills. No longer "Catholic," but "German" was trump. Theodor Eschenburg, *Das Kaiserreich am Scheideweg: Bassermann, Bülow und der Block* (Berlin, 1929), p. 46; Crothers, *The German Elections*, p. 181.

11. Alex R. Vidler, *The Modernist Movement in the Roman Church: Its Origins & Outcome* (Cambridge, 1934), pp. 200 and 202–203; Schroeder, *Aufbruch*, pp. 353 and 369. For an example of the confusion between the terms, see Hugo Holzamer, *Turm und Block: Bestrebungen über die Hauptaufgaben der deutschen Katholiken in den konfessionellen Kämpfen der Gegenwart* (Trier, 1912), pp. vi–vii.

12. Schroeder, *Aufbruch*, pp. 369, 388–389 and 403; Pastor, *Tagebücher*, entry of 18 Dec. 1902, p. 397.

13. *Der Katholizismus und das 20. Jahrhundert im Lichte der kirchlichen Entwicklung der Neuzeit* (Stuttgart, 1902).

14. Pastor, *Tagebücher*, entry of 10 Sept. 1912, p. 558.

15. Ehrhard, *Der Katholizismus und das 20. Jahrhundert*, pp. 357ff; quoted in Schroeder, *Aufbruch*, pp. 396 and 401.

16. Pastor, *Tagebücher*, entry of 18 Dec. 1912, p. 397.

17. Schroeder, *Aufbruch*, pp. 388–389.

18. The address was published under the title *Der Katholizismus als Prinzip des Fortschrittes*, 6th ed. (Würzburg, 1897). For additional details, see J.-B. Pelt, "Un théologien novateur en Allemagne," *Revue du clergé français*, V (15 Jan. 1898), 310–326. Cf. Josef Schmidlin, *Papstgeschichte der neuesten Zeit*, Vol. III (Munich, 1936), pp. 94–104.

19. Ernesto Buonaiuti, *Le Modernisme Catholique*, trans. René Monnot (Paris, 1927), pp. 154–155.

20. His nondoctrinal approach clearly separated Schell from the Modernists.

21. Hutten-Czapski, *Sechzig Jahre Politik*, I, 436.

22. Joseph Schnitzer, *Der katholische Modernismus*, Vol. III: *Die Klassiker der Religion* (Berlin, 1912), pp. 7–8.

23. Jean Rivière, *Le Modernisme dans l'Église: Étude d'histoire religieuse contemporaine* (Paris, 1929), p. 288.

24. Ibid.; Pastor, *Tagebücher*, entry of 4 Nov. 1906, p. 461.

25. Schroeder, *Aufbruch*, p. 377; Rivière, *Le Modernisme*, p. 293. See also A. ten Hompel, *Indexbewegung und Kulturgesellschaft: Eine historische Darstellung auf Grund der Akten* (Bonn, 1908). Martin Fassbender of the Centrum party was an adherent of the League. However it was also alleged that Hertling was a member. Cf. Pastor, *Tagebücher*, entry of 2 Mar. 1908, p. 490. Even though the count disavowed sympathy for the movement in Münster, he refused to make public his position on the matter. See correspondence between Hertling and Cardinal Raffaele Merry del Val, 13, 16, and 20 July 1907; BAK, *Nachlass* Hertling, Folio 36, Bl. 26 and 29.

26. Report from Otto von Mühlberg, 20 Mar. 1911; PAAA, Päpstl. Stuhl No. 6, Bd. 3.

27. *Das Cölner Osterdienstags-Protokoll: Ein Beitrag zur Würdigung latenter Kulturgegensätze im Katholizismus der Gegenwart* (Cologne, 1909), p. 7.

28. Chiefly responsible for lifting the question from the level of expediency to that of high principle was Hermann Roeren. See his *Zentrum und Kölner Richtung* (Trier, 1912). This emphasis did not entail a shift in priorities. The "Parity Question" was still the central problem for Roman Catholics.

29. See Roeren's *Zentrum und Kölner Richtung* and *Veränderte Lage des Zentrumsstreites*; Karl Marie Krueckemeyer's "Ist das Zentrum eine konfessionelle Partei?" HpBl, CXXXVIII (1907), and [Emil Ritter], *Das Zentrum eine konfessionelle Partei?* Heft 3 der Politischen Bibliothek der Windthorstbunde (Cologne, 1910).

30. In the opinion of the "Berliners," high churchmen in particular, "the Catholic religion should not confine itself merely to religious practices, but it must permeate and determine all of man's actions, private and 'public.' " Mühlberg to Bethmann Hollweg, 20 Mar. 1911; PAAA, Päpstl. Stuhl No. 6, Bd. 3. Because the interpretation of religious and ethical rectitude was the prerogative of the hierarchy, any definition of the party in ethical terms increased the episcopate's dominion over the Centrum party.

31. Cf. Hoensbroech, *Rom und das Zentrum*, pp. 91–96.

32. Hans Rosenberg, *Grosse Depression und Bismarckzeit*, pp. 120ff.

33. This development was especially important regarding the emerging class-consciousness of the Roman Catholic working classes. See Chapters V and VI.

34. Rosenberg, *Grosse Depression*, pp. 120ff; Thomas Nipperdey, *Die Organisation der Parteien vor 1918*, Vol. XVIII: *Beiträge zur Geschichte des Parlamentarismus und der politischen Parteien* (Düsseldorf, 1959), pp. 283f.

35. The basic, but partisan account, is Emil Ritter, *Die katholisch-soziale Bewegung Deutschlands im neunzehnten Jahrhundert* (Cologne, 1954). Ritter relies heavily on the Pieper Manuscript; StAMö, 15/1–3. Cf. Herbert Gottwald, "Volksverein für das katholische Deutschland (VKD) 1890–1933," in *Die bürgerlichen Parteien in Deutschland*, II, 810–834, and V. I. Lenin, "Organization of the Masses by the German Catholics," *Collected Works*, trans. Andrew Rothstein, 45 vols. (Moscow, 1960–1970), XXXVI, 244–246.

36. Nipperdey, *Die Organisation*, p. 281.

37. Ludwig Bergsträsser, "Der Riss im Zentrumsturm," *Akademische Blätter: Zeitschrift des Kyffhäuser-Verbandes der Vereine Deutscher Studenten*, XXV (16 Nov. 1910), 243; Meerfeld, *Die Deutsche Zentrumspartei*, p. 68.

38. Peter Molt, *Der Reichstag vor der improvisierten Revolution*, Vol. IV: *Politische Forschungen* (Cologne, 1963), pp. 267–268.

39. Bertram, *Die Wahlen*, pp. 27–28, n. 1; Meerfeld, *Zentrumspartei*, p. 67; Bergsträsser, "Riss im Zentrumsturm," 246.

40. Mühlberg to Bethmann Hollweg, 27 Nov. 1913; PAAA, Päpstl. Stuhl No. 6, Bd. 6.

41. Krueckemeyer, "Köln und Koblenz," 6.

42. Count Hans von Praschma to Hertling, 3 June 1908; BAK, *Nachlass Hertling*, Folio 36, Bl. 48.

43. See Hoeber, *Streit um den Zentrumscharakter*, pp. 66–67; Krueckemeyer, *Zentrum und Katholizismus*, p. 121.

44. "Drei Programmsätze," HpBl, CXLIII (16 Jan. 1909), 162–167; Krueckemeyer, "Köln und Koblenz," 2. At the end of March reprints of the article "Drei Programmsätze" were covertly sent to several individuals, together with the query if they were prepared to attend a clandestine meeting to discuss these issues. Deuerlein, "Verlauf und Ergebnis," 115; Hoeber, *Streit um den Zentrumscharkter*, p. 29; Krueckemeyer, "Köln und Koblenz," 3. For the text of the invitation, see *Nachlass* Bachem; HASK, Abt. 1006, No. 284a. This was not the first such meeting. Sometime in 1897 a conclave with similar goals took place in Cologne. Roeren was one of the leaders. But nothing came of it. See letter dated 14 Mar. 1911; HASK, *Nachlass* Bachem, Abt. 1006, No. 309.

45. With the appearance of the 23 June 1909 issue of the *Kölnische Volkszeitung*, the proceedings of the Easter Tuesday Conference became public knowledge. An anonymous participant gave the newspaper his stenographic notes, the text of which was then published. Subsequently this material was published separately under the pseudonum "Athanasius," a name used by Joseph Görres in his famous political tract protesting the Prussian government's actions in the "Cologne Troubles" of 1837. See *Das Cölner Osterdienstags-Protokoll*. Several typewritten copies were also circulated bearing the title *Protokoll der kirchliche-sozialen Konferenz am Osterdienstag, den 13. April 1909, im Köln* (Oberhausen, 1909). For details, consult Krueckemeyer, "Köln und Koblenz," 18–19. For the rejoinder by one of the participants, Hermann Roeren, see "Zur Klarstellung," a document privately circulated among the executive committee of the Prussian Centrum party as well as among other concerned persons. It is reprinted in *"Köln:" Eine innere Gefahr*, pp. 96–110; see also Roeren, *Veränderte Lage*, pp. 28, 31, and 86. Roeren denied the authenticity of the *Protokoll* as a clumsy work full of untruths and contradictions. But his explanations were deemed unsatisfactory. See Roeren to Carl Bachem, 27 June 1909; Carl Bachem to Roeren, 30 June 1909; Roeren to Carl Bachem, 3 July 1909; and Carl Bachem to Roeren, 5 July 1909; HASK, *Nachlass* Bachem, Abt. 1006, No. 284a.

46. *Das Cölner Osterdienstags-Protokoll*, p. 7; Deuerlein, "Verlauf und Ergebnis," 120; Hoeber, *Streit um den Zentrumscharakter*, p. 74; Krueckemeyer, "Köln and Koblenz," 4–5 and 67–69; Krueckemeyer, *Zentrum und Katholizismus*, pp. 170–171.

47. Krueckemeyer, "Köln und Koblenz," 66–67; Hoeber, *Streit um den Zentrumscharakter*, p. 79.

48. Friedrich Galen to Hertling, 13 Aug. 1909; BAK, *Nachlass* Hertling, Folio 37.

49. Memorandum, 30 Apr. 1903; HASK, *Nachlass* Bachem, Abt. 1006, No. 187.

50. Quoted in *Memoirs of Prince von Bülow*, I, 676.

51. Meerfeld, *Der Krieg der Frommen*, p. 15; Ritter, *Die katholisch-soziale Bewegung*, p. 327. Kopp's expression "Die Verseuchung des Westens" appeared in his letter to Amalie von Schalscha-Ehrenfeld, the head of the Catholic Womens' League. For a discussion of the impact of this letter when it became public knowledge in 1910, see Christoph Weber, "Kardinal Kopp's Brief von der 'Verseuchung des Westens,' " *Archiv für schlesische Kirchengeschichte*, XXVI (1968), 327–334. A copy of the letter is located in HASK, *Nachlass* Bachem, Abt. 1006, No. 294.

52. Hohenlohe, *Denkwürdigkeiten*, p. 397; Eugen von Jagemann, *Fünfund-siebzig Jahre des Erlebnis und Erfahrens (1849-1924)* (Heidelberg, 1925), pp. 156-157.

53. Kopp to Korum, 16 Aug. 1910; BAT, *Nachlass* Korum, Abt. 108, No. 48; Karl Bachem, *Zentrumspartei*, VII, 198.

54. Published as "Zentrum und kirchliche Autorität" in *Gegen die Quertreiber: Kundgebung der Deutschen Zentrumspartei im Städt. Saalbau zu Essen am 15. Februar 1914* (Essen, n. d. [1914]), pp. 12-42.

55. Karl Bachem, *Zentrumspartei*, VII, 246 and 257-258.

56. Ritter to Hertling, 24 June 1914; BHStA, Abt. II, Geheimes Staatsarchiv, MA I 929, Bl. 44. He, Hertling noted, "has illuminated the situation very well" and "it would really be tragi-comedy if Wacker who has done so much work for the Catholic church . . . must now spend his last days under the censor." See letter to Ritter, 19 Feb. 1914; BHStA, Abt. II, Geheimes Staatsarchiv, MA I 929, Bl. 33. This was not the only countermeasure employed by the Vatican. After complaints concerning the Cologne faction's efforts to give the Centrum the character of a political party reached Rome, the Curia demanded an explanation. Monsignor Umberto Benigni (the head of the anti-Modernist *Sodalitium Pianum*) criticized the "Cologners," creating the atmosphere of a "black terror" and "witch hunt." "The advisors of the pope," it was said, "had no idea at all of how Catholics and Protestants in Germany live with one another, can live together, and must live together." Carl Bachem to Felix Porsch, 12 May 1908; Porsch to Carl Bachem, 18 May 1908; HASK, *Nachlass* Bachem, Abt. 1006, No. 277; Bishop Adolf Bertram to Carl Bachem, 12 July 1908; ibid.; Hertling to Ritter, 6 Mar. 1912 and 11 June 1912; BHStA, Abt. II, Päpstl. Stuhl, No. 903; Hermann Cardauns, "Die Kehrseite des Kampfes gegen die Modernistenschnuffler," HpBl, CXLV (June 1910); Meerfeld, *Der Krieg der Frommen*, pp. 20-21.

57. Rehm, *Deutschlands politische Parteien*, p. 47.

58. Heinrich Köhler, *Lebenserinnerungen des Politikers und Staatsmannes, 1878-1949*, Vol. XI: *Veröffentlichungen der Kommission für Geschichtliche Landeskunde in Baden-Württemberg* (Stuttgart, 1964), p. 150.

59. Rehm, *Deutschlands politische Parteien*, p. 55.

60. Hoensbroech, *Rom und das Zentrum*, p. 97; Molt, *Der Reichstag*, p. 174.

61. See Pieper Manuscript, StAMö, 15/3, pp. 872-874, and Ritter, *Die katholisch-soziale Bewegung*, p. 328; Spael, *Das katholische Deutschland*, p. 23. For good, concise biographies of two of these three clerical labor leaders, see Hubert Mockenhaupt, "Heinrich Brauns (1868-1939)," in *Zeitgeschichte in Lebensbildern*, pp. 148-159, and the same author's essay "Franz Hitze (1851-1921)," in ibid., pp. 53-64. A biography of Pieper does not exist.

62. Krueckemeyer, "Köln und Koblenz," 7; Franz Schnabel, "Kardinal Kopps Bedeutung," 12.

63. Bergsträsser, "Riss im Zentrumsturm," 243.

64. Bertram, *Die Wahlen*, p. 162.

65. Data obtained from August Plate, *Handbuch für das Preussische Abgeordnetenhaus* (Berlin), editions of 1904 and 1908.

66. For information pertaining to the membership of the Reichstag, consult *Amtliches Reichstags-Handbuch* (Berlin), editions of 1903, 1907, and 1912.

67. Miscellaneous notes from *Klarheit und Wahrheit*; AAW, *Nachlass*

Porsch, Ia 4; extracts from *Cölner Correspondenz*, 6 May 1912; AAW, *Nachlass* Porsch, Ia 5. Italics in original.

68. Krueckemeyer, *Zentrum und Katholizismus*, p. 285. Italics in original.

69. Ibid., pp. 287–289.

70. Ibid., pp. 289–292.

71. *"Köln:" Eine innere Gefahr*, pp. 20, 32–33, and 35; Hoeber, *Streit um den Zentrumscharakter*, pp. 116–117.

72. *"Köln:" Eine innere Gefahr*, p. 36.

73. Whatever the similarity in viewpoint, however, Roeren hastened to disclaim all connection with Schopen's pamphlet. Roeren to Julius Bachem, 26 May 1910; HASK, *Nachlass* Bachem, Abt. 1006, No. 291a.

74. Meerfeld, *Deutsche Zentrumspartei*, p. 5; Ohr, *Das Zentrum*, p. 69; Roeren, *Kölner Richtung*, pp. 73–74, n. 1.

75. The novel was subsequently translated into English: Clara Viebig, *The Sleeping Army: A Story of Prussian and Pole*, trans. Gilbert Waterhouse (London, 1929), p. 111.

76. Hermann Mosler to Alexander Reuss, 16 Feb. 1886; BAT, *Nachlass* Reuss, Abt. 105, No. 1532. Italics in original.

77. The best general study of Germany's treatment of its Polish minority during this period remains Richard W. Tims, *Germanizing Prussian Poland: The H-K-T Society and the Struggle for the Eastern Marches in the German Empire, 1894–1919*, Vol. 487: *Studies in History, Economics and Public Law* (New York, 1941). A Polish problem on a smaller scale also existed in the Ruhr. See Hans-Ulrich Wehler, "Die Polen im Ruhrgebiet bis 1918," in *Moderne deutsche Sozialgeschichte*, pp. 437–455.

78. Biographical details can be found in Helmut Neubach, "Felix Porsch (1853–1930)," in *Zeitgeschichte in Lebensbildern*, pp. 113–128, and in the following two articles by Gerhard Webersinn: "Dr. Felix Porsch: Vizepräsident des Preussischen Landtages," *Jahrbuch der Schlesischen Friedrich-Wilhelms-Universität zu Breslau*, XIII (1968), 232–283, and "Felix Porsch als Kirchenrechtler, Sachwalter der Gerechtigkeit," *Archiv für schlesische Kirchengeschichte*, XXVII (1969), 130–146. Neither the Neubach sketch nor the Webersinn essays, however, are based on the *Nachlass* Porsch deposited in the Episcopal Archives of Wroclaw.

79. Felix Porsch's memorandum, 13 May 1907; AAW, *Nachlass* Porsch, Ib la, pp. 1–2.

80. Ibid. "There is missing," Porsch wrote, "a Centrist press in the Polish language. The only Polish Centrist paper, the Gazeka Katolika, has about 1,200 to 1,400 subscribers . . . as opposed to a total Greater Polish press of almost 100,000 subscribers . . . ." See also Stutz to Kopp, 16 Feb. 1906; AAW, *Nachlass* Kopp, IA 24a 17, B. No. 5186.

81. Porsch's memorandum, 13 May 1907; AAW, *Nachlass* Porsch, Ib la.

82. Porsch to Papal Nuncio in Munich, 7 May 1904; AAW, *Nachlass* Kopp, IA 24a 20.

83. *Ausgewählte Reden des Staatsministers a.D. und Parlamentariers Dr. Ludwig Windthorst gehalten in der Zeit von 1851–1891*, 3 vols. (Osnabrück, 1902–1903), III, 146.

84. Porsch to Papal Nuncio in Munich, 7 May 1904; AAW, *Nachlass* Kopp, IA 24a 20; see also memorandum entitled "Die polnische Bewegung in Oberschlesien," May 1904(?); AAW, *Nachlass* Kopp, IA 24a 20.

85. For biographical details, consult Hermann Ehren, *Graf Franz von Ballestrem: Ein Lebensbild* (Breslau, 1935) and K. H. Rother, "Franz Graf von Ballestrem," in *Schlesische Lebensbilder*, Vol. I: *Schlesier des neunzehnten Jahrhunderts*, edited by Friedrich Andreae *et al* (Breslau, 1922), pp. 247-251. See also Theodor Häbich, *Deutsche Latifundien: Bericht und Mahnung*, 3d ed. (Stuttgart, 1947), p. 125.

Ballestrem also made large financial contributions to Centrist activities. He gave 1,500 marks, for example, to a special fund for the Catholic Day arranged by Porsch. Franz von Ballestrem to Porsch, 6 Dec. 1910; AAW, *Nachlass* Porsch, IV 16 No. 5.

86. *Protokoll der Verhandlungen des VI. Kongresses der christlichen Gewerkschaften Deutschlands.* Abgehalten vom 22.-24 Juli 1906 in Breslau (Cologne, 1906), pp. 120-121.

87. Ehren, *Ballestrem*, pp. 22-25 and 27.

88. Quoted in Karl Bachem, *Zentrumspartei*, VI, 188. Similar epithets can be found in [Bernhard Karl?] Stephan, *Der Beuthener Prozess im Lichte der Wahrheit oder Wahrheitsgetreue Enthüllungen aus der polnischen Politik in Oberschlesien: Ein Beitrag zum Verständnis des oberschlesischen Wirren* (Berlin, 1903), p. 103. Ballestrem's policy was in harmony with the government's intentions. Polish workers were not permitted to have their own labor organizations, even if under the control of the Roman church. See Minister of Interior to Kopp, 9 Feb. 1902; AAW, *Nachlass* Kopp, IA 24a 20. For a similar argument, see Prince von Hohenzollern-Sigmaringen to Gottlieb von Jagow, 19 Apr. 1914; PAAA, Päpstl. Stuhl No. 26, Bd. 3. Because the Poles were denied national "parity," they even spurned the interconfessional trade unions. Jan Kapitza to Kopp, 2 May 1906; AAW, *Nachlass* Kopp, IA 24a 20. For Kapitza's [Polish spelling: Kapica] role in Upper Silesian politics, see Emil Szramek, "Ks. Jan Kapica: Zyciorys a Zarazem Fragment z Historji Górnego Slaska" in *Roczniki Towarzystwa Przyjaciól Nauk na Slasku* (Katowice 1931) pp. 1-86. I am indebted to Professor Andrej Brozek for calling this essay to my attention.

89. See SVZ, XXXV, 307 (10 July 1903), p. 4 and XXXV, 340 (29 July 1903), p. 6; Porsch's copy of election manifesto, 20 May 1906; AAW, *Nachlass* Porsch, III 9.

90. Markwart, "Das oberschlesische Zentrum und seine Presse," *Die Wartburg*, X, 28 (7 July 1911), 251.

91. Holtz (Regierungs-Präsident) to Minister of Interior, 14 Aug. 1903; AAW, *Nachlass* Porsch, III 9.

92. Johannes Altkemper, *Deutschtum und Polentum in politisch-konfessioneller Bedeutung* (Leipzig, 1910), p. 205; Ernst Sontag, *Adalbert (Wojciech) Korfanty: Ein Beitrag zur Geschichte der Ansprüche auf Oberschlesien*, Vol. VII: *Beihefte zum Jahrbuch der Albertus-Universität Königsberg/Pr.* (Kitzingen-Main, 1954), p. 20; Paul Weber, *Die Polen in Oberschlesien: Eine statistische Untersuchungen* (Berlin, 1913), p. 2.

93. Weber, *Die Polen*, pp. 2-3.

94. Altkemper, *Deutschtum und Polentum*, p. 209.

95. Kapitza to Kopp, 2 May 1906 and Porsch to Papal Nuncio in Munich, 7 May 1904; AAW, *Nachlass* Kopp, IA 24a 20.

96. Aus Schlesien [Felix Porsch], "Die schlesische Zentrumspartei," HpBl, CXLVIII (1911), 875.

97. See his essay, "Zur Polenfrage," FZB, Neue Folge, XXII, 1-2 (1903), 1-63.

98. Ibid., 1-2, 57, 59, and 61-62. Italics in original.

99. "Just on account of the language difficulty in Polish-speaking Upper Silesia the clergy" became "the Centrum's actual middleman." Porsch to Papal Nuncio in Munich, 7 May 1904; AAW, *Nachlass* Kopp, IA 24a 20. Similar sentiments were expressed in Porsch's memorandum, 13 May 1907; AAW, *Nachlass* Porsch, Ib 1a. Cf. Stephan, *Der Beuthener Prozess*, p. 220.

100. Pastor [Pfarrer] Hahnel to Canonicus, 14 Feb. 1907; AAW, *Nachlass* Kopp, IA 24a 18. Testifying to the growing problem of clerical loyalty to the Centrum are Kapitza's reports to Kopp, 15 June 1905; AAW, *Nachlass* Porsch, III 9 and 2 May 1906; AAW, *Nachlass* Kopp, IA 24a 20. See also Sontag, *Korfanty*, p. 23, and Stephan, *Der Beuthener Prozess*, p. 9.

101. Weber, *Die Polen*, pp. 2 and 3, n. 1. Die-hard Polish nationalists were badly shaken. "The [Polish] party staff in Beuthen . . . lost its head as a result of the election," Kapitza gleefully noted. Adalbert (Wojciech) Korfanty was "completely crushed" and Adam Napieralski, another Polish nationalist, felt "the ground slip from under his feet." Kapitza to Kopp, 3 Feb. 1912; AAW, *Nachlass* Kopp, IA 24a 18. Polish collaboration with the Centrum, it must also be admitted, was also designed to hamper German Roman Catholic cooperation with the Berlin government. Any alliance between Berlin and the German Centrists, the Poles concluded, led to a strengthening of "Germandom." That development could only work to the disadvantage of Polish interests. Altkemper, *Deutschtum und Polentum*, p. 214.

102. Carl Bachem to Porsch, 30 July 1909 and Carl Bachem's memorandum, 29 Aug. 1909; HASK, *Nachlass* Bachem, Abt. 1006, No. 284a.

103. Zenz, *Geschichte der Stadt Trier*, pp. 146-147 and 147, n. 87.

104. Josef Bellot, *Hundert Jahre politisches Leben an der Saar unter preussischer Herrschaft (1815-1918)*, Vol. XLV: *Rheinisches Archiv. Veröffentlichung des Instituts für Geschichtliche Landeskunde der Rheinlande an der Universität Bonn* (Bonn, 1954), p. 214.

105. Ibid., pp. 226-227. Roeren subjected the government to merciless criticism concerning policies and scandals related to German Southwest Africa in 1906. His role in the exposure of these scandals generated ferocious hostility toward him and his party. The controversy led the government to dissolve the Reichstag and call for elections (the "Hottentot" elections) of January 1907. See Epstein, "German Colonial Scandals," 637-663.

106. René Boch, his National Liberal opponent, received less than 4,500 votes. The Social Democratic candidate ran a poor third; he received only 408 votes.

107. When Wilhelm Marx stood as a Centrist candidate for Trier 6 (Ottweiler-St. Wendel) in 1907, he identified the Centrum as a political rather than a sectarian organization. Hearing this description of the party, a local cleric and party functionary advised Marx "to refrain from touching upon these things." Such ideas, he added reproachfully, "would surely irritate the people and they wouldn't understand it" in any case. Marx's reminiscences, n. d.; HASK, *Nachlass* Marx, Abt. 1070, No. 220.

108. Bellot, *Saar*, pp. 12 and 169; Molt, *Der Reichstag*, p. 132.

109. Bellot, *Saar*, p. 107.

110. Seeking to break the liberal hold on the district, the Centrum organi-

zation in Saarbrücken concluded that a sectarian party, confessional unions, and clerical leadership were a political liability. The local party therefore lent its support to interconfessional unions to rally more workers to the Centrum. A rival newspaper, the *Saar-Post*, was also formed in opposition to the clerical *Saarbrücker Volkszeitung*. See ibid., p. 219.

111. Marx's reminiscences, n. d.; HASK, *Nachlass* Marx, Abt. 1070, No. 220.

112. Ibid.

113. Ibid.; Bellot, *Saar*, pp. 242-243.

114. See Treitz, *Korum*, p. 137.

115. For this Centrist's role in the "Centrum conflict" consult Klaus Epstein, "Erzberger's Position in the Zentrumsstreit before World War I," *The Catholic Historical Review*, XLIV (Apr. 1958), 1-16. The best biography of Erzberger is Klaus Epstein, *Matthias Erzberger and the Dilemma of German Democracy* (Princeton, 1959).

116. Erzberger, "Der stille Kulturkampf," 51-52 and 55.

NOTES TO CHAPTER 5

Neither "Mastery From Above"
Nor "Class Struggle From Below"

1. "Organization of the Masses," 246. The remark was made in 1913.

2. See *Bericht über die Verhandlungen des zweiten Deutschen Arbeiter-Kongresses*. Abgehalten am 20., 21. und 22. Oktober 1907 in Berlin (Cologne, 1907), pp. 187-188 and 194-195. Silesia was a special case in point. Printed reports contained complaints, for instance, "that in Upper Silesia many children run around barefoot and the dwellings leave much to be desired."

3. *Protokoll der Verhandlungen des VI. Kongresses*, p. 105.

4. Ibid., pp. 11, 95, and 111-112; *Bericht über die Verhandlungen des zweiten Deutschen Arbeiter-Kongresses*, pp. 64-65; similar sentiments can be found in WAZ, XIV, 12 (23 Mar. 1912), p. 71.

5. August Pieper to August Brust, 24 Apr. 1923; StAMü, *Nachlass* Pieper, No. A 486, Mappe 35.

6. *Protokoll der Verhandlungen des VI. Kongresses*, p. 116.

7. Ibid., p. 90.

8. *Protokoll der Verhandlungen des V. Kongresses der christlichen Gewerkschaften Deutschlands*. Abgehalten vom 17.-20. Juli 1904 in Essen-Ruhr (Cologne, n.d.), pp. 9-10 and 13; *Protokoll der Verhandlungen des VIII. Kongresses der christlichen Gewerkschaften Deutschlands*. Abgehalten vom 6.-10. Oktober in Dresden (Cologne, 1912), p. 302.

9. *Protokoll der Verhandlungen des VI. Kongresses*, p. 114.

10. Ibid.; *Bericht über die Verhandlungen des zweiten Deutschen Arbeiter-Kongresses*, pp. 64-65.

11. *Bericht über die Verhandlungen des zweiten Deutschen Arbeiter-Kongresses*, pp. 64-65.

12. "Der 'Berliner' Ansturm abgeschlagen," ZcGD, XII, 13 (24 June 1912), 194.

13. "Dresden-Essen," ZcGD, XII, 25 (9 Dec. 1912), 396.

14. Krueckemeyer, "Köln und Koblenz," 10-11.

15. *Protokoll der Verhandlungen des ausserordentl. Kongresses*, p. 64.

16. *Bayerische Staatszeitung*, II (16 Mar. 1914), p. 2.

17. Pieper to Franz Brandts, 23 Feb. 1904; HASK, *Nachlass* Bachem, Abt. 1006, No. 215. Coexisting with Roman Catholic and interconfessional labor unions were the Evangelical Worker Associations. Of their 140,000 members in 1908, only about 1,000, chiefly from the Berlin area, declared themselves in favor of joining forces with the Christian Trade Unions. See J. Windolph, *Der deutsche Protestantismus und die christlichen Gewerkschaften* (Berlin, 1909), p. 93. In terms of percentage, using the data of 1911 and 1912, only one-sixth of the interconfessional unions' membership was non-Catholic. For details, see *Gutachten*, Oct. 1911 and June 1912; BHStA, Abt. II, Bayer. Gesandtschaft; Päpstl. Stuhl, No. 904, Bl. 90, p. 2 and Bl. 97, p. 8.

18. *Protokoll der Verhandlungen des ausserordentl. Kongresses*, pp. 13–15. Nor did all Roman Catholic workers belong to the interconfessional unions. Of the estimated three million Roman Catholic workers in Germany in 1904, only about 200,000 or six to seven percent were members of the Christian Trade Unions. [Jakob Treitz], *Kann und darf ich für eine Arbeiter-Bewegung auf katholischer Grundlage eintreten? Ein ruhiges Wort an Freund und Gegner unter den Katholiken von J. Carbonarius* (Trier, 1904), p. 72.

19. Cf. Rolf Weber, "Zur historischen Beurteilung Bischof Kettelers: Seine sozial- und nationalpolitische Konzeption in den sechziger Jahren," in *Die grosspreussisch-militaristische Reichsgründung 1871: Voraussetzungen und Folgen*, Vol. I, edited by Horst Bartel and Ernst Engelberg ([East] Berlin, 1971), pp. 438–453.

20. Hansen, *Preussen und Rheinland*, p. 232.

21. August Erdmann, *Die christlichen Gewerkschaften insbesondere ihr Verhältnis zu Zentrum und Kirche* (Stuttgart, 1914), pp. 29–30; Kisky, *Der Augustinus-Verein*, p. 177.

22. Erdmann, *Die christlichen Gewerkschaften*, p. 65.

23. Ibid., pp. 84–85; George Marshall Dill, Jr., "The Christian Trade Unions and Catholic Corporatism in Germany, 1916–1924" (Ph.D. Dissertation, Harvard University, 1949), p. 51; Maslowski, *Was ist die Deutsche Zentrumspartei?* p. 38.

24. For Stegerwald's career, see Josef Deutz, *Adam Stegerwald* (Cologne, 1952); Rudolf Morsey, "Adam Stegerwald (1874-1945)," in *Zeitgeschichte in Lebensbildern*, pp. 206–219; and Helmut J. Schorr, *Adam Stegerwald: Gewerkschaftler und Politiker der christlich-sozialen Bewegung in Deutschland* (Recklinghausen, 1966). A popular account is Ludwig Altenhofer, *Stegerwald: Ein Leben für den kleinen Mann* (Bad Kissingen, 1965). See *25 Jahre christliche Gewerkschaftsbewegung, 1899-1924, Festschrift* (Berlin-Wilmersdorf, 1924) for Stegerwald's autobiographical account of his activities.

25. Schorr, *Adam Stegerwald*, p. 30.

26. Membership statistics are imprecise and incomplete for both the Christian Trade Unions and the League of Catholic Worker Associations. But the following comparison reveals the competition between the two organizational forms:

Christian Trade Unions		*Worker Associations (Berlin)*
1900	152,000	-
1903	189,900	-
1904	203,161	-
1906	c. 245,000	-
1907	-	116,579
1908	260,767	123,000
1909	280,061	127,000
1910	316,115	128,000
1911	350,574	128,000
1912	330,476	130,000

Some eighty percent of the Christian Trade Union membership was confined to western and southern Germany.

Sources: Jos. Becker, "Der Verband der katholischen Arbeitervereine (Sitz Berlin) im Jahre 1913," ZcGD, XIV, 15 (20 July 1914), 235–236; [Heinrich Brauns], *Christliche Gewerkschaften oder Fachabteilungen in katholischen Arbeitervereine? Ein Wort zur Aufklärung von Rhenanus* (Cologne, 1904), p. 64; August Erdmann, *Die christliche Arbeiterbewegung in Deutschland*, 2d ed. (Stuttgart, 1909), p. 631; *Protokoll der Verhandlungen des V. Kongresses*, p. 32; *Prokoll der Verhandlungen des VI. Kongresses*, p. 34; *Protokoll der Verhandlungen des VIII. Kongresses*, p. 28; Schorr, *Stegerwald*, p. 30; *Die Verteidigung des Kartellverbandes der kath. Arbeitervereine West- Süd- und Ostdeutschlands gegen 'Sitz Berlin'* (n.p., 1912), pp. 4 and 6; ZcGD, XII, 16 (5 Aug. 1912), 248; ZcGD, XIV, 5 (2 Mar. 1914), 76.

27. Ritter, *Die katholisch-soziale Bewegung*, p. 325.

28. Karl Bachem, *Zentrumspartei*, VII, 192; Erdmann, *Die christlichen Gewerkschaften*, p. 136; Krueckemeyer, *Zentrum und Katholizismus*, p. 236.

29. StAMö, Pieper Manuscript, 15/3, p. 808.

30. See Franz Kempel, *Die "christliche" und die "neutrale" Gewerkvereins-Bewegung, beurteilt an der Hand des Rundschreibens 'Rerum Novarum' des Papstes Leo XIII. vom 17. Mai 1891 und des Hirtenschreibens der preussischen Bischöfe an ihre Geistlichkeit vom 22. August 1900* (Mainz, 1901), pp. 124–126.

31. Gerald D. Feldman, *Army, Industry, and Labor in Germany, 1914–1918* (Princeton, 1966), p. 325.

32. Paul Fleischer, "Ueber Wesen und Zweck des Berliner Verbandes," *Der Arbeiterpräses*, X, 6 (June 1914), 166.

33. [Treitz], *Kann und darf ich?*, pp. 38–39.

34. [Brauns], *Christliche Gewerkschaften oder Fachabteilungen?*, p. 37.

35. [Treitz], *Kann und darf ich?*, p. 39.

36. *Protokoll der Verhandlungen des VI. Kongresses*, p. 90. Italics in original. Also delineating these basic and fundamental differences was Johann Giesberts who said: "We [the München-Gladbach faction] represent the economic independence of the worker estate and demand for it the same freedom of movement and the same rights and jurisdiction of its organizations as are conceded to all other classes and occupational groups. By way of contrast, the Craft Associations maintain the system of tutelage in economic questions." See *Freide im Gewerkschaftsstreit? Kritische und Antikritische zum Streit über die Grundlagen der christlichen Gewerkschaften* (Cologne, 1909), pp. 62–63.

37. Mühlberg to Bethmann Hollweg, 3 Mar. 1912; PAAA, Päpstl. Stuhl No. 26, Bd. 1.

38. Quoted in Erdmann, *Die christlichen Gewerkschaften*, p. 136; see also StAMö, Pieper Manuscript, 15/3, p. 810; Schroeder, *Aufbruch*, p. 359.

39. *25 Jahre christliche Gewerkschaftsbewegung*, pp. 12–13.

40. Ritter, *Die katholisch-soziale Bewegung*, pp. 318–319 and 328.

41. "Die Stellung des Geistlichen in den Gewerkschaften des Berliner Verbandes," *Der Arbeiterpräses*, IX, 5 (May 1914), 162.

42. [Treitz], *Kann und darf ich?*, p. 6.

43. *Protokoll der Verhandlungen des VI. Kongresses*, p. 114.

NOTES TO CHAPTER 6

Political Economy Contra Labor Encyclical

1. Quoted in StAMö, Pieper Manuscript, 15/3, p. 812.

2. *Der Kölner Gewerkschaftsprozess: Die Grundsätze der christlichen Gewerkschaften in gerichtlicher Beleuchtung. Herausgegeben vom Generalsekretariat des Gesamtverbandes der christlichen Gewerkschaften* (Cologne, n.d.), p. 93.

3. [Brauns], *Christliche Gewerkschaften oder Fachabteilungen?*, p. 81. Italics in original.

4. "Zum Streit um die grundsätzliche Stellung der christlichen Gewerkschaften," ZcGD, XII, 7 (1 Apr. 1912), 102; "Zur jüngsten Etappe im Gewerkschaftsstreit," ZcGD, XIV, 3 (2 Feb. 1914), 44.

5. For this theme, see Heinrich Brauns, *Die Wahrheit über den Gewerkschaftsstreit der deutschen Katholiken: Kritik der gleichnamigen Broschüre Raimund Bayards* (M. Gladbach, 1912), p. 7; and "Finanzreform und christliche Gewerkschaften," ZcGD, IX, 17 (23 Aug. 1909), 257.

6. These charges were all the more wounding for being just. Endeavoring to neutralize these imputations of ineffectuality, the Trier faction published statistics concerning wage contracts negotiated since 1906. See "Ist die katholische Arbeiterorganisation fähig?" *Der Arbeiterpräses*, X, 2 (Feb. 1914), 100–128.

7. B., "Der Verband katholischer Arbeitervereine (Sitz Berlin) und seine Fachabteilungen im Jahre 1908," ZcGD, X, 2 (24 Jan. 1910), 25.

8. Deutz, *Adam Stegerwald*, p. 48.

9. *Bericht des zweiten Deutschen Arbeiter-Kongresses*, pp. 180 and 196.

10. *Protokoll der Verhandlungen des V. Kongresses*, p. 111.

11. See Hansen, *Preussen und Rheinland*, pp. 240, n. 1 and 241; Gerhard A. Ritter, *Die Arbeiterbewegung in Wilhelminischen Reich: Die Sozialdemokratische Partei und die Freien Gewerkschaften, 1890–1900*, Vol. III: *Studien zur europäischen Geschichte aus dem Friedrich-Meinecke-Institut der Freien Universität Berlin*, 2d ed. (Berlin, 1963), p. 69.

12. Archibald Hurd and Henry Castle, *German Sea-Power: Its Rise, Progress, and Economic Basis* (New York, 1914), p. 261.

13. "Eine erzbischöfliche Kundegebung über Arbeitervereine und Gewerkschaften," WAZ, XVI, 2 (8 Jan. 1914), p. 5; Ritter, *Die katholisch-soziale Bewegung*, pp. 332–333.

14. Memorandum, 5 Dec. 1910; HASK, *Nachlass* Bachem, Abt. 1006, No. 307.

15. Bellot, *Saar*, pp. 234–235; Cardauns, *Aus dem Leben*, pp. 119 and 168–169.

16. Erdmann, *Die christliche Arbeiterbewegung*, pp. 396 and 522; Hansen, *Preussen und Rheinland*, p. 233.

17. Quoted in Crothers, *German Elections*, p. 138.

18. Erdmann, *Die christliche Arbeiterbewegung*, p. 525; Hansen, *Preussen und Rheinland*, p. 242.

19. Raimund Bayard [Hermann Paul Fleischer], *Die Wahrheit über den Gewerkschaftsstreit der deutschen Katholiken*, Vol. I: *Die Frage der Zuständigkeit der kirchlichen Autorität für gewerkschaftlichen Organisationen als solche* (Trier, 1911), p. 19.

20. Ibid., p. 11.

21. Ibid., pp. 51 and 68–69; Hansen, *Preussen und Rheinland*, p. 233.

22. Quoted in StAMö, Pieper Manuscript, 15/3, pp. 812–813.

23. Karl Bachem, *Zentrumspartei*, VII, 192.

24. Quoted in StAMö, Pieper Manuscript, 15/3, p. 812.

25. Kempel, *Die "christliche" und die "neutrale" Gewerkvereins-Bewegung*, pp. 153–156. Italics in original.

26. Bayard, *Die Wahrheit über den Gewerkschaftsstreit*, p. 21. To the charge that the interconfessional unions were little different from the Free Trade Unions of Social Democracy, August Brust later replied: " 'In practice one can rarely distinguish the Christian trade unionist from the Free.' " Nevertheless, he countered, one can also say that " 'in practice one can only rarely distinguish the Christian entrepreneur from the Manchesterist National Liberal.' " Brust to Pieper, 29 Feb. 1924; StAMü, *Nachlass* Pieper, No. A 486, Mappe 35.

27. Bayard, *Die Wahrheit über den Gewerkschaftsstreit*, pp. 22, 23, 70, and 79. Italics in original.

28. Kempel, *Die "christliche" und die "neutrale" Gewerkvereins-Bewegung*, pp. 124–126. See also Ritter, *Die katholisch-soziale Bewegung*, p. 322.

29. Virtually a complete collection of these writings can be found in the StBMö. Although this list is not comprehensive, the basic arguments can be found in the following representative sample, arranged in order of publication: Franz von Savigny, *Arbeitervereine und Gewerkschaftsorganisationen im Lichte der Enzyklika Rerum Novarum* (Berlin, 1900); Kempel, *Die "christliche" und die "neutrale" Gewerkvereins-Bewegung;* [Treitz], *Kann und darf ich?;* [Brauns], *Christliche Gewerkschaften oder Fachabteilungen?; Christliche Gewerkschaften und Katholische Fachabteilungen im Saarrevier: Eine Mahnung von Vigilans* (St. Johann a. d. Saar, 1907); Heinrich Pesch, *Ein Wort zum Frieden in der Gewerkschaftsfrage* (Trier, 1908); Windolf, *Der deutsche Protestantismus;* Giesberts, *Friede im Gewerkschaftsstreit?;* J. Windolf, *Das Christentum der christlichen Gewerkschaften* (Berlin, 1910); Joseph Biederlack *Theologische Fragen über die gewerkschaftliche Bewegung* (Munich, 1910); Bayard, *Die Wahrheit über den Gewerkschaftsstreit;* Brauns, *Die Wahrheit über den Gewerkschaftsstreit; Die Verteidigung des Kartellverbandes;* and [Adam Stegerwald], *Im Kampf um die Grundsätze der christlichen Gewerkschaften. Vortrag von Generalsekretär A. Stegerwald nebst Stellungnahme des christlichen Gewerkschafts-Kongresses in Dresden zum Gewerkschaftsstreit* (Cologne, 1912).

30. Letter to Korum, 26 Dec. 1904; BAT, *Nachlass* Korum, Abt. 108, No. 21a (1904).

31. The debate was simply continued beyond Germany's frontiers in such newspapers as the *Massbode* in Rotterdam, the *Univers* in Paris, and the *Wiener kath. Sonntagsblatt* in Vienna. See *Der Kölner Gewerkschaftsprozess*, pp. 6–7. In general, the München-Gladbach faction was on the defensive during the period from 1910 to 1912. Like the Cologne wing of the Centrum party, it was concerned with maintaining the appearance of Roman Catholic unity for the impending Reichstag elections in January 1912. Much less polemical restraint was demonstrated after those elections. Franz X. Bachem to Porsch, 25 Jan. 1912; HASK, *Nachlass* Bachem, Abt. 1006, No. 334.

32. Ritter, *Die katholisch-soziale Bewegung*, pp. 316–317.

33. Ibid., pp. 318–319; *25 Jahre christliche Gewerkschaftsbewegung*, pp. 12–13.

34. Ritter, *Die katholisch-soziale Bewegung*, p. 328.

35. Erdmann, *Die christliche Arbeiterbewegung*, p. 624. The *Trierische Landeszeitung* was edited by Georg Friedrich Dasbach, a priest and Centrist deputy.

36. Kopp to Pieper, 9 Sept. 1910 and 25 Sept. 1910 and Franz X. Bachem to ?, 17 Sept. 1910; HASK, *Nachlass* Bachem, Abt. 1006, No. 294; see also StAMö, Pieper Manuscript, 15/3, pp. 810–811, and Ritter, *Die katholisch-soziale Bewegung*, p. 327.

37. In the decade before the First World War a new political movement appeared in France, the Christian Democratic Sillon. Led by Marc Sangnier, the Sillon movement rejected control by the hierarchy, became interconfessional, and sought a reconciliation between the Roman church and the Republic. Unable to rally sufficient support, the movement was suppressed in 1910 by Pope Pius X. Kopp threatened the German interconfessional unions with the fate of the Sillon group. For a comprehensive and excellent study of the French case, see Jeanne Caron, *Le Sillon et la démocratie chrétienne, 1894–1910* (Paris, 1966).

38. August Berndorff to Thomas Esser, 6 June and 13 June 1912; HASK, *Nachlass* Bachem, Abt. 1006, No. 320a; "Bericht des Ausschusses des Gesamtverbandes für 1912," ZcGD, XIII, 6 (17 Mar. 1913), 82–83.

39. Quoted in Meerfeld, *Der Krieg der Frommen*, pp. 33–34 and 51.

40. Ibid., p. 34.

41. Mühlberg to Bethmann Hollweg, 6 Nov. 1912; PAAA, Päpstl. Stuhl No. 26, Bd. 2.

42. Dill, "Christian Trade Unions," pp. 65–66. The full text of the encyclical appears in Erdmann, *Die christlichen Gewerkschaften*, pp. 154–159. This papal pronouncement was fully exploited by the Trier faction which quickly published and disseminated a translation entitled *Singulari quadam: Rundschreiben des Papstes Pius X. über die Gewerkschaftsfrage* (Berlin, 1912).

43. During 1912 membership apparently began to decline because of ecclesiastical pressure and the Christian Trade Unions' failure to participate in the Ruhr strike during that year. Profiting from this development were the Social Democrats. "For many years," said the mayor of Mayen, a small town near Coblenz, "it appeared as if the Social Democratic unions could not establish a firm toehold here." This hope was deceptive, he admitted, because "the Free Trade Unions and as a result Social Democracy have in recent years won here

a considerable number of members—far in excess of 400." Abschrift: Der Bürgermeister der Stadt Mayen [Vertraulich] , 8 Nov. 1913; BAT, *Nachlass* Korum, Abt. 108, No. 34, Bl. 1–2.

44. *Protokoll der Verhandlungen des VII. Kongresses,* p. 265.

45. For a biographical sketch of Sonnenschein, see Theodor Eschenburg, *Die improvisierte Demokratie: Gesammelte Aufsätze zur Weimarer Republik* (Munich, 1963), pp. 110–142.

46. Kopp to Porsch, 17 Nov. 1912; SA, *Nachlass* Stegerwald, Bl. 17; Giesberts to Stegerwald, 18 Nov. 1912; ibid., Bl. 11.

47. Erdmann, *Die christlichen Gewerkschaften,* p. 108; Meerfeld, *Der Krieg der Frommen,* p. 7.

48. Krueckemeyer, "Köln und Koblenz," 57–58 and 61–62.

49. For the transcript of the proceedings, see *Der Kölner Gewerkschaftsprozess.* A useful interpretive essay is "Ein klärender Prozess," WAZ, XVI, 1 (3 Jan. 1914), p. 3.

50. Meerfeld, *Der Krieg der Frommen,* pp. 41–42 and 51; Ritter, *Die katholisch-soziale Bewegung,* p. 332.

51. Yet even this group, when it became a question of its existence, was not above tactical compromise with Social Democracy. Typifying this pragmatism was Bitter's election to the Reichstag in 1907. He was actually jobbed into office as a result of an electoral alliance between the local Centrum party in Osnabrück-Bersenbrück and the Social Democrats. Franz Flaskampf, *Die Reichstagswahlen im Kreise Wiedenbrück (1867–1912),* Heft 88: *Quellen und Forschungen zur westfälischen Geschichte* (Rheda, 1960), pp. 15, 17, 22–23, 25, 29–31, and 34.

NOTES TO CHAPTER 7

Christian Trade Unions: A National Necessity

1. Bethmann Hollweg to Mühlberg, 16 Feb. 1914; PAAA, Päpstl. Stuhl No. 26, Bd. 3.

2. Quoted in StAMö, Pieper Manuscript, 15/3, p. 818.

3. Mühlberg to Bethmann Hollweg, 27 Nov. 1913; PAAA, Päpstl. Stuhl No. 6 Geheim, Bd. 6.

4. Ibid.; Ritter to Hertling, 28 Feb. 1914; BHStA, Abt. II, Bayer. Gesandtschaft, Päpstl. Stuhl, No. 905; Mühlberg to Bethmann Hollweg, 13 Mar. 1914; PAAA, Päpstl. Stuhl No. 26, Bd. 3.

5, Ritter, *Die katholisch-soziale Bewegung,* p. 328; Weber, "Kardinal Kopp's Brief," 328.

6. Ritter to Hertling, 7 Mar. 1914; BHStA, Abt. II, Päpstl. Stuhl, No. 905; Deuerlein, "Der Gewerkschaftsstreit," 74 and 76; Meerfeld, *Der Krieg der Frommen,* pp. 54–55; Ritter, *Die katholisch-soziale Bewegung,* p. 333.

7. Report from Bavarian envoy in Rome, 31 Oct. 1914; BHStA, Abt. II, Bayer. Gesandtschaft, Päpstl. Stuhl, No. 904; Politische Aufzeichnung, 28 July 1914; BHStA, Abt. II, Bayer. Gesandtschaft, Päpstl. Stuhl, No. 906.

8. Ludwig Volk has written a brief biographical sketch. See his article "Adolf Kardinal Bertram (1859–1945)," in *Zeitgeschichte in Lebensbildern,* pp. 274–286.

9. Ritter to Hertling, 18 Apr. and 25 Apr. 1914; BHStA, Abt. II, Bayer. Gesandtschaft, Päpstl. Stuhl, No. 917; Politische Aufzeichnung, 28 July 1914; BHStA, Abt. II, Bayer. Gesandtschaft, Päpstl. Stuhl, No. 906.

10. Report from Ritter, 23 Mar. 1914; BHStA, Abt. II, Geheimes Staatsarchiv, MA III 2567/2; Pastor, *Tagebücher*, entry of 24 Feb. 1912, p. 542.

11. The details of some of these efforts can be found in Carl Bachem's memorandum, 12 Oct. 1910; HASK, *Nachlass* Bachem, Abt. 1006, No. 296; letter to Fischer, 1910; ibid.; report to Munich, 5 Oct. 1913; BHStA, Abt. II, Bayer. Gesandtschaft, Päpstl. Stuhl, No. 904.

12. Karl Buchheim, *Geschichte der Christlichen Parteien in Deutschland* (Munich, 1953), pp. 320-321. The *Sodalitium Pianum* was not formally abolished until 1921.

13. Ritter, *Die katholisch-soziale Bewegung*, p. 318.

14. Karl Bachem, *Zentrumspartei*, IX, 140; Schmitz, *Kardinal Fischer*, pp. 195 and 198.

15. *Memoirs of Count Bülow*, II, 102; Berndorff to Esser, 13 June 1912; HASK, *Nachlass* Bachem, Abt. 1006, No. 320a. A succinct analysis of the strike can be found in Max Jürgen Koch, *Die Bergarbeiterbewegungen im Ruhrgebiet zur Zeit Wilhelms II. (1889-1914)*, Vol. V: *Beiträge zur Geschichte des Parlamentarismus und der politischen Parteien* (Düsseldorf, 1954), pp. 85-108. See also Dieter Fricke, *Der Ruhrbergarbeiterstreik von 1905* ([East] Berlin, 1955).

16. Maslowski, *Was ist die Deutsche Zentrumspartei?*, p. 41; Morsey, "Stegerwald," p. 209. Miners from the Christian Trade Unions participated in this strike.

17. Carl Bachem's memorandum, 12 Oct. 1910; HASK, *Nachlass* Bachem, Abt. 1006, No. 296; letter from a Court Chaplain in Freiburg to Stegerwald, 4 Dec. 1912; SA, Bl. 40; Bishop Michael Faulhaber to Hertling, 24 Feb. 1914; BHStA, Abt. II, Bayer. Gesandtschaft, Päpstl. Stuhl, No. 905; Mühlberg to Bethmann Hollweg, 4 July 1914; PAAA, Päpstl. Stuhl No. 26, Bd. 4.

18. Listening to an address delivered by Heinrich Fournelle in December 1912, a witness said it had the ring of *"an appeal to the Pope against the German bishops."* One got the distinct impression, this witness continued, that the episcopate was being threatened with Rome. See report from Berlin, 12 Dec. 1912; HASK, *Nachlass* Bachem, Abt. 1006, No. 329. Italics in original.

19. Mühlberg to Bethmann Hollweg, 4 July 1914; PAAA, Päpstl. Stuhl No. 26, Bd. 4.

20. Morsey, "Stegerwald," p. 209.

21. Mühlberg to Bethmann Hollweg, 4 July 1914; PAAA, Päpstl. Stuhl No. 26, Bd. 4. The details of the proceedings are recorded in *Protokoll der Verhandlungen des ausserordentl. Kongresses*.

22. Quoted in Ritter, *Die katholisch-soziale Bewegung*, pp. 332-333.

23. Krueckemeyer, "Köln und Koblenz," 10-11.

24. Carl Bachem's memorandum, 12 Oct. 1910; HASK, *Nachlass* Bachem, Abt. 1006, No. 296. Pieper himself won the Prussian government's confidence. He "seemed to me," reported the envoy to Rome, "to be the main leader of the 'Cologne faction' and Cardinal Fischer's intellectual adviser." Furthermore, it was alleged that Pieper was outspoken in his German nationalist attitude. Mühlberg to Bethmann Hollweg, 17 Nov. 1910; PAAA, Päpstl. Stuhl No. 26, Bd. 1.

25. "Die christliche Gewerkschaften im Jahre 1913," ZcGD, XIV, 14 (6 July 1914), 216; *Protokoll der Verhandlungen des ausserordentl. Kongresses*, pp. 24-26.

26. The fact that these interconfessional unions split working-class unity in 1912 was the reason for bitter socialist attacks against such organizations. See *Der Kölner Gewerkschaftsprozess.*

27. For a recent and brief biographical sketch, see Karl Erich Born, "Arthur Graf Posadowsky-Wehner, 1845-1932," in *Männer der deutschen Verwaltung* (Cologne, 1963), pp. 221-228.

28. Karl Erich Born, *Staat und Sozialpolitik seit Bismarcks Sturz: Ein Beitrag zur Geschichte der Innenpolitischen Entwicklung des Deutschen Reiches, 1890-1914,* Vol. I: *Historische Forschungen* (Wiesbaden, 1957), pp. 171ff.

29. Robert Musil, *The Man without Qualities,* trans. Eithne Wilkins and Ernst Kaiser (New York, 1953), p. 102.

30. See, for example, *Bericht des zweiten Deutschen Arbeiter-Kongresses,* pp. 19-22, and *Protokoll der Verhandlungen des VII. Kongresses,* pp. 45-52.

31. Hertling to Ritter, 24 June 1911; BAK, *Nachlass* Hertling, Folio 38; Minister of Education to Foreign Minister, 2 Feb. 1912; PAAA, Päpstl. Stuhl No. 26, Bd. 1.

32. Carl Bachem's memorandum, 13 Dec. 1912; HASK, *Nachlass* Bachem, Abt. 1006, No. 329.

33. Dispatch from Chancellor to Prussian envoy, 16 Feb. 1914; PAAA, Päpstl. Stuhl No. 26, Bd. 3.

34. Ritter to Hertling, 23 Feb. 1914; BHStA, Abt. II, Bayer. Gesandtschaft, Päpstl. Stuhl, No. 905; Morsey, *Die Deutsche Zentrumspartei,* p. 42, n. 2; Ritter, *Die katholisch-soziale Bewegung,* p. 328.

35. Advocating cooperation between the Christian and Free Trade Unions in 1906, Giesberts justified such action on the belief that it would compel the socialists to set aside "their propagandistic class struggle objectives." *Protokoll der Verhandlungen des VI. Kongresses,* p. 97; quoted in Fricke, *Ruhrbergarbeiterstreik,* pp. 131-132.

36. Minister of Education to Foreign Minister, 2 Feb. 1912; PAAA, Päpstl. Stuhl No. 26, Bd. 1.

37. Mühlberg to Bethmann Hollweg, 21 Feb. 1914; PAAA, Päpstl. Stuhl No. 26, Bd. 3; Ritter to Hertling, 23 Feb. 1914; BHStA, Abt. II, Bayer. Gesandtschaft, Päpstl. Stuhl, No. 905; report from Ritter, 23 Mar. 1914; BHStA, Abt. II, Geheimes Staatsarchiv, MA III 2567/2; Ritter to Hertling, 25 Apr. 1913; BHStA, Abt. II, Akten der Bayerischen Staatskanzlei, MA I 929. One other factor, it was said, also induced the Roman church to accept the Christian Trade Unions. With the disappearance of Christian Democracy in Italy, the existence of such labor unions in Germany appeared less menacing in the eyes of the Vatican. See StAMö, Pieper Manuscript, 15/3, pp. 818-819.

38. See, for instance, his letters to Baron von Ritter, 24 June 1911; BAK, *Nachlass* Hertling, Folio 38 and 5 July 1912; BHStA, Abt. II Päpstl. Stuhl, No. 903, Bl. 196.

39. Hertling to Ritter, 5 July 1912; BHStA, Abt. II, Päpstl. Stuhl, No. 903, Bl. 196 and Bl. 211 with enclosures; see also Ritter to Hertling, 2 Mar. 1914; BHStA, Abt. II, Bayer. Gesandtschaft, Päpstl. Stuhl, No. 905. Hertling also used the official Bavarian state newspaper—the *Bayerische Staatszeitung*—to support the Christian Trade Unions. For details, consult "Ein Regierungsblatt zum Gewerkschaftsstreit," WAZ, XVI, 10 (7 Mar.

1914), 15, and " 'Bayerische Staatszeitung' und christliche Gewerkschaften," WAZ, XVI, 13 (28 Mar. 1914), 77.

40. Hertling to Ritter, 27 Mar. 1913; BHStA, Abt. II, Bayer. Gesandtschaft, Päpstl. Stuhl, No. 904; Prince of Hohenzollern-Sigmaringen to Gottlieb von Jagow, 19 Apr. 1914; PAAA, Päpstl. Stuhl No. 26, Bd. 3; Ritter to Hertling, 25 Apr. 1913; BHStA, Abt. II, Geheimes Staatsarchiv, Akten der Bayerischen Staatskanzlei, MA I 929, Bl. 14a; Faulhaber to Hertling, 24 Feb. 1914; BHStA, Abt. II, Bayer. Gesandtschaft, Päpstl. Stuhl, No. 905.

41. Ritter to Hertling, 2 Mar. 1914; BHStA, Abt. II, Bayer. Gesandtschaft, Päpstl. Stuhl, No. 905.

42. Heinrich Brauns to Franz Hitze, 14 June 1912; HASK, *Nachlass* Bachem, Abt. 1006, No. 320a.

43. Carl Bachem's memorandum, 12 Oct. 1910; HASK, *Nachlass* Bachem, Abt. 1006, No. 296.

44. Letter to Cardinal State-Secretary, 20 Feb. 1904; HASK, *Nachlass* Bachem, Abt. 1006, No. 187.

45. Carl Bachem's notes, 30 Oct. 1908; HASK, *Nachlass* Bachem, Abt. 1006, No. 304; see also Carl Bachem's memorandum, 25 July 1912; HASK, *Nachlass* Bachem, Abt. 1006, No. 321.

46. Letter to Cardinal State-Secretary, 20 Feb. 1904; HASK, *Nachlass* Bachem, Abt. 1006, No. 187; Pieper to Franz Brandts, 23 Feb. 1904; HASK, *Nachlass* Bachem, Abt. 1006, No. 215; unsigned letter to Fischer, 1910; HASK, *Nachlass* Bachem, Abt. 1006, No. 296, pp. 3 and 6–7.

47. Carl Bachem to [Peter?] Spahn, 11 Oct. 1910; HASK, *Nachlass* Bachem, Abt. 1006, No. 296.

48. *Christliche Gewerkschaften und Katholische Fachabteilungen im Saarrevier*, pp. 13–14 and 29–30.

49. Carl Bachem to [Peter?] Spahn, 11 Oct. 1910; HASK *Nachlass* Bachem, Abt. 1006, No. 296.

50. For biographical information, see Hugo Stehkämper, "Wilhelm Marx (1863–1946)," in *Zeitgeschichte in Lebensbildern*, pp. 174–205.

51. *Gegen die Quertreiber*, p. 50. In the printed text of this speech, Marx's words appear in bold typeface. For the effects of the party's pronouncement, see " 'Sitz Berlin' und Zentrumspartei," WAZ, XVI, 9 (28 Feb. 1914), 52.

52. Report from Berlin, 12 Dec. 1912; HASK, *Nachlass* Bachem, Abt. 1006, No. 329.

NOTES TO CHAPTER 8

The Centrum is a Political Party

1. Letter to Kopp, 2 May 1906; AAW, *Nachlass* Kopp, IA 24a 20.

2. Ritter to Hertling, 7 Mar. 1914; BHStA, Abt. II, Päpstl. Stuhl, No. 905.

3. According to the census of 1910, the Roman Catholic population was concentrated in the following areas:

State/Province		Roman Catholic	Evangelical
West Prussia		844,566	764,719
Posen		1,347,958	605,312
Silesia		2,765,394	2,120,361
Westphalia	Prussia	1,845,263	1,733,413
Rhineland		4,472,058	1,877,582
Hohenzollern		64,770	3,040
Bavaria		4,612,920	1,844,736
Württemberg		696,031	1,582,745
Baden		1,206,919	769,866

Source: *Statistik des Deutschen Reiches*, Vol. 178 (Berlin, 1910), p. 106.

4. Nipperdey, *Die Organisation der deutschen Parteien*, p. 292. Never did the Centrum run candidates in every German constituency. In the elections of 1903, for example, Centrist candidates were entered into the race for 161 out of 397 seats and won 100. Nine years later, in 1912, the Centrum put up 206 candidates but secured only 90 seats. A truly national party like the Social Democrats, on the other hand, ran 390 candidates in 1903, 392 in 1907, and 397 in 1912. Karl Bachem, *Zentrumspartei*, VI, 190; Ritter, *Die Arbeiterbewegung*, p. 67, n. 97.

5. Matthias Erzberger, *Das Deutsche Zentrum*, 2d ed. (Amsterdam, 1912), pp. 96–97; Maslowski, *Was ist die Deutsche Zentrumspartei?*, p. 32; Molt, *Der Reichstag*, p. 369. Although the national committee was not established until 1914, the decision to create such an institution was made in 1911. Provincial and state organizations enjoyed complete independence. Unity, such as it was prior to 1914, was represented in the Centrum's Reichstag delegation. For the early history of the Silesian Centrum organization, see Paul Mazura, *Die Entwicklung des politischen Katholizismus in Schlesien: Von seinen Anfängen bis zum Jahre 1880* (Breslau, 1925).

6. Erdmann, *Die christlichen Gewerkschaften*, p. 597; *25 Jahre christliche Gewerkschaftsbewegung*, p. 21.

7. Erdmann, *Die christliche Arbeiterbewegung*, p. 239.

8. For an incisive biography see Hermann Renner, *Georg Heim: Der Bauerndoktor. Lebensbild eines "ungekrönten Königs"* (Munich, 1960).

9. Statistics bear witness to this situation. *Volksverein* membership in 1914 among Roman Catholic males in the various representative provinces and states was:

State/Province	Percent	Membership
Westphalia	30.8	163,683
Hanover	26.4	27,068
Oldenburg	26.0	7,058
Pfalz	21.6	22,459
Württemberg	21.2	39,597
Rhineland	20.0	247,123
Baden	19.2	61,840
Bavaria	8.4	–

State/Province	Percent	Membership
East Prussia	0.8	504
Silesia	3.2	—

Source: Ritter, *Die katholisch-soziale Bewegung*, p. 231.

10. Report, 14 Nov. 1910; BHStA, Abt. II, Päpstl. Stuhl, No. 903, No. 48.

11. The problem of continuing discrimination in Baden is exhaustively covered in Stadelhofer, *Der Abbau der Kulturkampfgesetzgebung*.

12. Bertram, *Die Wahlen*, p. 28, n. 1; Köhler, *Lebenserinnerungen*, p. 108; Meerfeld, *Die Deutsche Zentrumspartei*, p. 67; Ritter, *Die katholisch-soziale Bewegung*, p. 183.

13. Bertram, *Die Wahlen*, p. 23; Molt, *Der Reichstag*, pp. 127–128; Abbé E. Wetterlé, *Behind the Scenes in the Reichstag: Sixteen Years of Parliamentary Life in Germany*, trans. George Frederic Lees (New York, 1918), pp. 250–251. Oppersdorff owned over 12,000 hectares of land. See Häbich, *Deutsche Latifundien*, p. 128. "His wife, educated in Rome, born as is well-known a Radziwell," read a Prussian report, "is animated by Polish feelings as well as by burning ambition and is considered here the pacemaker for her husband's high-flying plans." Mühlberg to Bethmann Hollweg, 4 June 1912; PAAA, Päpstl. Stuhl No. 26, Bd. 1. See also SVZ, XLIII, 251 (3 June 1911), p. l.

14. Hertling to Ritter, 25 Feb. 1914; BHStA, Abt. II, Bayer. Gesandtschaft, Päpstl. Stuhl, No. 905; Deuerlein, "Der Gewerkschaftsstreit," 71; Meerfeld, *Der Krieg der Frommen*, pp. 25–26; Ritter, *Die katholisch-soziale Bewegung*, p. 327.

15. Hertling to Anna von Hertling, 26 Oct. 1911; BAK, *Nachlass* Hertling, Folio 21; Krueckemeyer, *Zentrum und Katholizismus*, pp. 292–293. The Centrum's dissatisfaction with the count can be traced in SVZ, XLIII, 251 (3 June 1911), p. 1 and SVZ, XLIII, 253 (4 June 1911), pp. 1–2. Only Roeren voted in favor of Oppersdorff's acceptance into the Centrum's Reichstag delegation.

16. It was Marx's opinion that "the so-called Catholic faction was chiefly represented by *Geheimrat* Roeren." Marx's reminiscences, n.d.; HASK, *Nachlass* Marx, Abt. 1070, No. 220.

17. Quoted in ibid.

18. Bellot, *Saar*, p. 327; Deuerlein, "Verlauf und Ergebnis," 122; Hoeber, *Der Streit um den Zentrumscharakter*, pp. 133–134; Roeren, *Zentrum und Kölner Richtung*, p. 114. Roeren's letter of resignation is reprinted in Hoeber, *Der Streit um den Zentrumscharakter*, pp. 133–134 and Bergsträsser, *Der politische Katholizismus*, II, No. 62, 384–387.

19. SVZ, XLIV, 444 (27 Sept. 1912), p. 1; Krueckemeyer, *Zentrum und Katholizismus*, pp. 300–301.

20. *Gegen die Quertreiber*, p. 50; KVZ, LV, 120 (10 Feb. 1914), p. 1.

21. Meerfeld, *Der Krieg der Frommen*, p. 59.

22. Treitz, *Korum*, p. 226; Zenz, *Geschichte der Stadt Trier*, p. 39.

23. Meerfeld, *Der Krieg der Frommen*, p. 25. Those who did not subscribe to the Centrum's recent pronouncement, Marx declared in April 1914, ought to be treated as "expellees." See Zenz, *Geschichte der Stadt Trier*, p. 39, n. 40.

24. Krueckemeyer, "Köln und Koblenz," 82–84. See also Bergsträsser, *Der politische Katholizismus*, II, No. 59, 375–376.

25. Krueckemeyer, *Zentrum und Katholizismus*, p. 324.

26. Meerfeld, *Der Krieg der Frommen*, pp. 23 and 62. Kaufmann's activities were further circumscribed by his expulsion, at the order of Cardinal Fischer in April 1911, from the Cologne Archdiocese.

27. According to Oppersdorff, Kopp by 1911 was so concerned that the *Germania* was becoming more and more dependent on the *Kölnische Volkszeitung*, that the prince-bishop threatened to sell his stock in the publication. See KVZ, LV, 270 (26 Mar. 1914), p. 1.

28. The Centrum, unlike the Social Democrats, never possessed an official party press. Rather, the party was supported by a number of independent newspapers—the Bachem family's *Kölnische Volkszeitung*, for example. See Ludwig Bergsträsser, *Geschichte der politischen Parteien in Deutschland*, 10th ed. (Munich, 1960), pp. 40f.

29. Krueckemeyer, *Zentrum und Katholizismus*, pp. 294–296.

30. Ibid., p. 296.

31. The Cardinal's essay appeared in the 27 November 1909 issue of *Germania*. In it Kopp accused Spahn and the liberal Roman Catholic journal *Hochland* of "de-Catholicizing" intellectuals, a task, he added gratuitously, which the *Volksverein* performed for the working classes. Pastor, *Tagebücher*, entry of 27 Jan. 1910, p. 513; Meerfeld, *Der Krieg der Frommen*, pp. 24–26.

32. Adding to this frustration was the Cologne faction's growing support from the Roman Catholic press abroad. Something like 159 newspapers in France, England, the Netherlands, and Spain, wrote a confidant in Rome to Carl Bachem, published articles *"in our favor."* Peregrinus to Carl Bachem, 1 June 1912; HASK, *Nachlass* Bachem, Abt. 1006, No. 329a. Italics in original.

33. Both sides became involved, although the most unbridled attacks were made by the "Berliners." In order of appearance, the most important of these pamphlets and tracts were: Hoeber, *Der Streit um den Zentrumscharakter;* Krueckemeyer, *Zentrum und Katholizismus;* Roeren, *Zentrum und Kölner Richtung;* Julius Bachem, *Das Zentrum;* Karl Bachem, *Zentrum, katholische Weltanschauung und praktische Politik;* and Roeren, *Veränderte Lage des Zentrumsstreits.*

34. Epstein, "Erzberger's Position," 9; Krueckemeyer, *Zentrum und Katholizismus*, p. 223; see also Pastor, *Tagebücher*, entry of 27 Jan. 1910, p. 513.

35. Epstein, "Erzberger's Position," 9–10. Spahn's attitude toward the Poles was of special interest because of his previous critical attitude. See his article "Polenpolitik" in *Hochland*, V, 2 (Apr. 1908), 83–103. In that essay he deplored the Centrum's compromising attitude toward the Poles.

36. Collective letter to Martin Spahn, 22 Aug. 1910; BAK, *Nachlass* Hertling, Folio 37.

37. Epstein, "Erzberger's Position," 9–10; see [Georg Graf von Oppersdorff], *Eine Gewissensfrage: Ist Martin Spahn Zentrumsmann? Material zur Begründung des Augsburger Briefes der 14 Reichstagsabgeordneten an den Reichstagskandidatur Herrn Prof. Dr. Spahn in Strassburg* (Berlin, 1910).

38. Peregrinus to Carl Bachem, 28 Oct. 1910; HASK, *Nachlass* Bachem, Abt. 1006, No. 307. Italics in original.

39. Printed letter to Centrist Reichstag delegation, 28 Nov. 1910; HASK, *Nachlass* Marx, Abt. 1070, No. 436; Oppersdorff's reply to Spahn's letter, 8 Dec. 1910; ibid.; Hertling to Anna von Hertling, 22 Nov. 1910, 7 Dec. 1910, and 18 Dec. 1910; BAK, *Nachlass* Hertling, Folio 20. Even while Spahn was presenting his case before the Centrum's leaders in Berlin, Oppersdorff pressed

his attack. See Oppersdorff to Hertling, 8 Dec. 1910; HASK, *Nachlass* Marx, Abt. 1070, No. 436. Spahn was admitted into the parliamentary delegation by a vote of 49 out of 70, with 4 abstentions.

40. Guido von Bergen to Bethmann Hollweg, 28 Sept. 1910; PAAA, Päpstl. Stuhl No. 26, Bd. 1; Marx's reminiscences, n.d.; HASK, *Nachlass* Marx, Abt. 1070, No. 220; Meerfeld, *Der Krieg der Frommen*, pp. 14 and quotation on p. 57.

41. Lerchenfeld to Hertling, 30 Jan. 1914; BHStA, Abt. I, Akten des Bayerischen Ministeriums für Soziale Fürsorge, Bd. 1, MAr b 384, Bl. 11; Ritter to Hertling, 31 Jan. 1914; BHStA, Abt. II, Bayer. Gesandtschaft, Päpstl. Stuhl, No. 905; Marx's reminiscences, n.d.; HASK, *Nachlass* Marx, Abt. 1070, No. 220; Meerfeld, *Der Krieg der Frommen*, pp. 14 and 57–61; Scholz, "Georg Kardinal Kopp," 530.

42. Quoted in Meerfeld, *Der Krieg der Frommen*, pp. 16–17.

43. Quoted in ibid., pp. 39–40; Krueckemeyer, *Zentrum und Katholizismus*, p. 293; excerpts copied for Porsch from *Klarheit und Wahrheit;* AAW, *Nachlass* Porsch, Ia 4.

44. Hertling to Ritter, 25 Feb. 1914 and 28 Mar. 1914, Ritter to Hertling, 1 Apr. and 22 Apr. 1914; BHStA, Abt. II, Bayer. Gesandtschaft, Päpstl. Stuhl, No. 905; Oppersdorff to Porsch, 15 June 1911; editor of SVZ to Porsch, 11 July 1911; StBMö, printed letters, pp. 2 and 15–16.

45. Ritter to Hertling, 31 May 1914; BHStA, Abt. II, Geheimes Staatsarchiv, MA I 929.

46. Porsch to Hertling, 27 Mar. 1914; BHStA, Abt. II, Bayer. Gesandtschaft, Päpstl. Stuhl, No. 905.

NOTES TO CHAPTER 9

Conclusion and Appraisal

1. *Das Cölner Osterdienstags-Protokoll*, p. 12.

2. The Conservative leader Ernst von Heydebrand later admitted that he had grossly overestimated the possibility of harmonious cooperation with the Centrists. Walter Koch, *Volk und Staatsführung vor dem Weltkriege: Beiträge zur Geschichte der nachbismarckischen Zeit und des Weltkriegs*, Heft 29, Neue Folge, Heft 9 (Stuttgart, 1935), p. 15.

3. Quoted in Bertram, *Die Wahlen*, p. 15; see also Koch, *Volk und Staatsführung*, p. 47; Karl Bachem, *Zentrumspartei*, VII, 329.

4. Wallraf was a relative by marriage to Konrad Adenauer, the future Chancellor of the Federal Republic of Germany.

5. Morsey, *Die Deutsche Zentrumspartei*, p. 43; Schauff, *Die deutschen Katholiken*, p. 74.

6. Rehm, *Deutschlands politische Parteien*, p. 86.

7. WAZ, XVI, 2 (8 Jan. 1914), p. 5.

8. Max Roeder, *Ist das Centrum eine Oppositionspartei?* (Amsterdam, 1913), p. 12.

9. *Das Cölner Osterdienstags-Protokoll*, p. 12. Italics in original.

10. Carl Bachem's notes, 5 Dec. 1912; HASK, *Nachlass* Bachem, Abt. 1006,

No. 307. Similarly in 1913, Carl Bachem complained to Porsch that Roeren's sectarian diatribes complicated the Centrum's collaboration with the Conservative party. Zeender, "Interconfessional Party," 427, n. 18.

11. For details pertaining to the tax controversy, see Epstein, *Erzberger*, pp. 79–82.

12. Dahrendorf, *Society and Democracy*, p. 72.

13. See Hans Dietzel, *Die preussischen Wahlrechtsreformbestrebungen von der Oktroyierungen des Dreiklassenwahlrechts bis zum Weltkrieg* (Emsdetten [Westf.], 1934), pp. 64–74; Koch, *Volk und Staatsführung*, pp. 41–42 and 47.

14. During the First World War, Fleischer (the Secretary of the Catholic Worker Associations [Berlin]) was a friend of Colonel Max Bauer, an associate of General Erich Ludendorff. All three of these men were opposed to a genuine labor movement. See Feldman, *Army, Industry, and Labor*, p. 325.

APPENDIX I

CONFESSIONAL PROPORTIONS AND ELECTORAL RESULTS IN
WESTPHALIA AND THE RHINE PROVINCE

Westphalia

District		Percentage of Catholic & Evangelical	1903	1907	1912
Münster	1 (Tecklenburg-Steinfurt-Ahaus)	73	C	C	C
	2 (Münster-Koesfeld)	90	C	C	C
	3 (Borken-Recklinghausen)	76	C	C	C
	4 (Lüdinghausen-Beckum-Warendorf)	93	C	C	C
Minden	1 (Minden-Lübbecke)	97 E	DK	DK	FVP
	2 (Herford-Halle)	96 E	DK	NL	NL
	3 (Bielefeld-Wiedenbrück)	73 E	C	SPD	U
	4 (Paderborn-Büren)	93	C	C	C
	5 (Warburg-Höxter)	87	C	C	C
Arnsberg	1 (Wittgenstein-Siegen)	85 E	AS	AS	C–S
	2 (Olpe-Meschede-Arnsberg)	94	C	C	C
	3 (Altena-Iserlohn)	70 E	FVP	FVP	FVP
	4 (Hagen)	74 E	FVP	FVP	FVP
	5 (Bochum-Gelsenkirchen-Hattingen)	51 E	SPD	SPD	NL
	6 (Dortmund)	53 E	SPD	SPD	SPD
	7 (Hamm-Soest)	53 E	NL	SPD	NL
	8 (Lippstadt-Brilon)	91	C	C	C

177

Rhine Province

District		Percentage of Catholic & Evangelical	1903	1907	1912
Cologne	1 (Stadt Köln)	77	C	C	SPD
	2 (Landkreis Köln)	83	C	C	C
	3 (Bergheim-Euskirchen)	96	C	C	C
	4 (Rheinbach-Bonn)	86	C	C	C
	5 (Siegkreis-Waldbroel)	77	C	C	C
	6 (Mülheim-Wipperfürth-Gummersbach)	69	C	C	C
Coblenz	1 (Wetzlar-Altenkirchen)	69 E	NL	AS	C–S
	2 (Neuwied)	61	C	C	C
	3 (Coblenz-St. Goar)	82	C	C	C
	4 (Kreuznach-Simmern)	55 E	NL	NL	NL
	5 (Mayen-Ahrweiler)	96	C	C	C
	6 (Adenau-Kochem-Zell)	88	C	C	C
Düsseldorf	1 (Lennep-Mettmann)	73 E	SPD	FVP	SPD
	2 (Städte Elberfeld-Barmen)	75 E	SPD	DRP	SPD
	3 (Solingen)	61 E	SPD	SPD	SPD
	4 (Düsseldorf)	68	C	C	SPD
	5 (Essen)	59	C	C	C
	6 (Mülheim a. d. Ruhr-Stadt Duisburg)	55	NL	SPD	NL
	7 (Mörs-Rees)	58	C	C	C
	8 (Kleve-Geldern)	91	C	C	C
	9 (Kempen)	95	C	C	C
	10 (Gladbach)	81	C	C	C
	11 (Crefeld)	80	C	C	C
	12 (Neuss-Grevenbroich)	89	C	C	C
Aachen	1 (Schleiden-Malmedy-Montjoie)	96	C	C	C
	2 (Eupen-Aachen Land-Burtscheid)	95	C	C	C
	3 (Stadt Aachen)	91	C	C	C
	4 (Düren-Jülich)	95	C	C	C
	5 (Geilenkirchen-Heinsberg-Erkelenz)	96	C	C	C

C	= Centrum	DK	=	Conservative
NL	= National Liberal	U	=	Unaffiliated (Posadowsky ran with Centrist support)
SPD	= Social Democrat			
C–S	= Christian-Social	AS	=	Anti-Semite
DRP	= Free Conservative	FVP	=	Progressive

Source: *Statistik des Deutschen Reiches*, Vol. 250:2 (Berlin, 1913), pp. 35–38 and 41–45.

APPENDIX II

CONFESSIONAL AND ETHNIC CONCENTRATIONS WITHIN UPPER
SILESIA

Administrative District			Percent Roman Catholic		Percent Polish	
Oppeln	1	(Kreuzburg-Rosenberg)	61		—	
	2	(Oppeln)	87	Stadtkreis	19.3	
				Landkreis	78.7	
	3	(Gr. Strehlitz-Kosel)	95		78.7	
	4	(Lublinitz-Tost-Gleiwitz)	91		80.9	
	5	(Beuthen-Tarnowitz)	92	Stadtkreis	37.5	Beuthen
				Landkreis	73.1	
	6	(Kattowitz-Zabrze)	92		70.7	Kattowitz
					68.7	Zabrze
	7	(Pless-Rybnik)	93		86.5	Pless
					82.5	Rybnik
	8	(Ratibor)	96		43.7	
	9	(Leobschütz)	91		—	
	10	(Neustadt)	92		44.6	
	11	(Falkenberg-Grottkau)	83		9.6	
	12	(Neisse)	93		—	

Source: *Statistik des Deutschen Reiches*, Vol. 150/151, Neue Folge, Vol. 111 (Berlin, 1903), p. 128; Vol. 250:2 (Berlin, 1913), pp. 24–25.

APPENDIX III

CONFESSIONAL PROPORTIONS AND ELECTORAL RESULTS IN THE
TRIER ADMINISTRATIVE DISTRICT

		Percent	*General Elections*		
Electoral District		*Catholic*	*1903*	*1907*	*1912*
Trier	1 (Daun-Prüm-Bitburg)	99	C	C	C
	2 (Wittlich-Berncastel)	84	C	C	C
	3 (Trier)	93	C	C	C
	4 (Saarburg-Merzig-Saarlouis)	96	C	C	C
	5 (Saarbrücken)	62	NL	NL	NL
	6 (Ottweiler-St. Wendel)	59	C	U	C

C = Centrum
NL = National Liberal
U = Unaffiliated

Administrative Districts 4, 5, and 6 comprised the Saar. Source: *Statistik des Deutschen Reiches*, Vol. 250:2 (Berlin, 1913), pp. 44–45.

BIBLIOGRAPHY

Introductory Remarks

Several problems confront the researcher interested in the Centrum party's history. The absence for so long of any centralized organization meant for the dispersal of records throughout Germany. Most of this material found its way into diocesan archives or private hands. This situation can make for difficulties in the accessibility of documents. Karl Trimborn's *Nachlass*, for example, is in the hands of his daughter and was unavailable to me. The Second World War and the political changes after 1945 created additional problems. Many records were destroyed by the bombings and the fighting during the final stages of the conflict. Following the division of Germany and the transfer of territories after 1945 essential material was also either lost or became difficult if not impossible of access. The *Volksverein*'s papers, thought to have been destroyed in 1933 after their seizure by the National Socialists, are now kept in the *Deutsches Zentralarchiv* in Potsdam. For reasons best known to themselves, the East German authorities refused my request to examine this collection.

Nevertheless, there exists an abundance of material. But it still remains widely scattered in various depositories (ecclesiastical, state, and private archives) in Germany and Poland. Because of this situation, this bibliography is not comprehensive. It includes only those archival materials I was able to locate or permitted to see. And it contains only those printed works most useful in the preparation of this book.

I. Primary Sources

A. Archival Material

Archiwum Archidiecezjalne we Wroclawiu

Nachlass Kopp, Sprachliche und politische Fragen in O/S.; IA 24a 17, IA
   24a 18, IA 24a 20.
Nachlass Porsch:
   Zentrum, Quertreiber, "Klarheit und Wahrheit:" (Grf. v. Oppersdorff.);
      Ia 4.
   Zentrum: Neuere Streitfragen; Ia 5.
   Oberschlesien; Ib 1a.
   Volksverein; II 13.
   Parität; II 14.
   Polen/Oberschlesien; III 9.
   General-Versammlung der Katholiken Deutschlands; IV 16 No. 5.

Bayerisches Hauptstaatsarchiv München, Abteilung Allgemeines Staatsarchiv

Acten des Bayerischen Ministeriums für Soziale Fürsorge, Betreff: Christliche Gewerkschaften; Bd. 1, Fach: 127 (1912–1913); MAr b 383.

Acten des Bayerischen Ministeriums für Soziale Fürsorge, Betreff: Christliche Gewerkschaften; Bd. 2, Fach: 127 (1914), MAr b 384.

Bayerisches Hauptstaatsarchiv München, Abteilung Geheimes Staatsarchiv

Bayer. Gesandtschaft, Berlin; No. 1074, Politische Berichte und Instruktion für das Jahr 1902.
Briefwechsel des Bayer. Gesandten Graf Lerchenfeld und Ministerpräsident Graf Hertling, 1912-13; MA I 955.
Briefwechsel des bayerischen Gesandten Graf Lerchenfeld mit dem Ministerpräsident Graf Hertling, 1913-1916, 2 vols.; MA I No. 957a, b.
Geheimes Staatsarchiv; MA III 2564 (1910); MA III 2689.
Geheimes Staatsarchiv; Der Parteitag des Zentrums am 28. Januar 1903 im kath. Kasino zu München; MA 99799.
Geheimes Staatsarchiv; Gesandtschaft beim Päpstl. Stuhle, Verschiedene Angelegenheiten; MA I 929.
Geh. Staatsarchiv München, Bayer. Gesandtschaft Berlin; Nos. 1080, 1086, and 1153.
Geh. Staatsarchiv München, Bayer. Gesandtschaft Berlin; Politische Berichte und Instruktionen [1911], No. 1083.
Geh. Staatsarchiv München; Bayer. Gesandtschaft, Päpstl. Stuhl; Nos. 902, 903, 904, 905, and 906.

Bistumsarchiv Trier

Nachlass Korum, Abt. 108,
Nos. 29a 1900, Bischofskonferenz
34 Sozialdemokraten
48 Gewerkschaftsstreit
74 Schriftwechsel mit anderen Diözesan (Breslau)
82 Schriftwechsel mit anderen Diözesan (Köln)
402 Confessionslose höhere Töchterschule
403 Persönliche Schriften an Bischof Korum (Trierer Schulstreit)
404 Pressangriffe (Trierer Schulstreit)
431 Arbeitervereine
Nachlass Treitz, Abt. 85, No. 1842.

Bundesarchiv Koblenz

Nachlass Cardauns. Aus dem Nachlass des Publizisten Cardauns: Briefe des Grafen Georg v. Hertling an Cardauns, Vol. 2: 1903-1918, Nr. 478-2.
Nachlass Hertling:
Errichtung einer katholisch-theologischen Fakultät an der Universität Strassburg, Vol. 1: 1899-1900; Vol. 2: 1901. Folios 31 and 32.
Briefe an die Gattin Anna geb. von *Biegeleben*. Vol. 6: 1900-1901; Vol. 12: 1910; Vol. 13: 1911-1912; Vol. 14: (1913-1916); Folios 14, 20, 21, and 22.

Angelegenheiten der Zentrumspartei, des deutschen Katholizismus und der deutschen Beziehungen zum Vatikan, Vol. 1: 1887-1903; Vol. 2: 1904-1906; Vol. 3: 1907/08; Vol. 4: 1909-1911; Vol. 5: 1912-1917. Folios 34, 35, 36, 37, and 38.

Historisches Archiv der Stadt Köln

Nachlass Bachem, Abt. 1006,

Nos.		
	76b	Paritätstabellen 1896
	76c	Beginn der Paritätsagitation
	85	Paritätsdenkschrift
	92a	Paritätsfrage
	92b	Paritätsfrage
	93	Paritätsfrage
	94	Paritätsfrage
	96	Posadowsky betr. Parität
	134-35	Affaire Spahn
	136	Fall Spahn
	146	Index u. Lehmann
	187	Trierer Fall
	215	Denkschrift nach Rom
	217	Eine Kundegebung Roms
	229	Briefe
	232	Christl. Gewerkschaften
	277	Charakter des Zentrums
	284a	Osterdienstagskonferenz
	285	Landesausschusssitzung der Zentrumspartei, 28 Nov. 09 und Entwurf Tr[imborns]
	291a	Zu "Cöln", eine innere Gefahr (Aktenstücke)
	294	Richtungsstreit [Briefe]
	295	Richtungsstreit-Briefe
	296	Richtungsstreit [Briefe]
	304	Unterredg. mit Nuntius Frühwirth in München am 30. Okt. 1908
	307	Allgemeines ab Nov. 1910
	308	Kampf gegen die "Kölner Richtung" Nov./Dez. 1910
	309	Kaufmann Ten.Hompel. Heiner
	320a	15. Delegiertentag der kath. Arb. Vereine (Sitz Berlin)
	321	Gewerkschaftsstreit
	328	Christl. Gewerkschaften
	329	Christl. Gewerkschaften
	334	Broschüre gegen die Quertreiber
	509	Hetze gegen Katholische Studenten Korporationen

Nachlass Marx, Abt. 1070,

Nos.		
	220	Der Fall Roeren
	221	Der Fall Roeren
	228	[Erinnerungsbericht]
	436	Zentrumsangelegenheiten

Politisches Archiv des Auswärtigen Amts, Bonn

Deutschland No. 125, Geheim, Die Centrumspartei, Bd. 4.

Elsass-Lothringen 3 No. 1, Bde. 1-9 (1894-1920) Geheime Akten betreffend: Die Universität in Strassburg.

Geheime Akten betreffend: Stellung der Kurie zu den christlichen Gewerkschaften, Bde. 1-4 (1909-14).

Päpstliches Stuhl No. 6, Geheim: Die Beziehungen zwischen *Preussen* und dem Vatikan, Bde. 1-6.

Päpstliches Stuhl No. 13a No. 1; Bde. 3-8: Die Aufhebung des Jesuiten-Gesetzes.

Staatsarchiv Koblenz

Ober-Präsidium der Rheinprovinz. Acta betreffend: Die Schullehrer-Seminarien in der Rheinprovinz; Abt. 403, No. 15207, Bd. 2.

Staatsarchiv Münster

Nachlass August Pieper: Nr. A 486·

Stadtarchiv Mönchengladbach

Pieper, August. "Geschichte des Volksvereins für das katholische Deutschland, 1890-1928." Typescript from handwritten draft of 1932: 15/1-3.

Stegerwald-Archiv

Nachlass Stegerwald. Band 1908-1919: Kirche und gewerkschaftliche Organisationen, Blätter 1, 3, 10, 11, 13, 14, 15, 16, 17, 24, 27, 28, and 42.

B. Published Documents

1. Public Documents

Stenographische Berichte über die Verhandlungen des Reichstags.

Stenographische Berichte über die Verhandlungen des Landtages, Haus der Abgeordneten.

Statistik des Deutschen Reiches.

Vol. 150/151, Neue Folge, Vol. III: *Die Volkszählung am 1. Dezember 1900 im Deutschen Reich.* Berlin: Verlag von Puttkammer & Mühlbrecht, 1903. Vol. 250, 2: *Die Reichstagswahlen von 1912.* Berlin: Verlag von Puttkammer & Mühlbrecht, 1913.

Vierteljahrshefte zur Statistik des Deutschen Reichs.

Vol. XVI: *Statistik der Reichstagswahlen von 1907. Ergänzungsheft zu 1907.* Teil I: *Vergleichende Übersicht der Reichstagswahlen von 1903 und 1907 auf Grund der Berichte der Wahlkommissare* (Berlin, 1907).

Evert, Georg. "Die preussischen Landtagswahlen des Jahres 1903 und früherer Jahre," *Zeitschrift des königlich preussischen statistischen Landesamts,* XXIII (1905).

2. Reports of Congresses and Trials

Bericht über die Verhandlungen des zweiten Deutschen Arbeiter-Kongresses.
Abgehalten am 20., 21. und 22. Oktober 1907 in Berlin. Cologne: Christlicher Gewerkschaftsverlag (A. Stegerwald), 1907.

*Protokoll über die Verhandlungen des IV. Kongresses der christlichen Gewerk-
schaften Deutschlands.* Abgehalten vom 29. Juni bis 2. Juli 1902 in München.
N. p.: Verlag des Gesamtverbandes der christlichen Gewerkschaften Deutschlands, n. d.

*Protokoll der Verhandlungen des V. Kongresses der christlichen Gewerkschaften
Deutschlands.* Abgehalten vom 17.–20. Juli 1904 in Essen-Ruhr. Cologne:
Verlag des Generalsekretariats des Gesamtverbandes der christlichen Gewerk-
schaften Deutschlands, n. d.

*Protokoll der Verhandlungen des VI. Kongresses der christlichen Gewerkschaften
Deutschlands.* Abgehalten vom 22.–24. Juli 1906 in Breslau. Cologne: Verlag
des Generalsekretariats des Gesamtverbandes der christlichen Gewerkschaften
Deutschlands, 1906.

*Protokoll der Verhandlungen des VII. Kongresses der christlichen Gewerk-
schaften Deutschlands.* Abgehalten vom 18. bis 21. Juli 1909 in Cöln.
Cologne: Christlicher Gewerkschaftsverlag, 1909.

*Protokoll der Verhandlungen des VIII. Kongresses der christlichen Gewerk-
schaften Deutschlands.* Abgehalten vom 6.–10. Oktober in Dresden. Cologne:
Christlicher Gewerkschaftsverlag, 1912.

*Protokoll der Verhandlungen des ausserordentl. Kongresses der christl.
Gewerkschaften Deutschlands.* Abgehalten am 26. November 1912 in
Essen [Ruhr]. Cologne: Christlicher Gewerkschaftsverlag, 1912.

*Der Kölner Gewerkschaftsprozess: Die Grundsätze der christlichen Gewerk-
schaften in gerichtlicher Beleuchtung. Herausgegeben vom Generalsekretariat
des Gesamtverbandes der christlichen Gewerkschaften.* Cologne: Christlicher
Gewerkschaftsverlag, n. d.

3. Documentary Collections Related to Political Parties

Bergsträsser, Ludwig. *Der Politische Katholizismus: Dokumente seiner Entwicklung.* 2 vols. Munich: Drei Masken Verlag, 1921–1923.

Mommsen, Wilhelm, ed. *Deutsche Parteiprogramm.* Vol. I: *Deutsches Handbuch
der Politik.* 2d ed. Munich: Olzog Verlag, 1964.

Treue, Wolfgang, ed. *Deutsche Parteiprogramme seit 1861.* 4th ed. Vol. III.
Quellensammlung zur Kulturgeschichte. Göttingen: Musterschmidt-Verlag,
1968.

4. Official Reference Works

Amtliches Reichstags-Handbuch. Berlin: Gedruckt in der Hausdruckerei des
Reichstags. Editions of 1898, 1903, 1907, and 1912.

Plate, August. *Handbuch für das Preussische Abgeordnetenhaus.* Berlin:

Preussische Verlagsanstalt G.m.b.H. or W. Moeser Buchdruckerei. Editions of 1898, 1904, 1908, and 1913.

C. Contemporary Political Pamphlets and Books

Altkemper, Johannes. *Deutschtum und Polentum in politisch-konfessioneller Bedeutung.* Leipzig: Verlag von Duncker & Humblot, 1910.

[Anon.]. *Christl. Gewerkschaften und Kathol. Fachabteilungen im Saarrevier.* St. Johann a. d. Saar: Druckerei der "Saar-Post," 1907.

[Anon.]. *Die katholischen Fachabteilungen.* (Vortragsskizze für den Kursus der Gewerkschaftssekretäre in Düsseldorf.) N. p., n. d.

[Anon.]. *Die Verteidigung des Kartellverbandes der kath. Arbeitervereine West-, Süd- und Ostdeutschlands gegen 'Sitz Berlin.'* N. p., August 1912.

[Anon.]. "Drei Programmsätze," *Historisch-politische Blätter,* CXLIII (1909), 162–167.

[Anon.]. "Georg Kardinal Kopp," *Hochland,* XI, 2 (May, 1914), 237–240.

[Anon.]. *Wo stehen wir in der Gewerkschaftsbewegung?* Cologne: Verlag: Adam Stegerwald, n. d.

[Anon.]. "Zentrum und Katholizismus," *Historisch-politische Blätter,* CLI (1913), 778–787.

[Anon.]. *Zur Aufklärung der kath. Arbeiterschaft an die katholischen Arbeiter! Leset! Prüfet! Urteilt! Zeit- und Streitfragen. Weshalb sind die katholischen Fachabteilungen den Arbeiterinteressen nicht dienlich und darum überflüssig?* N. p., n. d.

Athanasius [A. ten Hompel]. *Das Cölner Osterdienstags-Protokoll: Ein Beitrag zur Würdigung latenter Kulturgegensätze in Katholizismus der Gegenwart.* Bonn: C. Georgi, 1909.

Aus Schlesien [Felix Porsch]. "Die schlesische Zentrumspartei," *Historisch-politische Blätter,* CXLVIII (1911), 857–862.

Bachem, Julius. *Das Zentrum, wie es war, ist und bleibt.* Vol. II: *Zeit- und Streitfragen der Gegenwart.* Cologne: Verlag und Druck von J. P. Bachem, 1913.

_____. *Die Parität in Preussen: Eine Denkschrift.* Cologne: Verlag und Druck von J. P. Bachem, 1897. 2d ed., 1899.

_____. "Nochmals: Wir müssen aus dem Turm heraus!" *Historisch-politische Blätter,* CXXXVII (1906), 503–513.

_____. "Wir müssen aus dem Turm heraus!" *Historisch-politische Blätter,* CXXXVII (1906), 376–386.

Bachem, Karl. *Zentrum, katholische Weltanschauung und praktische Politik: Zugleich eine Antwort auf die jüngste Broschüre von Geheimrat Roeren: "Zentrum und Kölner Richtung."* Krefeld: J. B. Kelinsche Buchdruckerei M. Buscher, 1914.

Bayard, Raimund [Hermann Paul Fleischer]. *Die Wahrheit über den Gewerkschaftsstreit der deutschen Katholiken.* Vol. I: *Die Frage der Zuständigkeit*

der kirchlichen Autorität für gewerkschaflichen Organisationen als solche.
Trier: Petrus-Verlag G.m.b.H., 1911.

Bergsträsser, Ludwig. "Der Riss im Zentrumsturm," *Akademische Blätter:*
Zeitschrift des Kyffhäuser-Verbandes der Vereine Deutscher Studenten,
XXV, 16 (16 Nov. 1910), 241–246.

Bernhard, Ludwig. *Die Polenfrage: Der Nationalitätenkampf der Polen in*
Preussen. 3d ed. Munich: Duncker & Humblot, 1920.

Biederlack, Joseph. *Theologische Fragen über die gewerkschaftliche Bewegung.*
Munich: Buchhandlung des Verbandes südd. kath. Arbeitervereine, 1910.

[Brauns, Heinrich] . *Christliche Gewerkschaften oder Fachabteilungen in*
katholischen Arbeitervereine? Ein Wort zur Aufklärung von Rhenanus.
Cologne: Verlag und Druck von J. P. Bachem, 1904.

Brauns, Heinrich. *Die Wahrheit über den Gewerkschaftsstreit der deutschen*
Katholiken: Kritik der gleichnamigen Broschüre Raimund Bayards.
M. Gladbach: Westdeutsche Arbeiter-Zeitung, 1912.

Brauweiler, Heinz. "Der Kern und die Bedeutung des 'Zentrumsstreits,' "
Hochland, XI (1914), 75–89.

Bremer. *Der Streit im Zentrum: Ein Wort zur Verständigung.* Münster i. W.:
Druck und Verlag der Regensbergschen Buchhandlung, 1913.

Das Zentrum eine politische, keine konfessionelle Partei. Heft 1: *Tagesfragen.*
Sonderabdrucke aus der Kölnische Volkszeitung. Cologne: Verlag der
Kölnischen Volkszeitung J. P. Bachem, 1907.

D. "Die katholische Geschichts-Professur in Strassburg," *Preussische Jahrbücher,*
CVI, 2 (Oct.–Dec. 1901), 384–387.

Dewitz, Landrat a.D. [Hermann] von. "Hemmnisse der Politik des Zentrums,"
Preussische Jahrbücher, CLV, 1 (Jan. 1914), 116–132.

Ehrhard, Albert. *Der Katholizismus und das 20. Jahrhundert im Lichte der*
kirchlichen Entwicklung der Neuzeit. Stuttgart: J. Roth, 1902.

Erdmann, August. *Die christliche Arbeiterbewegung in Deutschland.* 2d ed.
Stuttgart: Verlag von J. H. W. Dietz Nachf., 1909.

_____. *Die christliche Gewerkschaften insbesondere ihr Verhältnis*
zu Zentrum und Kirche. Stuttgart: Verlag von J. H. W. Dietz Nachf.
G.m.b.H., 1914.

Erzberger, Matthias. *Das Deutsche Zentrum.* 2d ed. Amsterdam: Verlag der
Internationale Verlagsbuchhandlung: "MESSIS," 1912. Eng. trans. *The*
German Center Party. Amsterdam: International Catholic Publishing Co.
"Messis," 1911.

_____. *Der Modernisteneid: Den Katholiken zur Lehr und Wehr.*
Andersdenkenden zur Aufklärung. Berlin: Germania, 1911.

_____. "Der stille Kulturkampf," *Frankfurter Zeitgemässe Broschüren,*
Neue Folge, XXXII, 1 (15 Oct. 1912), 1–56.

_____. *Der Toleranzantrag der Zentrumsfraktion des Reichstages.*
Osnabrück: Bernhard Wehberg, 1906.

_____. "Die Bedeutung des Zentrums für das Deutsche Reich," *Zeit-*
schrift für Politik, II (1909), 212–325.

_____. *Die Kolonial-Bilanz: Bilder aus der deutschen Kolonialpolitik*

auf Grund der Verhandlungen des Reichstags im Sessionsabschnitt 1905/06.
Berlin: Verlag und Druck der Germania, A.-G. für Verlag und Druckerei,
1906.

Frank, Oswald. *Deutschland und die Modernismusbewegung: Ein Jahr neu-*
deutscher Kirchengeschichte. Eine Revue über Kämpfer und Kampfplätze,
Recht und Unrecht in einem Brüderkreig. Wiesbaden: H. Rauch, 1911.

Gegen die Quertreiber: Kundgebung der Deutschen Zentrumspartei im Städt.
Saalbau zu Essen am 15. Februar 1914. Essen: Verlag und Druck Fredebeul
& Koenen, n. d. [1914].

Gerigk, Hubert. *Christliche Gewerkschaft oder Katholische Fachabteilung?*
(Separat-Abdruck aus der Neisser Zeitung.) 2d ed. Breslau: Verlag von G. P.
Aderholz' Buchhandlung, 1904.

Gerlach, Helmut v. *Das Parlament.* Vol. XVII: *Die Gesellschaft.* Frankfurt am
Main: Literarische Anstalt Rütten & Loening, 1907.

_____. *Die Geschichte des preussischen Wahlrechts.* Berlin: Buchverlag
der "Hilfe," G.m.b.H., 1908.

Gerloff, Wilhelm. *Die Finanz- und Zollpolitik des Deutschen Reiches nebst*
ihren Beziehungen zu Landes- und Gemeindefinanzen von der Gründung
des Norddeutschen Bundes bis zur Gegenwart. Jena: Verlag von Gustav
Fischer, 1913.

Giesberts, J. *Friede im Gewerkschaftsstreit? Kritisches und Antikritisches*
zum Streit über die Grundlagen der christlichen Gewerkschaften. Cologne:
Verlag und Druck von J. P. Bachem, 1909.

Goetz, Leopold Karl. *Das Centrum eine konfessionelle Partei? Ein Beitrag zu*
seiner Geschichte. Bonn: F. Cohen, 1906.

Görres, J. *Athanasius.* 4th ed. Regensburg: Verlag von G. Joseph Manz, 1838.

Hoeber, Karl. *Der Streit um den Zentrumscharakter.* Vol. I: *Zeit- und Streit-*
fragen der Gegenwart. Cologne: Verlag u. Druck von J. P. Bachem, 1912.

Hoensbroech, Paul Graf von. *Das Zentrum: Ein Fremdkörper im national-*
politischen und kulturellen Leben. Leipzig: Breitkopf & Härtel, 1914.

_____. *Das Papstum in seiner sozial-kulturellen Wirksamkeit.* 2 vols.
Leipzig: Breitkopf & Härtel, 1904–1905.

_____. *Der Evangelische Bund: Eine Kritik.* Berlin: C. A. Schwetschke
& Sohn, 1906.

_____. *Der Toleranzantrag des Zentrums im Lichte der Toleranz der*
römisch-katholischen Kirche. 3d ed. Berlin: Hermann Walther Verlagsbuchhandlung, 1903.

_____. *Der Zweck heiligt die Mittel: Eine ethischhistorische Untersuchung*
nebst einem Epilogus geleatus. 3d ed. Berlin: C. A. Schwetschke & Sohn,
1904.

_____. "Die Parität im Preussischen Staate," *Preussische Jahrbücher,*
LXXVI, 2 (June 1894), 314–344.

_____. "Mein Austritt aus dem Jesuitenorden," *Preussische Jahrbücher,*
LXXII, 1 (Apr.-June 1893), 300–327.

_____. *Rom und das Zentrum: Zugleich eine Darstellung der politischen*
Machtansprüche der drei letzten Päpste: Pius IX., Leos XIII., Pius X. und

der Anerkennung dieser Ansprüche durch das Zentrum. Leipzig: Druck und Verlag von Breitkopf & Härtel, 1910.

_____. *14 Jahre Jesuit: Persönliches und Grundsätzliches.* 4th ed. 2 vols. Leipzig: Druck und Verlag von Breitkopf & Härtel, 1911.

Holzamer, Hugo. *Turm und Block: Betrachtungen über die Hauptaufgaben der deutschen Katholiken in den konfessionellen Kämpfen der Gegenwart.* Teil I: *Die positiven Aufgaben der inneren Durchbildung und Verblendigung des Glaubens.* Trier: Petrus-Verlag, GmbH, 1912.

Kempel, Franz. *Die "christliche" und die "neutrale" Gewerkvereins-Bewegung, beurteilt an der Hand des Rundschreibens 'Rerum Novarum' des Papstes Leo XIII. vom 17. Mai 1891 und des Hirtenschreibens der preussischen Bischöfe an ihre Geistlichkeit vom 22. August 1900.* Mainz: Verlag von Franz Kirchheim, 1901.

Kipper, Josef. *Zum 50 jährigen Zentrums-Jubiläum: Politisches Zitaten-Lexikon.* Vol. II: *Schriftenreihe des Reichsgeneralsekretariats der Deutschen Zentrumspartei.* Berlin: Druck und Verlag der Opladener Druckerei u. Verlagsanstalt, G.m.b.H., n. d. [1911?].

Korum, Bischof Dr. [Michael] *Unerbauliches aus der Diözese Trier: Darlegung der Verhältnisse höherer Töchterschulen in Trier, St. Johann und Kreuznach, mit Akten belegt.* Trier: Druck und Verlag der Paulinus-Druckerei G.m.b.H., 1903.

Krueckemeyer, Heinrich Marie. "Der Streit um den Zentrumscharakter," *Historisch-politische Blätter*, CL, 1 (1912), 61–80.

_____. "Ist das Zentrum eine konfessionelle Partei?" *Frankfurter Zeitgemässe Broschüren*, XXVII, 9 (1908), 259–316.

_____. "Köln und Koblenz: Eine Darstellung der Osterdienstags-Konferenz und ihrer Folgeerscheinungen," *Frankfurter Zeitgemässe Broschüren*, XXIX, 1–2 (1910), 1–88.

_____. "Müssen wir aus dem Turm heraus?" *Historisch-politische Blätter*, CXXXVII (1906), 676–695.

_____. "Strömungen innerhalb der Zentrumspartei," *Die Grenzboten: Zeitschrift für Politik, Literatur und Kunst*, LXXI (12 June 1912), 351-355.

_____. *Zentrum und Katholizismus.* Amsterdam: Verlag der Internationalen Verlags-Buchhandlung: "Messis," 1913.

Lehmann, Max. "Römisch-katholische Zensur zu Anfang des 20. Jahrhunderts," *Preussische Jahrbücher*, CVII, 1 (Jan.–Mar. 1902), 1–9.

Leimpeters, Johann. *Die Komödie im Saargebiet.* Bochum: Selbstverlag des Verfassers, n. d. [1913?].

Lenin, V. I. "Organization of the Masses by the German Catholics," *Collected Works.* Trans. Andrew Rothstein. Vol. 36 (1900–1923). Moscow: Progress Publishers, 1966. Pp. 244–246.

Lossen, Wilhelm. *Der Anteil der Katholiken am akademische Lehramte in Preussen: Nach statistischen Untersuchungen.* Cologne: Verlag u. Druck von J. P. Bachem, 1901.

Montanus. *Das alte und das neue Zentrum.* Bonn: Kommissionsverlag von Peter Hanstein, 1910.

Maslowski, Peter. *Was ist die Deutsche Zentrumspartei? Klerikalismus und Proletariat.* Berlin: Vereinigung Internationaler Verlags-Anstalten G.M.B.H., 1925.

Massow, Wilhelm v. *Die deutsche innere Politik unter Kaiser Wilhelm II.* Stuttgart: Deutsche Verlags-Anstalt, 1913.

Mausbach, Joseph. *Die katholische Moral und ihre Gegner: Grundsätzliches und zeitgeschichtliche Betrachtungen.* Cologne: Verlag u. Druck von J. P. Bachem, 1912.

Meerfeld, Jean. *Der Krieg der Frommen: Materialen zum Zentrumsstreit.* Berlin: Verlag: Buchhandlung Vorwärts Paul Singer G.m.b.H. (Hans Weber, Berlin), 1914.

_____. *Die Deutsche Zentrumspartei.* Vol. III: *Sozialwissenschaftliche Bibliothek.* Berlin: Verlag für Sozialwissenschaft G.M.B.H., 1918.

_____. *Kaiser, Kanzler, Zentrum: Deutscher Verfassungsjammer und klerikaler Byzantismus.* Berlin: Verlag: Buchhandlung Paul Singer G.m.b.H., 1911.

Merkle, Sebastian. "Die katholische Kirche," in *Deutschland unter Kaiser Wilhelm II.* Vol. II. Berlin: Verlag von Reimar Hobbing, 1914. Pp. 1023–1050.

Michaelis, A. "Das Verhalten der Strassburger philosophischen Fakultät im Fall Spahn," *Der Lotse,* II, 1 (23 Nov. 1901), 225–231.

Mommsen, Theodor. "Universitätsunterricht und Konfession," in *Reden und Aufsätze.* Berlin: Weidmann, 1905. Pp. 432–436.

Muser, Oskar. *Der Ultramontanismus und das Zentrum.* Lahr i. B.: Druck und Verlag von Moritz Schauenburg, 1907.

Nieborowski, Paul. *Upper Silesia, Poland and Catholicism: An Investigation in Accordance with the Events of the Time.* Trans. M. H. Rhiem. Breslau: Grass, Barth & Comp. (W. Friedrich), 1919.

Ohr, Wilhelm. *Das Zentrum.* Vol. IV: *Deutsches Parteiwesen.* Munich: Buchhandlung Nationalverein, 1911.

[Oppersdorff, Georg Graf von]. *Eine Gewissensfrage: Ist Martin Spahn Zentrumsmann? Material zur Begründung des Augsburger Briefes der 14 Reichstagsabgeordneten an den Reichstagskandidaten Herrn Prof. Dr. Spahn in Strassburg.* Berlin: Carl Heymanns Verlag, 1910.

Pelt, J.-B. "Un théologien novateur en Allemagne," *Revue du clergé français,* V (15 Jan. 1898), 310–326.

Pesch, Heinrich. *Ein Wort zum Frieden in der Gewerkschaftsfrage.* Trier: Druck und Verlag der Paulinus-Druckerei, G.m.b.H., 1908.

_____. "Kirchliche Autorität und wirtschaftliche Organisation," *Stimmen aus Maria-Laach,* LXXV, 9 (Oct. 1908), 410–424.

Pieper, August. *Zum Gedächtnis von August Brust.* Heft 2: *Sonderabdruck aus "Führer-Korrespondenz."* M. Gladbach: No Pub., 1924.

Rehm, Hermann. *Deutschlands politische Parteien: Ein Grundriss der Parteienlehre und der Wahlsysteme.* Jena: Verlag von Gustav Fischer, 1912.

[Ritter, Emil]. *Das Zentrum eine konfessionelle Partei? Ein Beitrag zur Frage des interkonfessionellen Charakters.* Vol. III: *Politische Bibliothek.* Elberfeld: Wuppertaler Aktien-Druckerei, n.d. [1910?].

Roeder, Max. *Ist das Centrum eine Oppositionspartei? Eine Aktuelle Politische Skizze*. Amsterdam: Verlag der Internationalen Verlags-Buchhandlung: "Messis.," 1913.

Roeren, Hermann. "Der Toleranzantrag des Centrums," *Frankfurter Zeitgemässe Broschüren*, Neue Folge, XXI, 2 (1902), 1–63.

_____. *Veränderte Lage des Zentrumsstreits: Entgegnung auf die Kritik meiner Schrift Zentrum und Kölner Richtung*. Trier: Petrus-Verlag, 1914.

_____. *Zentrum und Kölner Richtung*. Trier: Petrus-Verlag, 1913.

_____. "Zur Polenfrage," *Frankfurter Zeitgemässe Broschüren*, N. F., Vol. XXII, 1–2 (1903), 1–63.

Rosenberg (Pastor prim. in Kempen-Posen). *Der polnische Clerus, das deutsche Zentrum und das evangelische Deutschtum. Vortrag gehalten im Zweigverein "Berlin" des evangelischen Bundes am 20. November 1908*. Lissa i. P.: Oskar Eulitz' Verlag G.m.b.H., n.d. [1908?].

Rost, Hans. *Die Katholiken im Kultur- und Wirtschaftsleben der Gegenwart*. Cologne: Verlag und Druck von J. P. Bachem, 1908.

_____. *Die Parität und die deutschen Katholiken*. Vol. III: *Zeit- und Streitfragen der Gegenwart*. Cologne: Verlag u. Druck von J. P. Bachem, 1914.

_____. *Die wirtschaftliche und kulturelle Lage der deutschen Katholiken*. Cologne: Verlag und Druck von J. P. Bachem, 1911.

Savigny, Franz von. *Arbeitervereine und Gewerkschaftsorganisationen im Lichte der Enzyklika Rerum Novarum*. Berlin: Germania, 1900.

Savigny, Leo von. *Das Zentrums Wandel und Ende*. Berlin: Hermann Walter Verlagsbuchhandlung, 1907.

Schell, Hermann. *Der Katholizismus als Prinzip des Fortschritts*. 6th ed. Würzburg: A. Göbel, 1897.

Schnitzer, Joseph. *Der katholische Modernismus*. Vol. III: *Die Klassiker der Religion*. Berlin-Schöneberg: Protestantischer Schriftenvertrieb G.m.b.H., 1912.

Spahn, Martin. *Das Deutsche Zentrum*. 2d ed. Vol. V: *Kultur und Katholizismus*. Mainz: Kirchheim'sche Verlagsbuchhandlung, n.d. [1906?].

_____. "Glossen zur katholischen Literaturbewegung," *Hochland*, VI (Aug. 1909), 600–605.

_____. "Polenpolitik," *Hochland*, V, 2 (Apr. 1908), 83–103.

_____. "Zur Geschichte der Zentrumspartei," *Hochland*, IX (June 1912), 294–309.

_____. "Zur Vorgeschichte der Zentrumspartei," *Hochland*, VIII (July 1911), 416–430.

Stegerwald, A. *Im Kampf um die Grundsätze der christlichen Gewerkschaften. Vortrag von Generalsekretär A. Stegerwald nebst Stellungnahme des christlichen Gewerkschafts-Kongresses in Dresden zum Gewerkschaftsstreit*. Cologne: Christlicher Gewerkschaftsverlag, 1912.

Stephen, [Bernhard Karl?]. *Der Beuthener Prozess im Lichte der Wahrheit oder Wahrheitsgetreue Enthüllungen aus der polnischen Politik in Oberschlesien: Ein Beitrag zum Verständnis der oberschlesischen Wirren*. Berlin: Verlagsanstalt Karl Hof, n.d. [1903?].

Strantz, Kurt von. "Die katholische Geistlichkeit und das Polentum in Oberschlesien," *Die Grenzboten: Zeitschrift für Politik, Literatur und Kunst,*
LX (1901), 625–630.

[ten Hompel, Adolf]. *Das Cölner Osterdienstags-Protokoll: Ein Beitrag zur
Würdigung latenter Kulturgegensätze im Katholizismus der Gegenwart von
Athanasius.* Bonn: Carl Georgi, 1909.

_____. *Indexbewegung und Kulturgesellschaft: Eine historische Darstel-
lung auf Grund der Akten.* Bonn: C. Georgi, 1908.

Tille, Alexander. *Der Soziale Ultramontanismus und seine "Katholischen Arbeitervereine."* Vol. IV: *Sozialwirtschaftliche Zeitfragen.* Berlin: Verlag von
Otto Elsner, 1905.

[Treitz, Jakob]. *Kann und darf ich für eine Arbeiter-Bewegung auf katholischer
Grundlage eintreten? Ein ruhiges Wort an Freund und Gegner unter den
Katholiken von J. Carbonarius.* Trier: Druck und Verlag der Paulinus-
Druckerei, G.m.b.H., 1904.

Verband der katholischen Arbeitervereine, ed. *Singulari quadam: Rundschreiben
des Papstes Pius X. über die Gewerkschaftsfrage.* Berlin: Verlag des "Arbeiter," 1912.

Vigilans. *Christliche Gewerkschaften und Katholische Fachabteilungen im Saarrevier: Eine Mahnung von Vigilans.* St. Johann a. d. Saar: Druckerei der
"Saar-Post," 1907.

Von einem Deutschen. *Die Kirchenpolitik der Hohenzollern von einem Deutschen.* Frankfurt a. M.: Neuer Frankfurter Verlag G.m.b.H., 1906.

Von einem Geistlichen [Edmund Schopen]. *"Köln:" Eine innere Gefahr für
den Katholizismus.* Berlin: Hermann Walther Verlagsbuchhandlung G.m.b.H.,
1910.

Vorstand des Verbandes der Bergarbeiter Deutschlands, ed. *Der christliche Ge-
werkverein der Bergarbeiter und die katholischen Fachabteilungen. Weiteres
zu dem Thema: "Christen unter sich."* Bochum: Druck und Verlag von H.
Hansmann & Co., 1908.

Weber, Paul. *Die Polen im Oberschlesien: Eine statistische Untersuchung.* Berlin: Verlagsbuchhandlung von Julius Springer, 1913.

Windolph, J. *Das Christentum der christlichen Gewerkschaften.* Berlin: Kommissionsverlag des "Arbeiter," 1910.

_____. *Der deutsche Protestantismus und die christlichen Gewerkschaften.*
Berlin: Verlag des "Arbeiter," 1909.

Zentrums-Album des Kladderadatsch, 1870–1910. Berlin: A. Hofmann &
Comp., 1912.

*Zum Zwist im Zentrumslager: Betrachtungen und Materialen über verstarkten
oder abgeschwächten Klerikalismus. Sonderabdruck von Aufsätzen eines
parlamentarischen Mitarbeiters der "Nationalliberalen Blätter."* Berlin:
Buchhandlung der Nationalliberalen Partei G.m.b.H., 1910.

D. Memoirs, Diaries, and Correspondence

Bachem, Julius. *Erinnerungen eines alten Publizisten und Politikers.* Cologne: Verlag und Druck von J. P. Bachem, 1913.

_____. *Lose Blätter aus meinem Leben.* Freiburg i. B.: Herdersche Verlagshandlung, 1910.

Baumgarten, Paul Maria. *Römische und andere Erinnerungen.* Düsseldorf: Neue Brücke Verlag, 1927.

Brentano, Lujo. *Mein Leben im Kampf um die soziale Entwicklung Deutschlands.* Jena: Eugen Diederichs Verlag, 1931.

[Bülow, Bernhard von]. *Memoirs of Prince von Bülow.* Trans. F. A. Voigt and Geoffrey Dunlop. 4 vols. Boston: Little, Brown and Company, 1931-1932.

Cardauns, Hermann. *Aus dem Leben eines deutschen Redakteurs.* Cologne: Verlag und Druck von J. P. Bachem, 1912.

Deuerlein, Ernst, ed. *Briefwechsel Hertling-Lerchenfeld, 1912-1917: Dienstliche Privatkorrespondenz zwischen dem bayerischen Ministerpräsidenten Georg Graf von Hertling und dem bayerischen Gesandten in Berlin Hugo Graf von und zu Lerchenfeld.* Vol. L (in 2 parts): *Deutsche Geschichtsquellen des 19. und 20. Jahrhunderts.* Boppard am Rhein: Harald Boldt Verlag, 1973.

Dyroff, Adolf, ed. *Reden, Ansprachen und Vorträge des Grafen Georg von Hertling mit einigen Erinnerungen an Ihn.* Cologne: Kommissionsverlag und Druck von J. P. Bachem, 1929.

Jagemann, Eugen von. *Fünfundsiebzig Jahre des Erlebens und Erfahrens (1849-1924).* Heidelberg: Carl Winters Universitätsbuchhandlung, 1925.

Hertling, Georg von. *Erinnergungen aus meinem Leben.* 2 vols. Kempten: Verlag der Jos. Kösel'schen Buchhandlung, 1920.

Hohenlohe-Schillingsfürst, Fürst Chlodwig zu. *Denkwürdigkeiten der Reichskanzlerzeit.* Edited by Karl Alexander von Müller. Stuttgart: Deutsche Verlags-Anstalt, 1931.

[Holstein, Friedrich von]. *The Holstein Papers: The Memoirs, Diaries and Correspondence of Friedrich von Holstein, 1837-1909.* Edited by Norman Rich and M. H. Fisher. 4 vols. Cambridge: At the University Press, 1955-1963.

Hutten-Czapski, Bogdan Graf von. *Sechzig Jahre Politik und Gesellschaft.* 2 vols. Berlin: Verlag von E. S. Mittler & Sohn, 1936.

Köhler, Heinrich. *Lebenserinnerungen des Politikers und Staatsmannes, 1878-1949.* Edited by Josef Becker. Vol. XI: *Veröffentlichungen der Kommission für Geschichtliche Landeskunde in Baden-Württemberg.* Stuttgart: W. Kohlhammer Verlag, 1964.

Lerchenfeld-Koefering, Hugo Graf. *Erinnerungen und Denkwürdigkeiten, 1843 bis 1925.* 2d ed. Berlin: Verlag von E. S. Mittler & Sohn, 1935.

Meinecke, Friedrich. *Ausgewählte Briefwechsel.* Edited by Ludwig Dehio and Peter Classen. Vol. VI: *Friedrich Meinecke Werke.* Stuttgart: K. F. Koehler Verlag, 1962.

_____. *Erlebtes, 1862-1919.* Stuttgart: K. F. Koehler Verlag, 1964.

Pastor, Ludwig Freiherr von. *Tagebücher, Briefe, Erinnerungen, 1854–1928.* Edited by Wilhelm Wühr. Heidelberg: F. H. Kerle Verlag, 1950.

Schmidt-Ott, Friedrich. *Erlebtes und Erstrebtes, 1860–1950.* Wiesbaden: Franz Steiner Verlag GMBH, 1952.

Spahn, Martin. "Selbstbiographie," in *Deutscher Aufstieg: Bilder aus der Vergangenheit und Gegenwart der rechtsstehenden Parteien.* Edited by Hans v. Arnim and Georg v. Below. Berlin: Franz Schneider Verlag, 1925. Pp. 479–488.

Stein, August. *Irenaeus: Aufsätze August Steins.* Frankfurt am Main: Verlag der Frankfurter Societäts-Druckerei G.m.b.H., 1921.

Vierhaus, Rudolf, ed. *Das Tagebuch der Baronin Spitzemberg geb. Freiin v. Varnbüler: Aufzeichnungen aus der Hofgesellschaft des Hohenzollernreiches.* 2d. ed. Vol. XLIII: *Deutsche Geschichtsquellen des 19. und 20. Jahrhunderts.* Göttingen: Vanderhoeck & Ruprecht, 1961.

Wetterlé, Abbé E. *Behind the Scenes in the Reichstag: Sixteen Years of Parliamentary Life in Germany.* Trans. George Frederic Lees. New York: George H. Doran Company, 1918.

Wallraf, Max. *Aus einem rheinischen Leben.* Hamburg: Hanseatische Verlagsanstalt, 1926.

[Wilhelm II]. *The German Emperor's Speeches: Being a Selection from the Speeches, Edicts, Letters, and Telegrams of the Emperor William II.* Trans. Louis Elkind. London: Longmans, Green, and Co., 1904.

Wilhelm II. *The Kaiser's Memoirs.* Trans. Thomas R. Ybarra. New York: Harper & Brothers Publishers, 1922.

E. Newspapers and Journals

1. Newspapers

Der Arbeiter: Organ des Verbandes der katholischen Arbeitervereine Nord- und Ostdeutschlands
Bayerische Staatszeitung
Frankfurter Zeitung
Germania
Kölnische Volkszeitung
Münchener Neueste Nachrichten
Schlesische Volkszeitung
Trierische Landeszeitung
Westdeutsche Arbeiter-Zeitung: Organ des Verbandes kath. Arbeiter- und Knappenvereine Westdeutschlands

2. Journals

Der Arbeiterpräses: Praktisches Handbuch für die Leiter und Freunde der katholisch-sozialen Bewegung

La Correspondence de Rome
Die Fackel
Frankfurter Zeitgemässe Broschüren
Historisch-politische Blätter für das katholische Deutschland
Hochland: Monatschrift für alle Gebiete des Wissens der Literatur und Kunst
Mitteilungen des Gesamtverbandes der christlichen Gewerkschaften Deutsch-
   lands (Beginning in 1905 title changes to *Zentralblatt des Gesamtverbandes*
   der christlichen Gewerkschaften Deutschlands)
Preussische Jahrbücher
Die Wartburg: Deutsch-evangelische Wochenschrift

II. Secondary Literature

A. Books

Alexander, Edgar. "Church and Society in Germany: Social and Political Movements and Ideas in German and Austrian Catholicism, 1789-1950," in
   Church and Society: Catholic Social and Political Thought and Movements,
   1789-1950. Edited by Joseph N. Moody. New York: Arts, Inc., 1953. Pp.
   325-583.
Altenhöfer, Ludwig. *Stegerwald: Ein Leben für den kleinen Mann.* N.p. [Bad
   Kissingen?] : Verlag für Politische Schriften, 1965.
Bachem, Julius and Karl Bachem. *Die kirchenpolitischen Kämpfe in Preussen*
   gegen die katholische Kirche insbesondere der "grosse Kulturkampf" der
   Jahre 1871-1887. Sonderabdruck der Artikel aus der dritten Auflage des
   Staatslexikons der Görres-Gesellschaft. Freiburg im Breisgau: Herdersche
   Verlagshandlung, 1910.
Bachem, Karl. *Josef Bachem, seine Familie und die Firma J. P. Bachem in Köln,*
   die Rheinische und die Deutsche Volkshalle, die Kölnischen Blätter und die
   Kölnische Volkszeitung: Zugleich ein Versuch der Geschichte der katholi-
   schen Presse und ein Beitrag zur Entwicklung der katholischen Bewegung
   in Deutschland. 2 vols. Cologne: Verlag und Druck von J. P. Bachem, 1912.
_____. *Vorgeschichte, Geschichte und Politik der Deutschen Zentrums-*
   partei. 9 vols. Cologne: Verlag J. P. Bachem G.M.B.H., 1927-1932.
Becker, Josef. *Liberaler Staat und Kirche in der Ära von Reichsgründung*
   und Kulturkampf: Geschichte und Strukturen ihres Verhältnisses in Baden,
   1860-1876. Vol. XIV: *Veröffentlichungen der Kommission für Zeitge-*
   schichte. Mainz: Matthias-Grünewald-Verlag, 1973.
Bellot, Josef. *Hundert Jahre politisches Leben an der Saar unter preussischer*
   Herrschaft (1815-1918). Vol. XLV: *Rheinisches Archiv. Veröffentlichungen*
   des Instituts für Geschichtliche Landeskunde der Rheinlande an der Universi-
   tät Bonn. Bonn: Ludwig Röhrscheid Verlag, 1954.
Bergsträsser, Ludwig. *Geschichte der politischen Parteien in Deutschland.* 10th
   ed. Vol. II: *Deutsches Handbuch der Politik.* Munich: Günter Olzog Verlag,
   1960.

Bertram, Jürgen. *Die Wahlen zum Deutschen Reichstag vom Jahre 1912: Parteien und Verbände in der Innenpolitik des Wilhelminischen Reiches.* Vol. XXVIII: *Beiträge zur Geschichte des Parlamentarismus und der politischen Parteien.* Düsseldorf: Droste Verlag, 1964.

Betz, A. *Beiträge zur Ideengeschichte der Staats- und Finanz-Politik des Zentrums (1870-1918[20]).* 2d ed. Regensburg: Verlagsanstalt vorm. G. J. Manz, 1930.

Born, Karl Erich. "Arthur Graf Posadowsky-Wehner, 1845-1932," in *Männer der deutschen Verwaltung.* Cologne: Grote, 1963. Pp. 211-228.

_____. *Staat und Sozialpolitik seit Bismarcks Sturz: Ein Beitrag zur Geschichte der Innenpolitischen Entwicklung des Deutschen Reiches, 1890–1914.* Vol. I: *Historische Forschungen.* Wiesbaden: Franz Steiner Verlag GMBH, 1957.

Buchheim, Karl. *Geschichte der Christlichen Parteien in Deutschland.* Munich: Im Kösel-Verlag, 1953.

_____. *Ultramontanismus und Demokratie: Der Weg der deutschen Katholiken im 19. Jahrhundert.* Munich: Kösel-Verlag, 1963.

Buchner, Max. *Kaiser Wilhelm II.: Seine Weltanschauung und die Deutschen Katholiken.* Leipzig: Verlag von K. F. Koehler, 1929.

Buonaiuti, Ernesto. *Le Modernisme Catholique.* Trans. René Monnot. Paris: Les Éditions Rieder, 1927.

Cardauns, Hermann. *Adolf Gröber.* Vol. XXX: *Eine Sammlung von Zeit- und Lebensbildern.* M. Gladbach: Volksvereins-Verlag GmbH., 1921.

_____. *Karl Trimborn: Nach seine Briefen und Tagebüchern.* Vol. XXXI: *Eine Sammlung von Zeit- und Lebensbildern.* M. Gladbach: Volksvereins-Verlag GmbH., 1922.

Caron, Jeanne. *Le Sillon et la démocratie chrétienne, 1894-1910.* Paris: Plon, 1966.

Craig, John Eldon. "A Mission for German Learning: The University of Strasbourg and Alsatian Society, 1870-1918." Ph.D. Dissertation. Stanford University, 1973.

Crothers, George D. *The German Elections of 1907.* Vol. 479: *Studies in History, Economics and Public Law.* New York: Columbia University Press, 1941.

Dahrendorf, Ralf. *Society and Democracy in Germany.* Garden City, N.Y.: Doubleday & Company, Inc., 1967.

Deutz, Josef. *Adam Stegerwald: Gewerkschaftler, Politiker, Minister, 1874–1945: Ein Beitrag zur Geschichte der christlichen Gewerksschaften in Deutschland.* Cologne: Bund-Verlag GMBH, 1952.

Dickmann, Fritz. "Das Problem der Gleichberechtigung der Konfessionen im Reich im 16. und 17. Jahrhundert" in *Friedensrecht und Friedenssicherung: Studien zum Friedensproblem in der neueren Geschichte.* Göttingen: Vandenhoeck & Ruprecht, 1971. Pp. 7-35.

_____. *Der Westfälische Frieden.* 2d ed. Münster: Verlag Aschendorff, 1965.

Dietzel, Hans. *Die preussischen Wahlrechtsreformbestrebungen von der*

Oktroyierung des Dreiklassenwahlrechts bis zum Beginn des Welt-Krieges.
Emsdetten (Westf.): Verlags-Anstalt Hein. & J. Lechte, 1934.

Dill, George Marshall, Jr. "The Christian Trade Unions and Catholic Corporatism in Germany, 1916-1924." Ph.D. Dissertation. Harvard University,
1949.

Dix, Arthur. *Die Deutschen Reichstagswahlen 1871-1930 und die Wandlungen
der Volksgliederung.* Vol. LXXVII: *Recht und Staat in Geschichte und
Gegenwart.* Tübingen: Verlag von J. C. G. Mohr (Paul Siebeck), 1930.

Donner, Hermann. *Die Katholische Fraktion in Preussen, 1852-1858.* Borna-
Leipzig: Buchdruckerei Robert Noske, 1909.

Dru, Alexander. *The Church in the Nineteenth Century: Germany 1800-1918.*
London: Burns & Oates, 1963.

Duhr, Bernhard. *Das Jesuitengesetz: Sein Abbau und seine Aufhebung. Ein
Beitrag zur Kulturgeschichte der Neuzeit. Ergänzungsheft zu den Stimmen
der Zeit.* Erste Reihe: *Kulturfragen.* Heft 7. Freiburg im Breisgau: Herdersche Verlagshandlung, 1919.

Dunne, Edward J. "The German Center in Empire and Republic: A Study in
the Crisis of Democracy." Ph.D. Dissertation. Georgetown University, 1950.

Ehren, Hermann. *Graf Franz von Ballestrem: Ein Lebensbild.* Breslau: Ost-
deutsche Verlagsanstalt, 1935.

Epstein, Klaus. *Matthias Erzberger and the Dilemma of German Democracy.*
Princeton: Princeton University Press, 1959.

Eschenburg, Theodor. *Das Kaiserreich am Scheideweg: Bassermann, Bülow
und der Block.* Berlin: Verlag für Kulturpolitik, 1929.

Feldman, Gerald D. *Army, Industry, and Labor in Germany, 1914-1918.*
Princeton: Princeton University Press, 1966.

Flaskamp, Franz. *Die Reichstagswahlen im Kreise Wiedenbrück (1867/1912).*
Heft 88: *Quellen und Forschungen zur westfälischen Geschichte.* Rheda:
Franz Scharpenberg, 1960.

Franz-Willing, Georg. *Kulturkampf gestern und heute: Eine Säkularbetrachtung,
1871-1971.* Munich: Verlag Georg D. W. Callwey, 1971.

Fricke, Dieter. *Der Ruhrbergarbeiterstreik von 1905.* [East] Berlin: Rütten
& Loening, 1955.

Goyau, Georges. *Bismarck et l'Église: Le Culturkampf (1870-1887).* 4 vols.
Paris: Librairie Académique Perrin et Cie, 1911-1913.

Grenner, Karl Heinz. *Wirtschaftsliberalismus und katholisches Denken: Ihre
Begegnung und Auseinandersetzung in Deutschland des 19. Jahrhunderts.*
Cologne: Verlag J. P. Bachem, 1967.

Grosche, Robert. "Der geschichtliche Weg des deutschen Katholizismus aus dem
Ghetto," in *Der Weg aus dem Ghetto: Vier Beiträge von Robert Grosche,
Friedrich Heer, Werner Becker, und Karlheinz Schmidthüs.* Cologne: Verlag
J. P. Bachem, 1955. Pp. 11-34.

Grosser, Dieter. *Vom monarchischen Konstitutionalismus zur parlamentarischen
Demokratie: Die Verfassungspolitik der deutschen Parteien im letzten Jahr-
zehnt des Kaiserreiches.* Vol. I: *Studien zur Regierungslehre und Internationalen Politik.* The Hague: Martinus Nijhoff, 1970.

Habich, Theodor. *Deutsche Latifundien: Bericht und Mahnung.* 3d ed. Stuttgart: W. Kohlhammer Verlag, 1947.

Hansen, Joseph. *Preussen und Rheinland von 1815 bis 1915: Hundert Jahre politischen Lebens am Rhein.* Bonn: A. Marcus & E. Webers Verlag, 1918.

Hanus, Franciscus. *Die preussische Vatikangesandtschaft, 1747-1920.* Munich: Pohl, 1954.

Harms, Bernhard, ed. *Volk und Reich der Deutschen: Vorlesungen gehalten in der Deutschen Vereinigung für Staatswissenschaftliche Fortbildung.* 3 vols. Berlin: Verlag von Reimar Hobbing in Berlin, 1929.

Hartmann, Albrecht. "Zentrum und Christliche Gewerkschaften von 1900 bis 1912." Ph.D. Dissertation. Free University of Berlin, 1952.

Hanssler, Bernhard, ed. *Die Kirche in der Gesellschaft: Der deutsche Katholizismus und seine Organisationen im 19. und 20. Jahrhundert.* Paderborn: Verlag Bonifacius-Druckerei, 1961.

Hoffmann, Hermann. "Georg von Kopp," in *Schlesische Lebensbilder.* Vol. II: *Schlesier des achtzehnten bis neunzehnten Jahrhunderts.* Edited by Friedrich Andreae *et al.* Breslau: W. G. Korn, 1926. Pp. 323-332.

Huber, Ernst Rudolf. *Deutsche Verfassungsgeschichte seit 1789.* 4 vols. Stuttgart: W. Kohlhammer Verlag, 1957-1969.

_____. "Joseph Görres und die Anfänge des katholischen Integralismus in Deutschland," in *Nationalstaat und Verfassungsstaat: Studien zur Geschichte der modernen Staatsidee.* Stuttgart: W. Kohlhammer Verlag, 1965. Pp. 107-126.

Hüsgen Eduard. *Ludwig Windthorst: Sein Leben, sein Wirken.* New ed. Cologne: Verlag und Druck von J. P. Bachem, 1911.

Hundhammer, Alois. *Geschichte des Bayerischen Bauernbundes.* Munich: F. A. Pfeiffer & Co., 1924.

Hurd, Archibald and Henry Castle. *German Sea-Power: Its Rise, Progress, and Economic Bases.* New York: Charles Scribner's Sons, 1914.

Jablonski, Leo. *Geschichte des fürstbischoflichen Delegaturbezirkes Brandenburg und Pommern.* 2 vols. Breslau: Druck von R. Nischkowsky, 1929.

Jacobs, Ferdinand. *Von Schorlemer zur Grünen Front: Zur Abwertung des berufsständischen und politischen Denkens.* Vol. I: *Schriften zur Ländlichen Bildung.* Düsseldorf: Verlag Haus Altenburg, 1957.

Kehr, Eckert. *Schlachtflottenbau und Parteipolitik, 1894-1901: Versuch eines Querschnitts durch die innenpolitischen, sozialen und ideologischen Voraussetzungen des deutschen Imperialismus.* Vol. 197: *Historische Studien.* Berlin: Verlag Emil Ebering, 1930.

Kisky, Wilhelm. *Der Augustinus-Verein zur Pflege der katholischen Presse von 1878 bis 1928.* Düsseldorf: Verlag des Augustinus-Vereins, 1928.

Kissling, Johannes B. *Geschichte der deutschen Katholikentage.* 2 vols. Münster: Verlag der Aschendorffschen Verlagsbuchhandlung, 1920-1923.

_____. *Geschichte des Kulturkampfes in Deutschen Reiche.* 3 vols. Freiburg in Breisgau: Herdersche Verlagshandlung, 1911-1916.

Koch, Max Jürgen. *Die Bergarbeiterbewegung im Ruhrgebiet zur Zeit Wilhelms II. (1889-1914).* Vol. V: *Beiträge zur Geschichte des Parlamentarismus und der politischen Parteien.* Düsseldorf: Droste-Verlag, 1954.

Koch, Walter. *Volk und Staatsführung vor dem Weltkriege: Beiträge zur Geschichte der nachbismarckischen Zeit und des Weltkriegs.* Heft 29, Neue Folge, Heft 9: Stuttgart: Verlag W. Kohlhammer, 1935.

Kremer, Willy. *Der soziale Aufbau der Parteien des Deutschen Reichstages von 1871–1918.* Emsdetten: Gedruckt in der Dissertations-Druckerei Heinr. & J. Lechte, 1934.

Lehmann, Max and Hermann Granier, eds. *Preussen und die katholische Kirche seit 1640: Nach den Acten des Geheimen Staatsarchives. Publikationen aus den K. Preussischen Staatsarchiven.* 9 vols. Leipzig: Hirzel, 1878–1902.

Lill, Rudolf. *Die Beilegung der Kölner Wirren, 1840 bis 1842: Vorwiegend nach Akten des Vatikanischen Geheimarchivs.* Vol. VI: *Studien zur Kölner Kirchengeschichte.* Düsseldorf: Schwann, 1962.

Löffler, Kl. *Geschichte der katholischen Presse Deutschlands.* Vol. L: *Soziale Tagesfragen.* M. Gladbach: Volksvereins-Verlag GmbH, 1924.

Lutz, Heinrich. *Demokratie im Zwielicht: Der Weg der deutschen Katholiken aus dem Kaiserreich in die Republik, 1914–1925.* Munich: Kösel-Verlag, 1963.

Majunke, Paul. *Geschichte des "Culturkampfes" in Preussen-Deutschland.* Paderborn: Druck und Verlag von Ferdinand Schönigh, 1886.

Mazura, Paul. *Die Entwicklung des politischen Katholizismus in Schlesien: Von seinen Anfängen bis zum Jahre 1880.* Breslau: Verlag von M. & H. Marcus, 1925.

Molt, Peter. *Der Reichstag vor der improvisierten Revolution.* Vol. IV: *Politische Forschungen.* Cologne: Westdeutscher Verlag, 1963.

Morsey, Rudolf. *Die Deutsche Zentrumspartei, 1917–1923.* Vol. XXXII: *Beiträge zur Geschichte des Parlamentarismus und der politischen Parteien.* Düsseldorf: Droste Verlag, 1966.

_____, ed. *Zeitgeschichte in Lebensbildern: Aus dem deutschen Katholizismus des 20. Jahrhunderts.* Mainz: Grünewald, 1973.

Müller, Franz. *Franz Hitze und sein Werk.* Hamburg: Hanseatische Verlagsanstalt, 1928.

Müller, Klaus. "Zentrumspartei und agrarische Bewegung im Rheinland, 1882–1903," in *Speigel der Geschichte: Festgabe für Max Braubach zum 10. April 1964.* Edited by Konrad Repgen and Stephan Skalweit. Münster, Westf.: Verlag Aschendorff, 1964. Pp. 828–857.

Neumann, Sigmund. *Die Deutschen Parteien: Wesen und Wandel nach dem Kriege.* Berlin: Junker und Dünnhaupt Verlag, 1932.

Nichtweiss, Johannes. *Die ausländischen Saisonsarbeiter in der Landwirtschaft der östlischen und mittleren Gebiete des Deutschen Reiches: Ein Beitrag zur Geschichte der preussisch-deutschen Politik von 1890 bis 1914.* Vol. IV: *Schriftenreihe des Instituts für Allgemeine Geschichte an der Humboldt-Universität-Berlin.* [East] Berlin: Akademie-Verlag, 1964.

Nipperdey, Thomas. *Die Organisation der deutschen Parteien vor 1918.* Vol. XVIII: *Beiträge zur Geschichte des Parlamentarismus und der politischen Parteien.* Düsseldorf: Droste Verlag, 1961.

Ranchetti, Michele. *The Catholic Modernists: A Study of the Religious Reform*

Movement, 1864–1907. Trans. Isabel Quigly. London: Oxford University Press, 1969.

Renner, Hermann. *Georg Heim: Der Bauerndoktor.* Munich: BLV Verlagsgesellschaft, 1960.

Ritter, Emil. *Die katholisch-soziale Bewegung Deutschlands im neunzehnten Jahrhundert und der Volksverein.* Cologne: Verlag J. P. Bachem, 1954.

Ritter, Gerhard A. *Die Arbeiterbewegung im Wilhelminischen Reich: Die Sozialdemokratische Partei und die Freien Gewerkschaften, 1890–1900.* 2d ed. Vol. III: *Studien zur Europäischen Geschichte aus dem Friedrich-Meinecke-Institut der Freien Universität Berlin.* Berlin-Dahlem: Colloquium Verlag, 1963.

Rivière, Jean. *Le Modernisme dans l'Église: Étude d'histoire religieuse contemporaine.* Paris: Librairie Letouzey et Ané, 1929.

Rosenbaum, L. *Beruf und Herkunft der Abgeordneten zu den deutschen und preussischen Parlamenten 1847 bis 1919: Ein Beitrag zur Geschichte des deutschen Parlaments.* Frankfurt am Main: Frankfurter Societäts-Druckerei G.m.b.H., Abteilung Buchverlag, 1923.

Rosenberg, Hans. *Grosse Depression und Bismarckzeit: Wirtschaftsablauf, Gesellschaft und Politik in Mitteleuropa.* Vol. II: *Veröffentlichung der Historischen Kommission zu Berlin beim Friedrich-Meinecke-Institut der Freien Universität Berlin.* Berlin: Walter de Gruyter & Co., 1967.

Rossmann, Kurt. *Wissenschaft, Ethik und Politik: Erörterung des Grundsatzes der Voraussetzungslosigkeit in der Forschung. Mit Erstmaliger Veröffentlichung der Briefe Theodor Mommsens über den "Fall Spahn" und der Korrespondenz zu Mommsens öffentlicher Erklärung über "Universitätsunterricht und Konfession" aus dem Nachlass Lujo Brentanos.* Vol. IV: *Schriften der Wandlung.* Heidelberg: Verlag Lambert Schneider, 1949.

Rother, K. H. "Franz Graf von Ballestrem," in *Schlesische Lebensbilder.* Vol. I: *Schlesier des neunzehnten Jahrhunderts.* Edited by Friedrich Andreae *et al.* Breslau: W. G. Korn, 1922. Pp. 247–251.

Sachse, Arnold. *Friedrich Althoff und sein Werk.* Berlin: Verlegt bei E. S. Mittler & Sohn, 1928.

Saul, Klaus. *Staat, Industrie und Arbeiterbewegung im Wilhelminischen Reich, 1903–14.* Vol. XVI: *Studien zur modernen Geschichte.* Düsseldorf: Bertelsmann Universitätsverlag, 1974.

Seidel, Richard. *Gewerkschaften und politische Parteien in Deutschland.* Vol. 298: *Weltgeist-Bücher.* Berlin: Weltgeist-Bücher Verl.-Ges., 1928.

Schauff, Johannes. *Die deutschen Katholiken und die Zentrumspartei: Eine politisch-statistische Untersuchung der Reichstagswahlen seit 1871.* Cologne: Verlag J. P. Bachem, 1928.

Schmidlin, Josef. *Papstgeschichte der neuesten Zeit.* Vol. III. Munich: Verlag Josef Kösel & Friedrich Pustet, 1936.

Schmidt, F. *Burghard von Schorlemer-Alst: Führer des Volkes.* Vol. XXI: *Eine Sammlung von Zeit- und Lebensbildern.* M. Gladbach: Volksvereins-Verlag, GmbH, 1916.

Schmidt, Erich. *Bismarcks Kampf mit dem politischen Katholizismus*. Teil I:
  Pius der IX. und die Zeit der Rüstung, 1848–1879. 2d ed. Hamburg:
  Hanseatische Verlagsanstalt, 1942.
Schmidt-Volkmar, Erich. *Der Kulturkampf in Deutschland, 1871–1890*.
  Göttingen: Musterschmidt-Verlag, 1962.
Schmitt, Carl. *Römischer Katholizismus und Politische Form*. Vol. XIII: *Der
  Katholische Gedanke: Veröffentlichungen des Verbandes der Vereine
  Katholischer Akademiker zur Pflege der Katholischen Weltanschauung*.
  Munich: Theatiner-Verlag, 1925.
Schmitz, Johann. *Antonius Kardinal Fischer, Erzbischof von Köln: Sein
  Leben und Wirken*. Cologne: Verlag und Druck von J. P. Bachem, 1915.
Schnabel, Franz. *Der Zusammenschluss des politischen Katholizismus in
  Deutschland im Jahre 1848*. Vol. XXIX: *Heidelberger Abhandlungen zur
  mittleren und neueren Geschichte*. Heidelberg: Carl Winter's Universitäts-
  buchhandlung, 1918.
_____. "Kardinal Kopps Bedeutung für den politischen Katholizismus
  in Deutschland," in *Abhandlungen und Vorträge, 1914–1965*. Edited by
  Heinrich Lutz. Freiburg: Herder, 1970. Pp. 1–13.
Schofer, Joseph. *Erinnerungen an Theodor Wacker*. Karlsruhe: Verlag der
  Badenia, 1922.
Scholz, Franz. "Georg Kardinal Kopp, 1881–1887, Bischof von Fulda, 1887–
  1914 Fürstbischof von Breslau," *Beiträge zur schlesischen Kirchengeschichte:
  Gedenkschrift für Kurt Engelbert*. Edited by Bernhard Stasiewski. Vol. VI:
  *Forschungen und Quellen zur Kirchen- und Kulturgeschichte Ostdeutsch-
  lands*. Cologne: Böhlau Verlag, 1969. Pp. 511–529.
Schorr, Helmut J. *Adam Stegerwald, Gewerkschaftler und Politiker der ersten
  deutschen Republik: Ein Beitrag zur Geschichte der christlich-sozialen
  Bewegung in Deutschland*. Recklinghausen: Kommunal-Verlag, 1966.
Schroeder, Oskar. *Aufbruch und Missverständnis: Zur Geschichte der reform-
  katholischen Bewegung*. Graz: Verlag Styria, 1969.
Schrörs, Heinrich. *Die Kölner Wirren: Studien zu ihrer Geschichte*. Berlin:
  F. Dümmlers Verlag, 1927.
Schwidetzky, Ilse. *Die polnische Wahlbewegung in Oberschlesien*. Vol. I:
  Schriften des Osteuropa-Instituts in Breslau. Breslau: F. Hirt, 1934.
Siebertz, Paul. *Karl Fürst zu Löwenstein: Ein Bild seines Lebens und Wirkens
  nach Briefen, Akten und Dokumenten*. Kempten: Verlag Josef Kösel &
  Friedrich Pustet, 1924.
Sontag, Ernst. *Adalbert (Wojciech) Korfanty: Ein Beitrag zur Geschichte der
  polnischen Ansprüche auf Oberschlesien*. Vol. VII: *Beihefte zum Jahrbuch
  der Albertus-Universität Königsberg/Pr.* Kitzingen-Main: Holzner-Verlag,
  1954.
Spael, Wilhelm. *Das katholische Deutschland im 20. Jahrhundert: Seine
  Pionier- und Krisenzeiten, 1890–1945*. Würzburg: Echter-Verlag, 1964.
Spahn, Martin. *Ernst Lieber als Parlamentarier*. Gotha: Friedrich Andreas
  Perthes Aktiengesellschaft, 1906.
Stadelhofer, Manfred. *Der Abbau der Kulturkampfgesetzgebung im Gross-*

herzogtum Baden, 1878-1918. Vol. III: *Veröffentlichungen der Kommission für Zeitgeschichte bei der Katholischen Akademie in Bayern.* Mainz: Matthias-Grünewald-Verlag, 1969.

Stegmann, Dirk. *Die Erben Bismarcks: Parteien und Verbände in der Spätphase der Wilhelminischen Deutschlands. Sammlungspolitik, 1897-1918.* Cologne: Kiepenheuer & Witsch, 1970.

Thielmann, Joseph. *Die Presse der katholischen Arbeitervereine Westdeutschlands.* Vol. VIII: *Schriftenreihe des Instituts für Zeitungswissenschaft.* Munich: Zeitungswissenschaftliche Vereinigung, 1934.

Tims, Richard W. *Germanizing Prussian Poland. The H-K-T Society and the Struggle for the Eastern Marches in the German Empire, 1894-1919.* Vol. 487: *Studies in History, Economics and Public Law.* New York: Columbia University Press, 1941.

Tirrell, Sarah R. *German Agrarian Politics after Bismarck's Fall: The Formation of the Farmers' League.* Vol. 566. *Studies in History, Economics and Public Law.* New York: Columbia University Press, 1951.

Treitschke, Heinrich von. *History of Germany in the Nineteenth Century.* 7 vols. Trans. Eden & Cedar Paul. London: G. Allen & Unwin, Ltd., 1915-1919.

Treitz, Jakob. *Michael Felix Korum: Bischof von Trier, 1840-1921.* Munich: Theatiner Verlag, 1925.

Trippen, Norbert. *Das Domkapitel und die Erzbischofswahlen in Köln, 1821-1929.* Vol. I: *Bonner Beiträge zur Kirchengeschichte.* Cologne: Böhlau Verlag, 1972.

25 Jahre christliche Gewerkschaftsbewegung, 1899-1924. Festschrift. Berlin-Wilmersdorf: Christliche Gewerkschaftsverlag, 1924.

Vidler, Alex R. *The Modernist Movement in the Roman Church: Its Origins & Outcome.* Cambridge: At the University Press, 1934.

Weber, Christoph. *Kirchliche Politik zwischen Rom, Berlin und Trier, 1876-1888: Die Beilegung des preussischen Kulturkampfes.* Vol. VII: *Veröffentlichung der Kommission für Zeitgeschichte bei der Katholischen Akademie in Bayern.* Mainz: Matthias-Grünewald-Verlag, 1969.

Weber, Rolf. "Zur historischen Beurteilung Bischof Ketterlers: Seine sozial- und nationalpolitische Konzeption in den sechziger Jahren," in *Die grosspreussisch-militaristische Reichsgründung 1871: Voraussetzungen und Folgen.* Vol. I. Edited by Horst Bartel and Ernst Engelberg. [East] Berlin: Akademie-Verlag, 1971. Pp. 438-453.

Wehler, Hans-Ulrich. "Die Polen im Ruhrgebiet bis 1918," in *Moderne deutsche Sozialgeschichte.* Vol. X: *Neue Wissenschaftliche Bibliothek.* Edited by Hans-Ulrich Wehler. Cologne: Kiepenheuer & Witsch, 1966. Pp. 437-455.

Wendorf, Hermann. *Die Fraktion des Zentrums im Preussischen Abgeordnetenhause, 1859-1867.* Vol. XL: *Leipziger Historische Abhandlungen.* Leipzig: Verlag von Quelle & Meyer, 1916.

Windell, George C. *The Catholics and German Unity, 1866-1871.* Minneapolis: University of Minnesota Press, 1954.

Zeender, John K. "The Center Party and the Growth of German National Power, 1890-1906." Ph.D. Dissertation. Yale University, 1952.

Zenz, Emil. "Das höhere Mädchenschulwesen in der Stadt Trier vom Beginn
    der preussischen Zeit bis zum Ende des ersten Weltkrieges, 1814-1918" in
    *Neusprachliches Gymnasium für Mädchen Trier: Vormals Städtische
    Studienanstalt. Festschrift zur Einweihung des neuen Schulgebäudes bei
    St. Barbara.* N. p.: No Pub., 1966. Pp. 36-43.
_____. *Geschichte der Stadt Trier in der ersten Hälfte des 20. Jahr-
    hunderts.* Vol. XII; *Ortschroniken des Trierer Landes.* Trier: No Pub., 1967.

B. Articles

Bornhak, Conrad. "Die Begründung der katholisch-theologischen Fakultät
    in Strassburg," *Elsass-Lothringisches Jahrbuch,* XII (1933), 249-269.
Bornkamm, Heinrich. "Die Staatsidee im Kulturkampf," *Historische Zeit-
    schrift,* CLXX (1950), 41-72, 273-306.
Deuerlein, Ernst. "Der Gewerkschaftsstreit," *Theologische Quartalschrift,*
    CXXXIX (1959), 40-81.
_____. "Verlauf und Ergebnis des 'Zentrumsstreits' (1906-1909),"
    Stimmen der Zeit, CLVI (May 1955), 103-126.
Epstein, Klaus. "Erzberger and the German Colonial Scandals, 1905-1910,"
    The English Historical Review, LXXIV (Oct. 1959), 637-663.
_____. "Erzberger's Position in the Zentrumsstreit before World War
    I," *The Catholic Historical Review,* XLIV (Apr. 1958), 1-16.
Ferber, Walter. "Der Weg Martin Spahns: Zur Ideengeschichte des politischen
    Rechtskatholizismus," *Hochland,* LXII (May–June 1970), 218-229.
Friedrich, Manfred. "Die Parteitage des Zentrums in Bayern," *Zeitschrift für
    bayerische Landesgeschichte,* XXXVI, 3 (1973), 834-876.
Hirsch, Paul. "Briefe namhafter Historiker an Harry Bresslau," *Die Welt als
    Geschichte,* XIV (1954), 223-241.
Just, Harald. "Wilhelm Busch und die Katholiken: Kulturkampfstimmung
    im Bismarck-Reich," *Geschichte in Wissenschaft und Unterricht,* XXV
    (Feb. 1974), 65-78.
Mommsen, Wilhelm. "Zur Methodik der deutschen Parteigeschichte," *Historische
    Zeitschrift,* CXLVII (1932), 53-62.
Morsey, Rudolf. "Die deutschen Katholiken und der Nationalstaat zwischen
    Kulturkampf und erstem Weltkrieg," *Historisches Jahrbuch,* XC (1970), 31-
    64.
_____. "Georg Kardinal Kopp, Fürstbischof von Breslau (1887-1914):
    Kirchenfürst oder 'Staatsbischof'? Ein Beitrag zur Geschichte des Fürst-
    bistums Breslau," *Wichmann-Jahrbuch für Kirchengeschichte im Bistum
    Berlin,* XXI/XXIII (1967-1968), 42-65.
_____. "Zwei Denkschriften zum 'Fall Martin Spahn' (1901): Ein Beitrag
    zur preussisch-deutschen Wissenschaftspolitik," *Archiv für Kulturgeschichte,*
    XXXVIII, 2 (1956), 244-257.
Nell-Breuning, Oswald von. "Der Volksverein für das katholische Deutschland,"
    Stimmen der Zeit, CLXXX, 7 (July 1972), 35-50.

Neubach, Helmut. "Schlesische Geistliche als Reichstagsabgeordnete, 1867–1918: Ein Beitrag zur Geschichte der Zentrumspartei und zur Nationalitätenfrage in Oberschlesien," *Archiv für schlesische Kirchengeschichte,* XXVI (1968), 251–278.

Neuner, Peter. " 'Modernismus' und kirchliches Lehramt: Bedeutung und Folgen der Modernismus-Enzyklika Pius' X," *Stimmen der Zeit,* CLXXXX, 10 (Oct. 1972), 249–262.

Nipperdey, Thomas. "Interessenverbände und Parteien in Deutschland vor dem Ersten Weltkrieg," *Politische Vierteljahresschift,* II (Sept. 1961), 262–280.

Philippi, H. "Beiträge zur Geschichte der diplomatischen Beziehungen zwischen dem Deutschen Reich und dem Heiligen Stuhle, 1872–1909," *Historisches Jahrbuch,* LXXXII (1962), 219–262.

Pikart, Eberhard. "Die Rolle der Parteien in Deutschen Konstitutionallen System vor 1914," *Zeitschrift für Politik,* IX (Neue Folge), 1 (Mar. 1962), 12–32.

Rachfahl, Felix. "Windthorst und der Kulturkampf," *Preussische Jahrbücher,* CXXXV (Jan.-Mar. 1909), 213–253, 460–490; CXXXVI (Apr.-June 1909), 56–73.

Röhl, J. C. G. "Higher Civil Servants in Germany," *The Journal of Contemporary History,* II, 3 (July 1967), 101–121.

Sheehan, James J. "Political Leadership in the German Reichstag, 1871–1918," *The American Historical Review,* LXXIV, 2 (Dec. 1968), 511–528.

Silverman, Dan P. "Political Catholicism and Social Democracy in Alsace-Lorraine, 1871–1914," *The Catholic Historical Review,* LII (Apr. 1966), 39–65.

Spahn, Martin. "Das Jahr 1906," *Das Deutsche Volk: Katholische Wochenzeitung für das gesamte deutsche Volkstum,* III, 29 (15 July 1928), p. 1.

Weber, Christoph. "Kardinal Kopp's Brief von der 'Verseuchung des Westens,' " *Archiv für schlesische Kirchengeschichte,* XXVI (1968), 327–334.

Webersinn, Gerhard. "Dr. Felix Porsch: Vizepräsident des Preussischen Landtages," *Jahrbuch der Schlesischen Friedrich-Wilhelms-Universität zu Breslau,* XIII (1968), 232–283.

_____. "Felix Porsch als Kirchenrechtler, Sachwalter der Gerechtigkeit," *Archiv für schlesische Kirchengeschichte,* XXVII (1969), 130–146.

Zeender, John K. "German Catholics and the Concept of an Interconfessional Party, 1900–1922," *Journal of Central European Affairs,* XXIII (Jan. 1964), 424–439.

_____. "The German Center Party during World War I: An Internal Study," *The Catholic Historical Review,* XLII (Jan. 1957), 441–468.

C. Reference Works

Fricke, Dieter, ed. *Die bürgerlichen Parteien in Deutschland: Handbuch der Geschichte der bürgerlichen Parteien und anderer bürgerlicher Interessenorganisationen vom Vormärz bis zum 1945.* 2 vols. Leipzig: VEB Bibliographisches Institut, 1968–1970.

Gottschalk, Joseph, ed. *Schlesische Priesterbilder*. Aalen/Württ.: Theiss, 1967.

Huber, Ernst Rudolf, ed. *Dokumente zur deutschen Verfassungsgeschichte*. 3 vols. Stuttgart: W. Kohlhammer, 1961–1966.

Kosch, Wilhelm. *Das Katholische Deutschland: Biographisch-Bibliographisches Lexikon*. 3 vols. Augsburg: Literarisches Institut von Haas & Grabherr, 1930–1938.

Nowack, Alfons. *Lebensbilder schlesischer Priester*. Breslau: O. Borgmeyer, 1928.

Schwarz, Max. *MdR: Biographisches Handbuch der Reichstage*. Hannover: Verlag für Literatur und Zeitgeschehen GmbH, 1965.

Specht, Fritz and Paul Schwabe. *Die Reichstagswahlen, 1867–1907*. 3d ed. Berlin: C. Heymann Verlag, 1908.

INDEX

209

Germany, government of; Prussia,
government of
Clergy, Roman Catholic: in Baden,
122; in Centrum party, 62–68, 74,
76, 77; in Christian Trade Unions,
90; and clerical caucus in Ratibor,
65
Coblenz, 9, 76, 77
Coblenz, conclave in, 60–61
Coburg-Gotha, 19
Collegium Germanicum, 10
Cölner Correspondenz, 103–104
Cologne, 9, 76, 94–95, 116; Archbishop of, 14; bishopric of, 46, 47
Cologne faction, 45, 54, 59, 121,
128, 130, 131, 157n56, 168n24;
appears as extension of Modernism
and Reform Catholicism, 55; criticized by opponents, 57, 66–67,
129–130; and disappointment in
Black-Blue bloc, 132; effect of
Kopp's death on, 119; influenced
by regional conditions, 45; made
Centrum party more venal, 137;
motives and methods of, 42, 46,
52, 56, 118, 126, 135, 136, 137–
138; and press, 128, 173n32; regional strength of, 123; and Reichstag elections in 1912, 166n31; and
relationship to Christian Trade
Unions, 91, 138; strength of, 122,
123; wins control of party, 119,
120–121, 122–128, 131. *See also*
"Centrum conflict"; Centrum party
"Cologne Troubles," 13, 15, 156n45
Concordat: of 1801, 24; of 1933,
135
Confederation, German, 7, 11, 12
Confederation, North German, 11
Conference, Easter Tuesday, 60, 65,
66, 103, 126, 156n45
Conference, Prussian Bishops', of
1900 in Fulda, 99; of 1910 in
Fulda, 99
Congress, Centrum party, of 1914
in Essen, 62
Congress, Christian Trade Union, of
1912 in Essen, 109–110; of 1912 in
Frankfurt am Main, 101
Congress, League of Catholic Worker

Associations (Berlin), of 1912 in
Berlin, 101
Congress of Vienna, 7, 9; Federal Act
of, 7, 8
Conservative party: alienated by Centrum's sectarianism, 34, 35, 45,
135–136; and Bülow bloc, 36; criticized by Berlin faction, 56, 135; relations with Centrum party, 34, 35,
36, 37, 39, 42, 45, 46, 55, 56, 132;
in Upper Silesia, 74. *See also* "Alliance of Knights and Saints"; Black-
Blue bloc
Constitution, Frankfurt, 9
Constitution, Prussian, 9, 15, 20
Counter Reformation, 3, 13, 132
Craft Associations, 99, 104, 113;
character of, 98; numerical strength
and economic effectiveness, 87, 101;
origins and purpose, 85; relationship
to Centrum party, 95; and Roman
Catholic church, 85–86; in the Saar,
86. *See also* "Trade-union conflict";
Trier faction; Worker Associations,
Catholic
"Creeping" Kulturkampf. *See* "Si-
lent" Kulturkampf
Cujus regio, ejus religio, 6
Curia, 57, 59, 62, 106, 112, 131,
157n56. *See also* Church, Roman
Catholic; Holy See

Danes, 16
Das katholische Deutschland, 128
Dasbach, Georg Friedrich, 166n35
Delbrück, Clemens von, 112, 114
Delsor, Nikolaus, 26
Depression, Great, of 1873–1896, 58
Deutsche Zeitung, 1
Discrimination: in Baden, 122; class,
79; ethnic, 68–71, 73; in post-
Kulturkampf era, 32; in Prussia, 9,
10; religious, 19, 31, 79. *See also*
"Academic" Kulturkampf; Ger-
many, government of; Prussia, gov-
ernment of; "Spahn case"; Trier
school conflict
Dortmund, 85
Droste-Vischering, Clemens August,